MARJORY STONEMAN DOUGLAS

VOICE
of the RIVER

Books by Marjory Stoneman Douglas

Adventures in a Green World:
    David Fairchild and Barbour Lathrop   1973
Florida: The Long Frontier   1967
Alligator Crossing   1959
Hurricane   1958
Freedom River   1953
Road to the Sun   1952
The Everglades: River of Grass   1947
    (Revised Edition 1987)

VOICE
of the RIVER

An Autobiography by
Marjory Stoneman Douglas
with John Rothchild

MARJORY
STONEMAN
DOUGLAS

Pineapple Press, Inc.
Sarasota, Florida

Pineapple Press, Inc.
P.O. Drawer 16008
Southside Station
Sarasota, Florida 34239

Library of Congress Cataloging-in-Publication Data

Douglas, Marjory Stoneman.
    Marjory Stoneman Douglas: voice of the river.

    1. Douglas, Marjory Stoneman. 2. Conservationists—Florida—Biography.
I. Rothchild, John. II. Title.
QH31.D645A3 1987   333.7'2'0924 [B]   87-2242
ISBN 0-910923-33-7: (hb.) — ISBN 0-910923-94-9 (pbk.)

Design by Frank Cochrane Associates, Sarasota, Florida
Typography by Lubin Typesetting and Literary Services, Sarasota, Florida

10 9 8 7 6 5 4

To Massachusetts, with love

Acknowledgments

Special thanks to: Joette Lorion; June and David Cussen; Don DeHut; Joe Browder; Mildred Merrick; Beth Dunlop; Linda Hardin; Christine Bell; Michelle Kavanaugh; Pat Tucker; Donald Klein and the law firm of Kline, Moore, and Klein; Susan Rothchild; Florida International Realty; Jennifer Krugman; and the following members of the Coral Gables High School National Honor Society: Vanessa Barton, Sara Espinosa, Marc Camacho, Alan Obregon, George Healy, Gloria Gonzalez, Andrea Rose, Dan Nicholls, Santiago Gato, Elena Figueroa, Reed Martin, and Mitchell Lysinger.

Contents

Introduction:
Notes from a Fan

by John Rothchild

The first time I saw Marjory Stoneman Douglas was in the gymnasium of the Everglades City school. It was 1973, sometime in late summer, known locally as the mosquito season. An incredible optimist in this town of 100 stone crabbers and a handful of odd Yankees, lost in the fog of mosquitoes at the edge of the Everglades National Park, had proposed to build a suburb. The optimist needed a bridge permit, which was the subject of this public hearing, sponsored by the U.S. Army Corps of Engineers.

The suburb idea stirred up environmentalists from both sides of the state, and they were fighting the bridge permit. We townspeople, most of us opposed to the development ourselves, were delighted when Mrs. Douglas appeared in her famous floppy hat. We'd heard that this power-ful woman, old enough to be prehistoric by Florida standards, would not allow any suburbs in the Everglades. In fact, it was rumoured that she'd more or less created the Everglades and was as fiercely protective as a parent for a child. I imagined her to be some sort of cross between Mother Teresa, Clare Boothe Luce, Rachel Carson, Athena, and Golda Meir. Somebody drove her out here all the way from Miami, an hour and a half and several decades of progress away.

There was no air-conditioning in the gymnasium and no screens on the windows. Whoever was in charge of matters of life and death had decided that heat was more threatening than bugs, so the windows and doors were left open. The audience slapped and scratched sitting down as the various speakers slapped and scratched standing up. One environmentalist after another described the fragility of nature, the subtle ecosystems of the Everglades, while attackers from the ecosystem buzzed around their ears until they could scarcely keep track of their thoughts.

Mrs. Douglas was half the size of her fellow speakers and she wore huge dark glasses, which along with the huge floppy hat made her look like Scarlett O'Hara as played by Igor Stravinsky. When she spoke, everybody stopped slapping and more or less came to order. She reminded us all of our responsibility to nature and I don't remember what else. Her voice had the sobering effect of a one-room schoolmarm's. The tone itself seemed to tame the rowdiest of the local stone crabbers, plus the developers, and the lawyers on both sides. I wonder if it didn't also intimidate the mosquitoes. What impressed me most is that Mrs. Douglas never needed to slap. At least, I never saw her slap. The request for a Corps of Engineers permit was eventually turned down. This was no surprise to those of us who'd heard her speak.

At the time of the meeting in the gymnasium, Mrs. Douglas was 83. I considered it a privilege to have witnessed Florida's greatest defender of the environment in the last stage of her long and exciting career. How ignorant can you get. It turns out this was the beginning of a long and exciting career. Mrs. Douglas wasn't fully activated as an environmentalist until she was 79. As she's gone on considerably from there, the speech I heard should be taken as one of her premature efforts. She's done more flying around the country, issuing press releases, lobbying in Tallahassee, campaigning against developers and hunters, speaking for the panthers and the birds, the mangroves and the wetlands, the Kissimmee River and the Everglades, as a 90-year-old than she did as an 80-year-old, while as a 70-year-old she was busy writing books.

In fact, Mrs. Douglas has had several careers, though this is easily overlooked since her efforts as a 90-year-old represent the work of a normal complete existence. This is embarassing for the allegedly active 40-year-old to contemplate, but it's true. Mrs. Douglas, moreover, does not ascribe anything to magic. As she explains in the pages that follow, life for any 80-year-old can be healthy and productive, but you have to take care of yourself and avoid indolence and self-indulgence, so you'll be even healthier and more productive in your nineties.

After that meeting in the Everglades, the next news of Mrs. Douglas came to me unexpectedly through the breezes. That is, my family and I wanted to build a sensible Florida house that was open to the breezes, avoiding the expense of an air conditioner. A sensible house was such an unpopular prospect that hardly an architect within 500 miles would consider designing one, any more than they'd draw a plan for a teepee or a yurt. At last we found a sympathetic architect in Marion Manley, an octogenarian who'd moved to Miami long before air-conditioning, early enough to remember the hurricane of 1926, as well as all the lesser breezes. She also remembered Mrs. Douglas.

Of course Marion Manley had to have known Marjory Stoneman Douglas. How could they have avoided each other — two free thinkers among the few thousand real-estate crazed South Florida inhabitants in the 1920s? Ms. Manley told me the juicy gossip, how Mrs. Douglas arrived in Miami in 1915 to move in with her father, and, horror of horrors, to get a divorce. Her father, Frank Stoneman, was the founder and editor of the Miami *Herald*. Ms. Manley described how later, when the architect was down on her luck, Mrs. Douglas took her into her little house in Coconut Grove and gave her the back room. This was during the Depression and after the big land bust.

1915! It might not mean much to New England, but a person who goes back that far in South Florida goes back through everything, back to the original undredged real estate, back to the original scoundrels, back to the beginning of Eastern standard time. From chatting with Ms. Manley, I realized that Mrs. Douglas was doubly valuable, not only as a defender of the Everglades, but also as the local Homer.

That's when I decided to read *The Everglades: River of Grass*, Mrs. Douglas's best known book. As an author whose own books have disappeared off shelves, and not, one gathers, from great popular demand, I uncovered another galling fact: Mrs. Douglas's work was published in 1947 and was still selling 10,000 copies a year. In it I got my first appreciation of her writer's side. Nowhere had I read such lyrical descriptions of the clouds and vapors across the Everglades, the whoop and swoop of birds, the imperceptible ebbs and flows along the course of what Mrs. Douglas called a river, and what so many others had foolishly dismissed as swamp.

When my family moved to Miami in 1980, one of my first projects was visiting this remarkable person. She'd just turned 90. She was living in her tiny house in Coconut Grove, just as she had since 1926. To get there, I had to drive through the middle of the business district, once a haven for beatniks and peyote-takers, now a fashionable stretch of liberal commerce. Beyond the business district are the residential sub-tropical jungles, and there among ranchettes, Alhambras, and displaced palazzos is her mushroom-roofed cottage. It is set back off the road behind a neighbor's house and partly hidden by bushes, looking like a herder's hut from the English sheeplands. There is no driveway, just lawn. I found out later why Mrs. Douglas never needed a driveway. She never saw the sense in cars, and never learned to drive one.

Inside is one big room with a 14-foot ceiling, semi-exposed beams, and moisture stains on ancient plaster walls. A desk and the floor surrounding it is cluttered with envelopes and legal pads. There's no television and of course no air-conditioning, since this is a sensible house open to breezes. In the corner is a metal fan, one of the few sops to modern convenience.

There are some end tables and an oval coffee table, the kind that most people would clutter with knickknacks. Mrs. Douglas's coffee tables are cluttered with papers and with awards: plaques from the state of Florida, goblets from Sierra Clubs, honorary citations from colleges and federal agencies. There are enough awards to fill a high-school trophy case, but they aren't displayed with forethought nor set out to impress. In fact, they're scattered about or half-hidden under manuscripts, proof that the recipient has better things to think about.

Books are everywhere: books in the shelves, books on the tables, books stacked on the couch and in the chairs, books in the usual book form, books on records, and books on tape sent by an agency for the blind. On one far table are several towers of books Mrs. Douglas has written, which she didn't begin doing until the age of 55. A cat sleeps on books. A little talking clock, one of the rare bits of evidence that this could be 1980, sits on a pile of books.

I couldn't avoid thinking this room is actually Mrs. Douglas's mind turned inside out. Nothing essential has changed since the presidency of Harding. Everything is simplicity and utility, with no devotion to false gods of housekeeping. Simplicity and utility, I discovered later, come from her seafaring Cornish ancestors on the one side and her rabble-rousing Quaker ancestors on the other. The pigheaded Bonapartists fit in there someplace as well.

Behind the big room is a small kitchen with no oven and no dishwasher. I peeked into the refrigerator, and it was nearly empty. From what I could see, Mrs. Douglas cooks on an old double hot plate. From the evidence in the refrigerator, I guessed that she'd survived on club soda and unsalted peanuts, plus the daily two ounces of Scotch that she was about to pour. She corrected me on her diet eventually. Though she admits to an impatience with cooking, she says she occasionally prepares a full meal. Like most high-powered professionals, she goes out to dinner several nights a week.

In back of the kitchen is the narrow sparse bedroom, where she's slept since she built the house. There's a little swinging door for the cats. Except for the constant cats and shorter stays by Ms. Manley and her Uncle Charlie, she's lived happily alone since raccoon coats and the Charleston. I made the mistake of asking if she were lonely, with a hint of syrup in my voice. "I didn't say lonely," she snapped. "I said alone. They're not the same, you know. A person can be alone but not lonely. In fact, a person should be alone from time to time. If you're never alone then you'll never know who you are."

She fixed me a bourbon to go with her Scotch. She moved about the kitchen with such ease — getting out the ice, pulling down the glasses, pouring the peanuts — that I almost forgot she was nearly blind. Then when I remembered and tried to help her set her glass on a coaster, she rebuffed my gesture as an insult. "They say I'm pigheaded," she cheerfully confessed. "Pigheadedness covers a multitude of virtues as well as sins." Already I was convinced of her formidable companionship. Heaven help her adversaries.

She sat me in the big stuffed chair next to the standing lamp, the one reserved for visitors. She turned the light on me as if I were a nightclub performer. The smaller chair she took for herself. Even through her dark glasses, she noticed that I hadn't put a coaster under my drink and had set it directly on a book — where else? "That's the trouble with men," she sniffed. "They never think coasters are important. What is it that men have against coasters?" Then we had a nice discussion about the cultural history of coasters. I began to sense that her sharp tongue was connected to a soft heart, and that she was genuinely fond of most people, and amused with all others. This was a major relief.

Soon we became friends. I found myself drawn to conversations at her house, to evenings with Mrs. Douglas, often preferring them to football or to evenings with my contemporaries, who start at a half-century later. At first, the two of us discussed books. Books are Mrs. Douglas's favorite topic. She liked to talk about books more even than she liked to talk about the Everglades. Of course she did most of the talking. "Do you remember old Mr. Traddle?" she'd ask. "Yes," I'd say, "from *Oliver Twist*." "No, not *Oliver Twist*," she'd correct. "*David Copperfield*. I know my Dickens. My grandmother used to read it to me . . . let's see . . . back in 1897."

I realized that books were not things to Mrs. Douglas. They were members of her household. She was still fuming about the "fiend in human form who borrowed my *Alice in Wonderland* and didn't bring it back." Although I never pursued this, I wouldn't be surprised if this unforgivable act predates Al Capone.

Classics were her special companions. Mrs. Douglas not only knew their exact whereabouts on the shelves or in the piles — a trick if you can't see them — she also had a terrifying memory for their contents. At least, it was terrifying to someone who claims to have a great memory because he can recall a few phone numbers. On one of my visits, we discussed the war in the Falkland Islands. In the middle of our chat, she pointed toward a dark corner of the room and announced: "Over there on the third shelf down, near the end of the row, more toward the right side, you'll find Darwin's *Voyage of the Beagle*. In the back of the book, maybe the third to last chapter, there's his description of the Falklands." I looked it up and she was right.

Hang around Mrs. Douglas long enough, and you begin to alter your normal perception of time. You soon discover that "war" means First World War — during which she served in Europe in the American Red Cross. She remembers it as well as she remembers any recent trip downtown. Actually, she remembers it better. "Mr. Bryan" is the great William Jennings Bryan whom she met early in the century at tea parties at his Miami villa. She's just as disturbed that Mr. Bryan argued the wrong side in the Scopes monkey trial as she is that President Reagan sent arms to Iran. The "shocking decision" that riles her the most turns out to be the Dred Scott decision of the 1840s. Though Mrs. Douglas doesn't go back quite that far — and you have to remind yourself of this — her Quaker ancestors do. The family tradition of social conscience is still alive in her today. Great-great-uncle Levi Coffin, the head of the famous Underground Railroad, fought to free the slaves just as Mrs. Douglas fights to free the Kissimmee River.

I was amazed to find her angry one day at something that *Harper's* magazine had just written about Harriet Beecher Stowe! How delightful to find an intelligent companion who at any mention of John Dos Passos can say, "I met him once but I didn't pay any attention," or can debunk the "new wave" in literature and mean Hemingway, or, when asked if she's seen Halley's Comet can dismiss the subject with "Oh, yes. The last time."

A couple of years ago I asked her advice on what to see in Rome. She went on for 15 minutes about the best sights, the places to stay, the things to do and the things not to do, and only because I'd begun to know her well did I think to ask: "When was the last time you were there?" "Nineteen nineteen, I think" was her answer.

This sort of long view is part of what makes Mrs. Douglas's story interesting. What's especially satisfying about her vivid recall is that nobody gets away with anything, going back to the founders of Miami. How about Henry Flagler, the railroad man and developer of Miami, and his engineering sidekick, Mr. Sewell? They probably hoped history would forget their destruction of the Indian mounds at the mouth of the Miami River, plus their laying out the city to resemble a railroad yard. How about old Governor Jennings and his little pet real estate project in the Everglades? How about the north Florida politicians, "wool-hat boys in the red dust beyond the Suwanee," who spat in their spitoons and voted down the women's suffrage amendment? History may have forgotten to date, but Mrs. Douglas remembers.

As far back as things go with Mrs. Douglas, they also go forward — so if the past hasn't escaped her, then neither will the future. I first realized this when — at the age of 95 — she told me she'd decided to brush up on her French. There was no particular reason for her to do this, except that talking about the war made her think about the last time she took French lessons, and she realized it was time for a sesquicentennial check up. I'm told she's contacted a local French teacher.

Another thing she's determined to do is find somebody to read her George Eliot's novel, *Middlemarch*, only because she missed it the first time back in high school. Then there's her W.H. Hudson book. She's not reading it, she's writing it. At the age of 78, and already losing her eyesight, she took on this big research project that required several trips to Argentina and several other trips to England. This she's accomplished without an advance from a publisher and with no particular encouragement from editors, as a part-time effort in addition to saving the Everglades. For the last decade or so, she's had a secretary come in once a week to take dictation and read back the Hudson manuscript. This goes on year in and year out, with no end in view. To me, a 40-year-old who gets exhausted from much less, it's another perverse example of her inexhaustible enthusiasm.

Beyond her general survival alone in her house, her reading, her French lessons, her flying blind around the world, Mrs. Douglas's excess energy spills over onto the unending list of environmental causes that extends from Lake Okeechobee to the Kissimmee River, from the endangered panther to the wood stork, from the coral reefs of Key Largo to the historic houses of Coconut Grove. And she does all this as a private citizen. To help her on these projects, she's got another secretary, not to mention the battalion of supporters she's enlisted across the state. She gets them by demanding they put their time and effort where their mouths are, and otherwise trapping them with her damnably infectious enthusiasms.

You can't sit down with Mrs. Douglas for too many idle conversations without sooner or later being dragged into something that takes work. In my case, this happened as follows. I went to visit her for one of our regular chats about nothing in particular, maybe Charles Dickens. In the middle of the Dickens, I made the mistake of mentioning I'd seen an article about the plight of the Florida panther. There'd been a cover story in the local Sunday magazine.

What infuriated Mrs. Douglas was that some bureaucrats in Tallahassee had begun to support the remaining panthers by shooting them with tranquilizer rifles and putting beeper collars around their necks. They followed the beeps from airborne helicopters, so they could map the panthers' territory. To Mrs. Douglas, the collaring program was a stupid as the Dred Scott decision and as reprehensible as the failure to ratify the women's suffrage amendment, not to mention the draining of the Everglades.

She knew it was stupid and reprehensible because of her own cats. Mrs. Douglas loves cats and has a long-term understanding with a former stray named Jimmy, who sleeps on the books. "If Jimmy hates collars," she pronounced, "so would any other cat. Cats are bothered by collars, especially the roaming-around kind of cat. A collar can get stuck on a branch and strangle a cat."

I told Mrs. Douglas I agreed with that collars were terrible for cats, and that the panther collaring program was stupid. Then I made the second mistake of mentioning I was going to Tallahassee on some magazine assignment. Five minutes later, I'd been signed up as her emissary on the panther question.

Tallahassee is the state capital, and when you go there as Mrs. Douglas's emissary, you realize how seriously a private citizen can be taken. For my own article, I had the usual difficulty in setting up interviews, and had to be fit in to busy schedules. But when I called on the Game and Fresh Water Fish Commission on behalf of Mrs. Douglas, they nearly overturned the agency to accomodate me. I was assigned a full-time panther expert who gave me a half-day's worth of lectures, slides, and special presentations, all calculated to convince Mrs. Douglas that collaring was good for panthers. I wasn't completely sold, but after meeting a lot of people who knew more about panthers than I did, I had to admit that collaring didn't sound so bad.

I reported this to Mrs. Douglas, and she dismissed everything I had to say with one of her devastating sniffs. It was obvious to her I'd been taken in by meddlesome bureaucrats who suffered from the "male hunting syndrome." We dropped the subject of panthers and for all I know, she found a better emissary.

Three years later, the collaring program was a subject for general hot debate. It was reported that one panther died after the collaring people shot it with a tranquilizer gun. The animal fell from the tree in which it was perched and broke its neck. The loss of one panther is a devastating one, given the few that remain.

Mrs. Douglas isn't through with this issue, of course. She wants the government to abolish hunting in the Big Cypress region where panthers roam. As it is, hunters kill the deer and wild pig that otherwise would be food for the panther. Her newest idea is to take the panther problem to the schoolchildren. With her encouragement, the children voted the panther the official state animal. Shouldn't the children be told that the state is putting collars on the panthers, and allowing hunters to shoot the panthers' food? "They've been trying to talk me out of it, but someday up there in Tallahassee they're going to get a lot of angry letters from children," she said.

"They call me a nice old woman but I'm not," she once joked. Anyone who plans to get off easy with the "yes-ma'am-isn't-that-nice?" approach is in for a comeuppance. Mrs. Douglas seems to have a nose for the yes-ma'am approach and a great distaste for it. Once, I saw a local television commentator try to sum up a discussion of growth versus the environment with a conciliatory flourish: "With wonderful people like Mrs. Douglas here watching out for our interests, we can solve all the problems of this fast-growing state." "No we can't," corrected you-know-who. "Of course we can," continued the announcer, now visibly miffed. "No we can't," insisted Mrs. Douglas. This went on until the announcer began to lose her temper, and finally cut the wonderful Mrs. Douglas off.

Although I was taken off the panther project, eventually we got around to this book. It started out rather innocently as an article I intended to write about Mrs. Douglas. Then as I began to tape-record her views on various subjects, I also heard about her troubled childhood in New England, her brief and bizarre marriage, her unexpected reunion with a long-lost father in Miami, her career as a journalist, her second career as a short-story writer, her third career as an author of full-length books, and her fourth career as Florida's most powerful environmentalist, and I realized we'd gotten in too deep for an article. In listening to her talk, I also realized that I wasn't the best person to cover Mrs. Douglas. As usual, she was.

Then we began to let the tape recorder run and she began to talk for 200 hours or so, which didn't take much encouragement. To me, the only frustration was sharing Mrs. Douglas and our tape-recorder time with the Everglades, the ongoing W.H. Hudson book, the French lessons, her considerable correspondence, numerous nights out to dinner, flying to Washington, Tallahassee or Seattle to accept endless awards, plus her expanding list of new environmental projects, such as stopping a developer from tearing down an historic house in Coconut Grove, stopping a large-scale land project in the upper Keys, and abolishing hunting in the Big Cypress swamp.

It took two years to produce 50 cassette tapes, recorded on both sides, which I've edited down to what you have in your hands. Without tipping off too much, let me tell you what's most interesting to me. Mrs. Douglas was an environmentalist long before the word existed, though as I've said, her ferocious involvement is recent. She was a feminist long before that word existed, and an early suffragette. In one way, she's a more uncompromising feminist than the up-to-date variety who go to bed with men. Mrs. Douglas had it with going to bed with men back a few years ago — that is, 1913.

Not that she's entirely a feminist: "I think the trouble with it is that feminist women have a way of getting silly. But in general I'm for it. I'd like to hear less talk about men and women and more talk about citizens. Why should they have a Women's Hall of Fame, as I heard they wanted to put me in the other day? Why not a Citizen's Hall of Fame? We're not men and women when it comes to our social relations." As for the men, she's had numerous admirers and platonic suitors of all ages who delight in her companionship, most recently Don DeHut, the next-door neighbor; Dr. Henry Truby the master of elocution; former governor and now newly-elected U.S. Senator Bob Graham; Johnny Jones of the hunter's lobby even though she hates his hunting; and, of course, yours truly.

Mrs. Douglas was a civil rights activist before that word existed, and helped raise the alarm there was no indoor plumbing in the ghettoes of Miami. All along, she's been a writer, or as she calls it, a "writing woman." Here is a great struggle in the writer who must decide whether to explore her own psyche or to explore the world, to go inward or outward. With her troubled family, there were all the ingredients for internal absorption, but Mrs. Douglas began the novel she never finished. Soon after that, she did her best writing about the Everglades.

I think of the Everglades as her novel, the place where she found unexpected beauty, the territory she discovered alone, and through it turned all her skepticism and unrest into something useful. To have been useful, a useful citizen, has been her greatest pleasure.

Here you'll find an unusual voice, at times prudishly Victorian, at times naively neo-Freudian ("I had a nervous breakdown and went to good old Dr. Dodge. He explained the whole thing. It was a conflict between my Ego and my Superego") and at times contentiously futuristic. It's a voice of sanity, a voice of good sense, a literal voice, a voice bemused. It's a voice that laughs at its owner. It's a clear voice of that kind that only a clear-headed person could develop, with no quiver, no waver, no hint of ambiguity or uncertainly. It's a high-pitched voice, an orator's voice that rings with fundamental conviction.

It's a voice of independence, a voice of reason, and a hopeful voice for those who fear growing old. It's a voice that hasn't given up, a voice that admits no uselessness, bitterness, and sedentary despair. It's the voice of a woman who is nearly 100 years old and has no complaints. Instead of complaints, she has cats, the Everglades, friends, talking-book tapes and enough projects to occupy three government agencies. Her secretaries arrive in the afternoons, and her phone rings incessantly. If it isn't a producer from NBC News who wants to discuss birds, it's an employee of the government who wants to discuss the Kissimmee River. At night, there's the inevitable dinner date.

The rest I'd better let her tell.

John Rothchild
Miami Beach, 1987

MARJORY STONEMAN DOUGLAS

———

VOICE of the RIVER

I

Early
Years

The hardest thing is to tell the truth about oneself. One doesn't like to remember unpleasant details, but forgetting them makes one's life seem disorganized. I'm not at all sure how to go along but I'll begin at the beginning.

I was born on April 7, 1890, in Minneapolis, Minnesota. We lived in the first apartment house in Minneapolis, called Netley Corner. I see myself sitting on the stairs going down to the kitchen, being fed out of a pan of warm, creamed potatoes. It is my only memory of that time. We soon moved to an address which must no longer exist, because nobody in Minneapolis seems to know anything about it. I was taught it very carefully, in case I got lost. It was 2121 Bryant Avenue South.

It was a small, wooden, two-story house with a vacant lot alongside it. There my earliest memory is sitting on the floor in my mother and father's bedroom, against a wall that was next to an open door, being horribly startled by my cousin Forrest Rundell, a year older and a bit of a bully, who pounced and yelled at me from above.

My father was Frank Bryant Stoneman. He had lived in Minnesota ever since he was a little boy. He was six-feet-two and broad-shouldered, the kind of man who got handsomer as he got older. He had a big Roman nose in proper proportion with his high forehead. He had brown hazel eyes, the same kind I have, not remarkable as eyes but his were very keen and intelligent. He carried himself well, a Westerner in height and in overall effect.

My mother was Florence Lillian Trefethen. She never used the Florence, she was always "Lillian." She was small, not more than five feet and a half, and a true French brunette. All the French side of her family came out in her. She had marvelous black hair, brown eyes like brown velvet, a lovely nose, a beautifully cut mouth and the beautiful teeth she inherited from my grandfather.

To me, she was particularly beautiful all her life. I am going to have difficulty telling about her, I'm still deeply emotionally involved. I will try not to show that I am so upset, but I think I've never been so close to anyone as I was to my mother, as soon I shall relate.

My mother was a musician. She'd been brought up in Taunton, Massachusetts. She'd come to Minneapolis with her brother, Uncle Charlie, who was younger and needed her mature companionship. They lived in a boarding house, and that's where my mother met my father. I don't know the whole story, but he took my mother out on a sleigh ride somewhere and proposed. After appropriate ceremony and after a reasonable length of time, they were married in the front parlor of the family house back in Taunton. The wall between the front hall and the parlor was cut down so my mother could march downstairs in her wedding dress. The newlyweds returned to Minneapolis, and I was born the next April.

Uncle Charlie continued to stay with us in Minnesota. Much later, he told me this story: One night in the middle of winter, when it was about 40 degrees below zero, there was a knock at the door and my father opened it. It was a stranger, who begged to come in for a minute to get out of the cold. My father thought he would freeze to death, and insisted he stay the night. He made a bed for the man down by the furnace in the basement. This astonished Uncle Charlie, because nobody in Massachusetts would ever let a stranger into the house. It was an indication that Minnesota was a much more rugged country than New England, that people like my father had adapted to a different way of life, in which one felt responsible for strangers.

About 1894 I would guess, when I was 4 or so, my father and mother — along with a group of friends from Minneapolis — took a train down to New Orleans, and a Plant Line steamer from New Orleans to Tampa and from there to Havana. It was some sort of business trip, but they brought me along. My first memory of Florida was being held up to pick an orange off of an orange tree in the gardens of the Tampa Bay Hotel. That's the hotel built by Henry Plant which put Tampa on the map. It's there 100 years later, a college now, still complete with its turrets and towers.

We stayed at the Tampa pier on the ship *Morro Castle* before heading to Havana. In Havana, we stayed at the Hotel Pasaje. I remember the taste of the guava jelly and the torch light processions. The Cubans were going on about freedom from Spain and were allowed to have torchlight processions to express their displeasure, which the Spaniards were powerless to prevent.

On the passage to Havana, I got seasick and was put up in stateroom. I woke up from being seasick — you feel lovely and relaxed and everything's wonderful. I could hear my father and mother talking on deck outside the open door, the room was filled with marvelous light, this wonderful white tropic light, I saw it and was thrilled by it. I never forgot the quality of the tropic light as if I had been looking for it all the years of gray Northern light; as I came back many years later I recognized it as something I had loved and missed and longed for all my life, one of the things that made me so happy about being in Florida.

MY MOTHER'S SIDE

My maternal ancestors were the Trefethens of Cornwall. I learned this little verse from my grandfather, Daniel Augustus Trefethen: "By the Tre, Tref, and Pen, you can tell all Cornish men." Of course, that includes not only Trefethens or Trevathens as they sometimes spelled it, but also Trelanics and Trelawneys and people whose names begin with Pen and all that.

My grandfather had the wonderful Cornish blue eye that I've seen many times in Cornwall itself. The blue eye was inherited by my mother's youngest sister and by my Uncle Charlie, who had a particularly charming version. Grandfather, I'm sure, was a typical Trefethen. He was short — they were all small people, I think — and he took such long steps that when he came walking down a street he looked as if he were bobbing up and down. Behind that walk was the Cornish tradition of courage, endurance, and the kind of quiet that carries on empires.

He was a hardworking man with a great heart and with such affection for his children and his grandchildren, such wonderful fatherliness about him that I am only too happy I was later brought up with him, under his roof.

The earliest Trefethens settled around Portsmouth and up the coast of Maine. The name was hardly known inland. They were seagoing people and never forgot their heritage. There were also Trefethens who served under Benedict Arnold when he was still a great general in the campaign in Canada, long before he became our great traitor.

Every sea in the world was known to the Trefethens. My great-great-grandfather sailed on ships from Maine around the Horn to China and back to Maine again a year or two later. My great-grandfather William Trefethen sailed the great circle, following the Gulf Stream to Europe, down the coast of France and Portugal and across on the Equatorial current, up from the West Indies back to the coast of Maine. Great-grandfather William Trefethen spoke to my grandfather when grandfather was a very young man about the fact there was hardly money left in the sea any more. He asked grandfather what he would like to do, and — typical Cornishman as he was — he said he'd like to go into metals. The only occupation Cornish men knew besides sailing was mining tin.

My grandfather was apprenticed to some people named Bowen in Attleboro, Massachusetts, taken into their family, and taught the brass business. When he came out of his apprenticeship, he went to the train station planning to go to Providence, Rhode Island. For some reason he got off the train in Taunton, Mass. to look around and to take a walk. He never got back on.

He walked down the street toward the middle of town where a beautiful green was surrounded by elm trees. On the way, he saw a brass foundry and stopped in. The brass foundry was owned by a man named Pierre Parady who offered him a job. Pierre Parady also had a younger sister, Florence. That's the beginning of my French side.

They'd spelled it "Paradis" back in France, but in New England it was spelled with a y at the end. The Paradys were Norman French. They were all Bonapartists who thought that Napoleon was the greatest man in the world. After the Battle of Waterloo when Napoleon was sent into exile, the French Bonapartists had a very hard time and many of them left, including the Paradys. They fled to Canada where my grandmother Florence was born. After that, they moved to Vermont.

They all spoke French — Norman French rather than Canadian French — which was always a point of pride with my grandmother. She once told me they originally came from a little town on the Seine not far from Rouen but she couldn't remember the name of it. I've since visited a place called Portmort right on the river about seven miles from Rouen and imagined that might be it.

Some friends of mine have an old farm there — quite a lot of land right on the river. There's a tiny little up-and-down house — I've always thought that could easily have been the kind of house where my grandmother's people came from. Not the best house in the village, but, oh maybe the second best or the third best where maybe a younger son or somebody . . . I really don't know. I wish grandmother could have remembered it.

Nevertheless, Florence was completely French and I've always rejoiced in that. To the day of her death, she spoke with something of a French accent. I've always valued the fact that on both sides of the family I was English and French — and I delighted especially in the French part.

Florence Parady was sent from Vermont down to Taunton to live with her brother because her family wanted to get her away from a man with whom she'd fallen in love. She must have been 16 or 17 at the time. She was apprenticed to some elderly ladies who had a millinery shop in Taunton and she promptly got involved with another man. It was Daniel Augustus Trefethen, my grandfather-to-be, who was then 19. I think she never forgave him for not being the tall handsome young man she'd originally loved, but she married him nonetheless.

My grandfather had fallen desperately in love with Florence himself. They got married a little before the Civil War. It was good timing, because when Pierre died, grandfather was able to take over the brass foundry.

Grandfather was never wealthy. He'd done well in the Civil War, making trench mortars for General Burnside, but after that the metals business moved West and grandfather refused to follow. He had to work very hard to keep up a faltering trade. The family was brought up to be thrifty.

At least they'd saved enough money to buy the house at 14 Harrison Street in Taunton, the family house for three generations to follow. It was a big house with connecting woodsheds and storerooms over wood-sheds, a wonderful place for children who could get off by themselves and lead their own lives, yet everybody knew where they were and that they were all right. How I came to be brought up there, I will tell about later.

My mother's oldest sister, Alice, was born about 1857 and my mother Lillian was born in 1859. My Aunt Fanny was born later and my Uncle Charlie was younger than she. The youngest was little Uncle Walter, who died at the age of seven in the great diphtheria epidemic that ravaged the entire country. This was my grandmother's greatest sorrow.

There was no public high school in Taunton when Aunt Alice was a teenager. She was sent to the Bristol Academy, sort of a private school. Soon after that, my grandfather, who was an alderman, served on the board that voted to build a public high school. I later attended this school, and was always proud of the fact that my grandfather's name was on the plaque honoring the founders.

My mother could have gone to high school but didn't because she was having trouble with one of her eyes. She had an operation, but it wasn't very successful. She was so musical that she wasn't interested in studying anything but music, anyway. At the age of seven, she had begun to play a little violin and was sent to Boston to study under a famous German musician, Julius Eichberg.

She had what they call perfect pitch: She could hear a note and name it. She played anything with strings. In the house, there were a guitar and two banjos and a mandolin and my mother played all of these naturally, instinctively. She could tune a series of glasses and play them or she could find sticks of different lengths to play tunes on. I'm not sure she didn't get some of that from grandfather, who had a beautiful speaking voice to go along with his Cornish blue eye and the most perfect set of teeth I've ever seen on a mortal individual. When he was 90, it was the first time he had to have a little filling. He also had a beautiful singing voice — but didn't sing very much.

They were all musical. My Aunt Fanny — who really was Fanny, not Frances — could play the piano, guitar, the banjo and the mandolin as well. My mother tried to get Uncle Charlie to play the cornet, but he had trouble with asthma, so he couldn't do it. Instead, he made a zither and he played that.

It was Uncle Charlie's asthma that indirectly brought my mother together with my father out West. Uncle Charlie was brilliant in school. My grandfather sent him to MIT, but he never finished because of his health. I think some of the asthma business was a reaction to my grandmother, because she was so obviously more interested in her daughters than in her son. Anyway, as a result of the asthma, the family doctor advised Uncle Charlie to move to a different climate, and he got a teaching job at the University of Minnesota. My mother, who was older and more sophisticated, was sent out there with him, which is when she met my father, Frank Bryant Stoneman.

MY FATHER'S SIDE

On my father's side were the Stonemans and the Whites. Most of the Whites came from the south of England. The Stonemans might have come either from Devon or from the Thames valley, where there are lots of Stonemans. But I suspect they came from Devon for the completely inadequate reason that somewhere in the Stoneman family there was a woman named Tamar. Tamar River, I'm told, is the easternmost boundary of Devon.

James Stoneman had a son, Joshua, who wanted to come to America. His father didn't want him to, so Joshua ran away to the nearest seaport which must have been Bristol. He sold his indenture to a ship captain for the passage. The ship captain sold the indenture to a doctor in Philadelphia who took Joshua home. Joshua was both a coachman and a medical assistant, and later became a doctor as well. Somehow, he made it to the southern part of Virginia, because my grandfather Mark Davis Stoneman was born there, in Galax. He married Aletha White, my grandmother on my father's side.

When the Whites came to this country I have no idea, but they settled in Guilford County, North Carolina, right across the state line from Galax. The Whites were all Quakers, many with Biblical names like Levi and Mordechi. There was some French on this side also. My grandmother's mother was Lovica Bondurant, which is Huguenot.

Presumably the Whites left England at the time when other Quakers left, either by force or by their own inclination to seek a country where they could believe what they pleased. Of all the religious people that sought refuge in America the Quakers are the most independent and the most pigheaded. I reflect my Quaker ancestry because I feel both independent and pigheaded as well. You know, pigheaded covers a multitude of virtues — as well as sins.

The Whites and the Stonemans didn't stay in Virginia and North Carolina for long. Soon they crossed the Ohio River into states where there were no slaves. Quakers went West because they didn't want to bring up children in slave-holding states. Indiana was settled by roving bands of Quakers who stuck together, as is the custom among pioneers.

My father was born in a Quaker colony in Spiceland, Indiana, east of Indianapolis, during the time my grandfather Mark Davis Stoneman served as a surgeon for the Northern forces in the Civil War. My grandfather was the kind of all-around frontier doctor typical of those days. There is some legend about his having taken formal medical training, but nobody is sure. Even though he was a Quaker he was allowed to take part in this war because it was for the emancipation of the slaves.

He was wounded at the battle of Shiloh, then recovered and was sent out with some troops to Ft. Snelling, in Minnesota, to quell an expected Indian uprising that never happened. Grandfather liked Minnesota very much. As soon as he got out of the army he went back to Indiana, collected my grandmother and the children, and took them to Minnesota with him. He became one of the pioneer doctors of Minneapolis. The rest of the Whites and Stonemans followed.

These were a courageous and quick-thinking people. They read books constantly, remembered what they read, and made up their own minds concerning it. The most famous person from this side of the family, and a great inspiration to me as a free thinker and an activist, was Levi Coffin. My great-great-aunt Katie White was married to Levi, which, I'm proud to say, makes him my great-great-uncle. Uncle Levi was the president of the Underground Railroad.

The Coffins were Quakers from Nantucket, who'd also migrated to Indiana. Uncle Levi ended up living in Indiana, in a town called Newport. He was an abolitionist, and said God didn't approve of slavery. Long before the Civil War, he'd made many trips through the South. He went everywhere in his Quaker clothes and hat, telling people that if any escaped slaves got to his house in Newport, they'd be taken in and cared for, and sent north to Canada where they could be free.

The rumor of their offer spread across the land. There was a law against inciting slaves to escape, but nobody could arrest the Quakers for breaking it. They were too smart for that. Technically, they never advocated escape, but merely informed the slaves of the good things that would happen if they did escape. The famous story of Eliza crossing the ice, told by Harriet Beecher Stowe in that badly written but enormously important book, *Uncle Tom's Cabin*, is true. Recently, it's been fashionable to doubt this, but I know that the doubters are wrong. The reason I know is that my great-great-aunt Katie was a friend of Harriet Beecher Stowe's and Aunt Katie told her the Eliza story in the first place. After Eliza crossed the ice with her baby, jumping desperately from one floe to the other, she was taken to Uncle Levi and Aunt Katie's place in Indiana.

Aunt Katie and Uncle Levi had a nice, warm room, kind of half underground, where Aunt Katie nursed Eliza's sick baby. They helped many other slaves as well. A few were brought upstream by William Beard, father of historian Charles Beard. Beard was a Quaker abolitionist as well. He and Uncle Levi once disguised some male slaves as

veiled women and took them to Chatham in Canada where they were
freed. Some years later, the two tall Quakers in funny clothes and hats
returned to Chatham. As they walked the streets, the doors opened and
people they'd rescued poured out to thank them. It was a wonderful
thing.

I'm as proud of this ancestry as I am of my French side. There's an
unending supply of great stories about Uncle Levi. He went through the
Southern states and bought free-labor cotton — cotton that was grown
where no slaves worked. He set up a free labor gin in Louisville, Ken-
tucky, then found free labor boats to take the free cotton up the river.
The free cotton finally was sent to England, where the weavers were in
sympathy with the abolitionist movement. In fact, they refused to weave
any cotton that had been picked by slaves. Uncle Levi's cotton was the
only cotton the weavers of England had during all the Civil War.

After the shocking Dred Scott decision of Chief Justice Roger B.
Taney, posses of Southerners could ride through Northern states to
recapture their slaves. Once Uncle Levi was standing by his house when
a slave, running from a posse, raced past his gate. Uncle Levi motioned
him in, and Aunt Katie hid the man down in the secret room. The posse
arrived and its spokesman said: "Mr. Coffin, have you seen an escaped
slave going by the gate?" Uncle Levi answered, "No escaped slave has
passed by this gate, but if thee will hurry down to the Louisville-and-
Northern station thee will get there before the train pulls out." The
men left.

Later, Aunt Katie scolded Uncle Levi for lying about how no slaves
had passed the gate. "I did not tell a lie," said Levi. "No escaped slave
passed this gate. He came *in* this gate. I presume you have him in the
house."

Another time, a judge of the local court was told that Uncle Levi was
sheltering escaped slaves and sent the sheriff to summon him. Levi went
to court, and the sheriff said: "Mr. Coffin, you have to take your hat off."
Levi said, "Friend, I do not take it off for anyone but God. If thee wants
it off thee will have to take it." The sheriff took Levi's hat off. Then, the
judge said, "I will not require you to take an oath because I know you
always speak the truth, but I understand you had certain escaped slaves
at your house last night."

"Certain people of color said they were escaped slaves," Uncle Levi
answered, "but in Indiana, the word of a slave is not taken as evidence.

I do not know whether they were escaped slaves or not. All I can tell you is they are not there now."

The judge had to let him go. At the door, the sheriff tried to give him back his hat. Uncle Levi replied, "Friend, thee has taken my hat and thee can have it."

There is a book, *Reminiscences of Levi Coffin*, that should be reprinted. People have forgotten what the Civil War was about. They should never forget. Slavery was a great curse on American history.

My grandfather Mark Davis Stoneman had several children. My father was the second, and evidently the most responsible. After he was born there was Aunt Katie (not to be confused with Levi Coffin's wife), Aunt Stella, and then Edward, Uncle Ned. Uncle Ned became a doctor and had a big influence on my life at a crucial point later.

After a few years in Minneapolis, Mark Stoneman felt the country was getting too filled with people and thought he'd like to go to California, which had opened up in 1848. But he died before he could get there, at the age of 53. Many frontier doctors died young. They never got much sleep, and exhausted themselves from having to do so much.

My father was a student at the University of Minnesota when his father died. Before that my father had gone to Carleton College, in the same class as Thorstein Veblen. Veblen was just a rawboned Scandanavian boy in those days, my father a rawboned Quaker boy. Neither liked Carleton College, because it was very religious, and people they met on the street said, "Have you found Jesus?" which embarrassed both of them for different reasons. Veblen continued at Carleton, my father transferred to the University of Minnesota, but soon had to leave to support the family.

His not finishing college always gave him an inferiority complex, that sense of feeling inadequate because he didn't have a degree. That was stupid, and later I scolded him about it, in the quiet Quaker manner. He was always a scholar at heart and in mind, a very self-educated man.

To make a living, he started teaching school in the Irish district of Minneapolis. He taught school in the daytime and in the evening he and the rest of the family cut cabbage to make sauerkraut. Eventually, he went off to Montana, where he thought he'd make his fortune. He and another man started the first grocery store in Billings.

By the age of 18, my father had converted to Episcopalianism. I think he felt the Quaker meetings were rather barren and dry and he rejoiced in the beautiful language of the Episcopal service. He was also a Mason. I don't know when he became a Mason, but it meant a great deal to him. He was instrumental in founding the first Masonic lodge in Billings.

The customers at the Billings grocery store were mostly Indians, who would come in and put down a silver dollar for a dollar's worth of sugar. Father learned to wrap the sugar in a flat piece of paper. I always wondered how he did it, and once he told me, "You kind of make a cornucopia of it and put the right amount of sugar in it and kind of fold it up." The Indians would put down another silver dollar and he would fold up another five pounds of sugar. Indians got good service from my father and his partner.

The two of them lived at the back of the store. At night father played checkers with a retired artillery officer who'd been all through the West, named Beanbelly Brown. My father liked to tell me about Beanbelly Brown. Apparently, Beanbelly always snookered my father — or whatever you do to win in checkers — and every time he won he said: "Well, Stoneman, I admire your courage but damn your judgment." I've always remembered this saying as very wise. To admire people's courage but to damn their judgment is to understand a great deal. That little bit of advice is about all my father took with him when he left Billings. He certainly hadn't made his fortune. He came back to Minneapolis to try again.

That's when father and his brother-in-law Forrest Rundell (Aunt Katie's husband) went into some sort of building and loan business. It was also about the time I was born. At first, everything went fine in this business — but not for long.

PROVIDENCE

My general impression is that Forrest Rundell was a promoter type, and he and my father either failed or were about to fail, and their company was going into bankruptcy. It's possible that they got caught up in the panic of 1893, which devastated that part of the West. Father was always very sensitive on this subject and never liked to talk about it.

At any rate, we moved to Providence, Rhode Island, when I was three. My father got some kind of job selling oil. I don't know what kind of oil it was or where he sold it — this was long before the days of gasoline. I'm sure he wasn't very good at selling oil, because my father wasn't interested in that kind of thing at all. He'd become a thoughtful and scholarly man.

We lived on East Manning Street in a very nice duplex. We had an upstairs and downstairs half, the other half occupied by people named Barney. I remember the Barney twins vaguely. When we were taking baths in the our back-to-back bathrooms, we could shout and dimly hear each other's voices.

The house had a large entrance hall and a small reception room to the right of the stairs going up. The door on the left led into a dining room with kitchen and butler's pantry behind that. Upstairs at the top of the landing was a sitting room. There were two large bedrooms, one bath, and a third little bedroom off the master bedroom that was mine. It had a white brass enamel bed, not much bigger than a cot, which I used until I got too big for it.

In the front of the upstairs was the living room with furniture that became so familiar, especially my father's big overstuffed chair, his half desk and half bookcase. Outside was a back yard that didn't amount to much. There was a side garden full of marigolds, but I never liked them on account of that queer, acrid smell.

My grandmother from Taunton let us have Mary McCabe who'd been with her for years and was as good as a member of the family. Mary McCabe came to Providence and lived upstairs in the guest bedroom, and slept in the best brass bed in splendor. Originally, she was from Dublin. She had a lovely soft Irish talking voice with a Dublin accent, and a plaintive Irish singing voice. A little drop cake frosted with chocolate was one of her kitchen specialities.

My mother's piano, a Steinway upright, stood in the reception room downstairs. It was used by the accompanist when my mother played the violin in her impromptu concerts. The chairs would be set in a big square in the front hall. Sometimes when I was being put to bed I could hear the music and the people's voices. My mother always began the concerts by saying that her little girl was upstairs and going to sleep. Then she played the Brahms lullaby.

Upstairs in the sitting room, father read to me, mostly from Hiawatha. When he came to Hiawatha building the canoe and saying to the birch tree, "Give me of your bark, oh birch tree," and the birch tree sighing and bending over to give up its bark, he was astonished by the fact that I burst into loud sobs. I couldn't make him understand I was sorry for the birch tree, because why should the birch tree have to give up his bark just because Hiawatha wanted to build a canoe? I couldn't stand it. I cried and I guess father skipped the canoe part after that.

I was given my very first book, which was *Alice in Wonderland*. It was a beautiful grey and silver edition with illustrations by Tenniel and I kept it until recent years when some fiend in human form must have borrowed it and not brought it back. Of course, I still have an annotated Alice in the house, because you couldn't do without Alice in the house. Actually, I was a little young for *Alice in Wonderland* when it first was read out loud to me, and I couldn't quite accept the idea of the rabbit with a waistcoat and a watch. I was a logical child and I'd never seen a rabbit like that, so I remained skeptical about the whole business.

By then I must have been five years old, already going to kindergarten. I was an only child. With the kind of attention that my father gave me, an only child can make quite a good deal of progress as a thoughtful individual. The incident that I remember most clearly was one which astonished my father and looking back I can see how it would. It was my first really independent thought.

I stood at the front window of that upstairs sitting room one evening. I was in my nightgown and I expected to be put to bed any minute. Father was in the big chair behind me and I was looking out the window, out over a lot of roofs and chimneys shining with frost in the moonlight.

We didn't have a fireplace, but as I stood there — this must have been after Christmas — I thought about Santa Claus having to climb down all those chimneys with a pack on his back and it suddenly occurred to me, well he couldn't possibly do it, that's all, he couldn't get through.

Suddenly, I turned to my father and said, "There isn't any Santa Claus, is there?" My father dropped his book and in very concentrated attention, I think he said something like, "Do you think there isn't any Santa Claus?" and I think I said something like, "No, there can't be any Santa Claus." To my father's eternal credit, he didn't deny it. He said, "You're right, probably there isn't any Santa Claus." He made no bones about it and I was always glad that he treated me in the Quaker fashion.

I took a little spill in Providence, one of those mishaps that grown-ups dismiss but children remember and think about the rest of their lives. I was playing on the sidewalk outside the house, stumbled, fell down, and hit my head on one of those metal manhole covers. I must have been stunned for a minute, but then I got up, ran back to the house and told my mother I'd cracked my head. She said, "Oh, you haven't cracked your head, there's no blood or anything, you're all right."

The funny thing is, I did crack my head. I've grown up being able to feel a little indentation in my skull between my eyebrows that goes up for an inch or two. I've called my various doctors' attention to it and they've said it was an injury of some sort. I wondered if it didn't affect the bone in my nose, which grew a little crooked so I have only one nostril that I breathe through easily. The left-hand nostril is not very open.

While I'm on the subject of my face, I ought to mention my eyes. I was born with the left eye crossed. My mother had trouble with her eye and had an unsuccessful operation. She always wore glasses and her eye would turn a little if she didn't. I was born with the same defect, and my mother was determined I would never have an operation because hers hadn't worked. They put glasses on me at the age of three. They were little gold rims. My parents would set them on my nose, I'd throw them on the floor, and they'd pick them up again. The process went on and on. One thing parents never get enough credit for is keeping track of the glasses.

Gold-rimmed glasses were the crowning unattractive feature on an unattractive child in general. When I was born — I'm ashamed to say although I didn't have much to do with it — I weighed 12 pounds. I was the most disgusting looking baby you could possibly imagine, a huge 12-pound thing with this great square head. My poor little mother was only five feet one inch, and why I didn't kill her being born I really don't know.

From then on, I was a fat little child and a fat little girl because in those days it was considered healthy to have fat children and I was plied with the best of butter, cream, pancakes, and everything fattening there was. To top it off, I had stringy, kind of mouse-colored hair.

My father's business was again unsuccessful and we had to move from East Manning Street somewhere on the outskirts of Providence. My grandmother Aletha Stoneman, plus Aunt Katie and her husband Forrest Rundell, lived across the street. There was a little lake nearby. I saw sunlight on the waves of the lake and was excited and exhilarated by the brightness and the air, the sunshine and the water.

It was in this second house in Providence that my mother and I formed a habit of walking out together in the early evening when it was a nice day. We'd walk around the block, or we'd walk around two blocks, always arm in arm or holding hands and looking at people's windows beginning to light up and talking about the people in the houses.

These walks were an important part of my closeness to my mother, as we seemed to have developed the same way of looking at things. Mother liked to sit by a window and look out and I always liked to sit by a window and look out. At East Manning Street, I would sit in my mother's lap in the chair in the bedroom and she would hold me and we would look out at the stars. Sometimes, we'd say the Lord's Prayer together. My mother was a good Episcopalian like my father, and she taught me the important prayers, and also the Ten Commandments and the Creed, which I repeated without understanding much about them. She was careful to see that I learned things by heart, just as my father was careful to see I had an inquisitive and skeptical background.

It was during this time in Providence that the terrible things that soon would happen to my mother began, in a very minor way, to reveal themselves. I don't think anybody in the family either recognized or understood the strain she had endured for a long time. In those days, the 1890s, there was a good deal of difference between the temperaments of New England, the East, and the West, of which Minnesota was a part. The Western people, my father's family, were in some ways more hardy, or otherwise they wouldn't have gone. Besides, they were Quakers and that made them pretty tough anyway. They adjusted easily to discomforts or handicaps and tried to do something about them, whereas in New England — or at least southeastern Massachusetts where my mother was brought up — the way of life was pretty well settled. Bad things didn't happen so much and consequently the people were more upset when they did.

So my father's family had no conception of the devastating effect all his business troubles, bankruptcy or whatever, had had on my mother. Living on the edge, or whatever it was, was completely alien to her idea of how a family should live. Also, I have to say that my father's mother, my grandmother Aletha, was a most disagreeable woman to have living across the street. She was sarcastic and rude to children. Even when I was very young I had no feeling of love for her. I don't remember that she ever put a hand on me in affection.

That she particularly disliked my mother and my mother particularly disliked her was an additional strain on my mother's delicate nervous system. All this contributed to the strange breakdown that I was the first to notice.

There was a side porch on the house extending onto a large lawn, where I enjoyed playing on the back steps. One day, I heard loud voices, looked up from where I was sitting, and saw my cousin, Forrest Rundell — who was about as tall as my mother — trying to hit her. She'd said something sarcastic about my grandmother, of whom my cousin was very fond, and he couldn't stand it. My mother was holding him off. She had beautiful arms and hands but they were the strong arms and hands of a violinist.

While the two of them struggled on the porch, my mother turned her head aside and laughed in an eerie, strained way It was the first time I'd heard such a laugh. It frightened me so much that I can still hear it today.

Sometime later, I woke up suddenly in the middle of the night in my own small bed, which in that house was in the corner of my parent's bedroom. My mother was crying over me, and my poor father was trying to reason with her to come back and go to sleep. My mother was accusing him of trying to kidnap me. He finally managed to quiet her and I went back to sleep and tried to forget all about it.

TAUNTON

It must have been late summer when I was playing on the porch steps again and my mother appeared with a suitcase. She put my hat and jacket on me and announced: "We're going to Taunton." We must have taken the train from Providence, although I don't remember that part. I only remember walking in the early dusk down Harrison Street to the house of my mother's parents, my grandparents in Taunton. We rang the bell because the door was always locked at that time of day and my Aunt Fanny came to answer it. She didn't seem surprised at all to see us. She said hello and stepped back, and we went into the hall, and the door was closed behind us.

They'd finished their supper, and we were taken at once upstairs to the second floor of the house. It had a sitting room on the southeast corner, a big sunny airy room we called the sewing room, because grandmother sewed there in the daytime. My aunt brought up a tray of supper and everybody was sitting in absolute silence. As I was about to begin to eat, I burst into loud sobs. I must have felt the sudden dislocation and sensed the deeper meaning that I couldn't intellectually understand. I was five years old at the time.

Finally, I was calmed down and put to bed. I don't know how long it was after that in days, but I remember waking up in bed with my mother. It was the big double bed in the room that was called the front chamber, a charming room with black walnut furniture but not overdone: the bed with its high headboard and footboard, a bureau with beautiful wooden scrollwork around the mirror, a marbletop table, and a marbletop side commode with a water pitcher and bowl (since the house had bathrooms, the pitcher and bowl no longer used). It was in the middle of the night, my mother was laughing and talking in a loud voice over on her side of the bed and I was terrified. I woke up to realize that my grandfather was sitting beside the bed, fully dressed even to his watch chain and he had me in his arms. I was in bed but he had his arms around me and I was pressed up against his wonderful heart.

My grandmother and aunt were sort of crouched outside the door because when they'd tried to come in my mother screamed at them and they hadn't dared to come in again. It was the beginning of what was called my mother's "nervous breakdown." Many times I heard them say it had something to do with a flaw in the nervous systems of my grand-father's family. There was somebody, maybe a brother of his, who had gone insane several times.

For a while, they had a trained nurse to look after my mother. Then I think she was considered to be in a very bad way and was taken for a short while to the Butler's Sanitarium in Providence. I don't know how long it was, but when she came back she was outwardly a different woman. She was subdued and woozy, and had very little initiative left. She'd developed an antipathy toward her mother, and she was having serious quarrels with Aunt Fanny, who was high-strung herself.

There was a terrible fight about the family Bible. My mother decided to put it on the parlor table — well, what difference could that make? My aunt couldn't stand it and she'd take the Bible and put it away someplace else. Then my mother would bring it back again, and there'd be bickering all over the place. I was so impatient with all the bickering that I felt like an outsider.

In the great family crisis, I was left to myself, naturally ignored. I was well taken care of, but I mooned around alone — a bystander to an excited, difficult time. My mother and I were still so close, and our closeness seemed to make up for everything.

My mother didn't seem to care that she and my father were separated. Part of her mental condition was her acceptance of the present. My grandmother and my aunt blamed my father for my mother's insanity, which of course was impossible. My poor father blamed for that, and we had left him in Providence! To add insult to injury, my grandfather and Uncle Charlie went right back there and loaded up a horse and wagon with all the furniture and carpets, because my mother had spent $1,000 of her own money on them. The carpets were later sold. I once went into the house of a friend in Taunton and was startled to see the familiar things that I had known so long.

After my mother's breakdown, I had some side effects of my own — from the shock of the illness, from leaving my father, and from complete-ly changing the whole picture of my life. There were the bad dreams from which often I woke myself, screaming. These bad dreams carried on for a good many years. Perhaps I may have waked myself partially but not entirely, because I remember walking around in a kind of haze in the darkness of the bedroom, still light enough in the moonlight to see myself in the long pier glass, a child in a nightgown walking around with her arms over her head and her hands kind of flapping. It was a half-waking, half-sleeping state of horror. It seemed as if there were some enormous thing by my left ear, some enormous thing that was going to explode with a loud noise at any minute.

Once I had one of those dreams, and my grandmother came into the room and took me out. She sat me in her lap, by the window, and talked to me soothingly and showed me the stars. She talked about how beautiful the stars were and how far away, and slowly the horror disappeared until I was sleepy and grandmother got me back to bed.

My grandparents' house on Harrison Street was, for the rest of my childhood, my home. I'll describe it as best I can. It was three stories — a big, high house with a lot of land, more than 100 feet frontage on the street. It had a vegetable garden and a lawn on one side and an enormous apple tree, four pear trees and a great big cherry tree on the other. In the Trefethen tradition, grandfather always had a green thumb.

The house was well-appointed in the early Victorian style. We had a table in the parlor made of onyx and black enamel — a perfectly dreadful thing but very stylish at the time. The parlor door that had been cut out for my parents' wedding was now closed off with heavy curtains, because it was not considered economical to heat the space. There was a big steam furnace down below. The sewing room was always hot from the sun coming in.

Above the front hall was a little bedroom we called the "writing room," even though nobody ever wrote in it. The bookcase was up there, filled with a wide collection of books, a set of Dickens that I still have, an old set of *Encyclopedia Brittanica*, all kinds of histories, like the history of the Johnstown flood and the Chicago fire, the complete Shakespeare in very tiny print in one big calf-bound volume that later I read and reread. There was also a collection of Byron's poems and a row of paperback novels.

My grandfather was proud of the fact we had the first inside bathroom on the street. It was quite luxurious for that day. Before that they'd used the two-holer in the back of the house where the woodsheds were connected.

An alley led to two little backhouses that were perfect for hide and seek. Up a little staircase was the storeroom for summer furniture, which also contained a huge tub — the original bathtub for the family. There was a pump to draw the water. Grandmother said I could do anything I wanted up there except burn the place down.

On the third floor of the house was a tremendous attic with several rooms that were used for bedrooms. The back bedroom had blue and white paper with rosebuds on it and overlooked the garden. That's where my grandmother and grandfather slept. The room next to that was Mary McCabe's — of course she'd been returned to Taunton with the furniture. The front bedroom had extra beds and cribs that children had outgrown, and was usually unoccupied. It was another place I could get away from grown-ups. Being an only child, I often felt there were too many grown-ups around for just me.

My Early Education

The mind of a child is like a dried-out sponge, ready to absorb every kind of substance there is around. That first fall in Taunton, when I was six, my grandmother enrolled me in the Barnam Street Elementary. It was quite a long walk for me. Miss Florence Francis was my teacher. Being in school was wonderful in itself, and doubly wonderful since it got me away from the strains of the house.

This was 1896, and by then the Massachusetts public school system was extremely good. There wasn't much that literate women could do except to teach school, and maybe that accounted for the wonderful teaching we had. I skipped the second grade for some reason and went right into third — even though I was bad at arithmetic. I didn't understand fractions. The teacher tried to demonstrate fractions by cutting up an apple. I don't know whether this had anything to do with my hating apples, but it may have. I've always hated apples as well as fractions, and a raw apple I simply cannot stand.

Somewhere back in the first grade I suddenly began to read. I don't remember the process, except that I was already reading in the back of the book while the rest of the class was poking along in the front. One of the stories was about two little girls and their dolls. The first little girl spent her money on a silk dress for the doll and didn't bother about the underwear or the practical winter clothes. The second little girl prepared her doll for cold weather with cotton pants, a cotton dress, and a flannel petticoat. This was supposed to show that the second little girl was much more sensible than the one who'd bought the silk dress.

I didn't think it was sensible. I didn't believe a doll needed a flannel petticoat because it didn't feel cold. I didn't believe a doll was a real person, and I thought the little girl who'd spent her money on the silk dress had more fun with her doll by making it prettier.

I suppose the dislocation of my life, being the child of a broken family, made me something of a skeptic and a dissenter. To this day, I'm still a skeptic and a dissenter, and don't believe everything people tell me. In 1896, I particularly didn't believe things that were said in bitterness about my father.

At home I played with dolls very little. There was only one I liked — a brunette because my mother was. Her name was Jeanne and her eyes opened and shut. One time, her eyes fell out and her hair came off in a kind of little scalp. I put the eyes back, stuffed the head with something called curled hair, used to stuff cushions, and glued the hair back on. Then I discovered I'd put in the eyes upside down so the lids showed at the bottom and they didn't work anymore. I was too lazy to change it and I didn't care.

My grandmother gave me another doll which she'd dressed up with embroidered skirts and so on, but I was lukewarm towards this doll. It had no particular character, but my little old Jeanne did, she was more like a companion really, sitting around while I was reading. Doll playing was never as important as reading. I could get up in the storeroom or in the attic, when most of the family was in the sitting room, and I could always read.

On my own, I'd discovered magazines. There was one called *St. Nicholas* magazine organized as a club. You'd get into the St. Nicholas League if the magazine printed your work. Supposedly Edna St. Vincent Millay had belonged to it, which inspired all us budding Millays to write poems and short little essays. I tried these things and was turned down, but I finally got in by inventing a puzzle, which I called "Double the Headings and Curtailings." I was awarded with the St. Nicholas gold medal. It was a great moment in my life when I got into the league.

When I was 8 or 9, I was expected to learn to play the piano. I was the only person in the family who wasn't musical, which I took completely from my father's long line of English and Quaker ancestors. They didn't know anything about music and had no musical memory. I'm that way myself. I'll hear something and have a vague idea I've heard it before, and it turns out to be the Ninth Symphony or something that's been played to me a million times.

I made the most awful sounds and mistakes on the piano and I just hated it. When I hit the wrong note everybody from attic to cellar would yell: "That's not sharp, that's flat!" How did they know? If only I could have a book and get lost in it until I was ready for school again. That's all I wanted.

It got to be quite a thing about my piano. One day my grandmother asked me if I'd practiced and I said, "No, grandmother, I haven't," and she went off in one of her French bad tempers and said, "When will the time ever come when you will practice without my telling you to?" I said, "Well, grandmother, I've never had the opportunity," and she flared up at that and shot back, "I will never speak to you about this for as long as I live." That was great because she didn't and I didn't, and I never practiced again.

Her sole interest in my learning the piano was merely that she wanted all her girls to be able to make their own living. In those days a woman either taught school or taught music — that was about it. Later, I was sent off to voice training. Of course I took to that like a duck to water and I am still elocutionizing at a great rate. I've certainly made a lot of speeches and it comes to me very easily. I never worried about an audience — I could talk to 500 people as well as to two people even as a child.

I had every sort of lesson even though the family fortunes were diminishing, and they had to rake and scrape very hard to give me these advantages. I didn't lack for anything that was pleasant and useful for a child to have. I got my first bicycle when I was about eight years old. Somebody called me to come outside, and I went down the back steps and out the big covered way into the big curved driveway. A man came down from the street with this little red bicycle, and I saw it and thought it was the most beautiful thing I'd ever seen. I asked somebody whose it was, and grandfather said, "Well, it's your bicycle," and that was just wonderful.

My grandmother felt I should join a gymnasium class, and she made me a gymnasium suit with little bloomers and a cute little sash. Once, she insisted I join a sketch club. Later, I went to dancing school on Friday afternoons. After the Barnam Elementary, I went to Cohannet Grammar School. Cohannet was named for a local Indian tribe. The school was right next to St. Thomas Episcopal Church where my grandmother and mother and aunt were members, and where I was taken also. It was an easy walk from where I lived.

There were large classes in those days, from 40 to 50 in a room. That is supposed to be very bad, but I think the education was still very good. The women who taught seemed to be perfectly capable of reaching that many children.

In sixth grade, I had Miss Dartt. She came from Vermont and had graduated from Wellesley. For some reason, she took a special interest in me. She came to call on my mother and always insisted I was going to Wellesley, which I did, eventually. It wasn't only her influence that got me there, but I heard about it early through her. The drawing teacher was Miss Ora Strange, another friend of the family. She'd wander from school to school with little pans of paints and watercolors, giving everybody a chance to be an artist. Dear Mr. Howse did the same with music. Any child could grow up finding something that he or she could do.

In school I was the one whom the teacher could never be sure of. Many times I didn't know the answer to something, but other times because of my reading, I would be the only one who knew. For instance, in Sunday School we studied some Biblical history and the rector would come around and ask questions. Once he asked: "Who was the Egyptian princess who rescued Moses from the bullrushes?" and then quickly added, "Of course, you wouldn't know that." I piped up: "She was the daughter of the Pharaoh." That convinced me that all my reading was worthwhile, even though my family thought I read too much. They thought I should be out playing, but you couldn't drag me away from books or books away from me.

I continued to read everything I could get my hands on. If there was nothing in the house, there were always the books in the blessed Carnegie Library. I read a lot of things I didn't understand, but that didn't stop me. When I got the measles I sat up in bed and read *Swiss Family Robinson*. I think I read one or two novels of Scott's. I read the encyclopedia, anything, it didn't matter what.

THE IMMEDIATE FAMILY

Outwardly, my life went on normally, although the family itself was not a very normal picture. There was my mother, struggling along woozily as best she could. My mother didn't have much say about running the house and in her moments of irresponsibility or in a kind of whimsicalness she continued to do odd little things that would irritate Aunt Fanny. Sometimes, it made an uncomfortable situation, which is why my mother and I kept to ourselves downstairs while the rest of the family often stayed upstairs. Things worked out better that way.

My mother gradually became more dependent on me. It was as if my mother had become my child and I was trying to protect her from criticism and prevent family quarrels. I became quite mature in that, a maturity that was forced on me and had certain effects. The year we moved in, my mother insisted I should have a Christmas tree. My aunt said they hadn't bothered with Christmas trees since my mother and her other sister Alice had left home. We got a tree that year, but as time went on, I found that I had to take charge of such things. It's almost as if I had to carry out my mother's wishes and struggle to maintain the happy family appearance, though that's not exactly what we had.

As I got older, my aunt and I used to take our bicycles and ride out to the open woodlands where we chopped down our Christmas trees with a hatchet. I don't know if we stole the trees or not. I hope not, but I'm afraid that sometimes we did. I decorated the trees, and insisted on having presents for everyone. I took care that each person had a present, and I had to do it on fifty cents or a dollar for the whole family. It was a great problem. This, too, was part of my early maturity. I had to sort of take over the family's social life in that way.

Next to my mother, the most important person to me was my French grandmother. Though she was capable of violent emotion, she had a great sense of humour, plus an interested and eager mind. We'd sit up in the sewing room and she'd tell me stories. She was a great reader of Dickens and told me the story of Nicholas Nickelby very early, but her best stories were about bears. The rest of the family would supposedly be reading, but I'd look up and find them all involved in the bears, instead.

When I was old enough to go to church with her on Sunday morning she'd be sailing alongside in her black silk dress, repeating: "Observe the New England scene." She'd lived in New England most of her life, yet she had the enthusiasm of just having arrived.

She also had a kind of scorn for the sheer hardworking ability of my grandfather, and felt she could have done a lot better. If she had gone to college, she could have been a brilliant businesswoman, but it was not the custom for a married woman to have any kind of business.

She made clothes for everybody. She loved to sew. She made all my dresses: I had to stand still and be fitted indefinitely because as a dress was made it was fitted as it went along. The beautiful and complicated concoctions she'd made for my mother's first concerts were still in the closet. They had velvet, satin, and ruffles, lace and what was called passementerie, very complicated braidwork. There was an orange-corded silk dress with black trim. There was a dress trimmed with red velvet, which my grandmother was secretly the most proud of. She was a very ambitious woman in the French way, ambitious for her girls. Mother particularly had been her great delight, before all the terrible things had happened.

Of course, there was hardly any choice about the clothes during the time I was growing up. Since we didn't have much money, it was a matter of getting by as frugally as we could. The dresses from a girl across the street, Grace Billings, were handed down to me as she outgrew them. People in Taunton weren't ashamed of wearing one another's clothes. I wore Grace Billings's clothes with pleasure. She had a cousin who sent her little bronze kid gloves and ankle tie shoes from Paris. Since she was too big for them, I got them at once. I don't suppose I've ever looked as elegant before or since. Once, in one of Grace's dresses I found a pocketful of Scotch drops that had survived a wash. I thought this was very lucky.

Then there was my grandfather, who worked hard in a business that was dying in New England as the profitable foundries moved West. He went to Boston every Thursday. He dressed up in his good suit and his second-best hat and his gold watch chain and called on customers. That's the way you did it; without any advertising, you had a discreet and gentlemanly relationship to clients. He always went to the Faneuil Hall Market and had lunch at the old place called Durgin-Park.

In summers, he loved to get up early in the morning and hoe. I heard his hoe clicking against the stones in the corn patch before any of us had had breakfast. The morning glories would have run up the tall bean poles when the sun had just arisen; they would have leaped from one pole to the other and would be in full blossom in that early sunrise, and the orioles would be singing in the high elm trees and everything would be fresh. My grandfather was there in all my growing up and he was a great influence, a quiet little man with a wonderful sense of love for his family.

My Aunt Fanny was in many ways my caretaker, and the caretaker of the entire family. In those days in New England, the youngest daughter was almost always sacrificed in this way. She didn't marry and stayed at home to help the parents in their later years. Up and down our street were at least 13 old maids, sometimes two to a family. So many men had been killed in the Civil War and so many others had gone West, there were 60,000 unmarried women in New England alone. This made it a very female society. I was brought up in that. The only men I really knew until I got to high school were my grandfather and my Uncle Charlie, who used to take me sailing in the boat down Narragansett Bay.

Aunt Fanny had plenty of chances with men, actually. She was attractive and they'd flock around and then she'd snub them in one way or another. She wanted nothing to do with them. Also, she would have made a fine mathematics scholar. She'd gone through high school and had some training in bookkeeping, so she took care of the books of my grandfather's brass foundry. She worked part-time on the books of a bank owned by some friends. She would have loved to work full-time at a bank, but she had to stay home.

Her great passion was the bicycle club of young ladies. The young ladies of the bicycle club wore skirts that came down only to the ankle. I remember hers distinctly. It was a light brown cloth skirt with quite a smart flare and she wore puttees — gators that go over the shoes — and she had the little short Eton jacket over the striped shirtwaist and a little narrow stiff starched collar and starched cuffs and some kind of a brown felt hat that turned up one side with a feather in it. Aunt Fanny and I would go bicycling around the country finding nut trees so we could bring back the nuts.

Eventually, she got interested in astronomy. She got star books and a regular monthly star map and became an accomplished amateur astronomer. She knew all about the magnitudes and the declinations.

When I'd come home on my college vacations, and she'd be sitting up at night caring for my grandmother or for my grandfather, she'd say: "Look out over the roof and you'll see a very bright star two degrees north of the chimney. That is Deberon and it's in the constellation such and such." She taught me about Orion and the Pleiades.

The stars were a great comfort to her, especially when the house was not happy. Frequently it wasn't, and Aunt Fanny was somewhat to blame. She had a bad and sudden temper and was always blowing up about something she didn't like. Her temper was never checked, and she and my mother had a strong and ongoing antipathy.

On the other hand, Aunt Fanny was a jolly companion when she wasn't cross as two sticks. She had a good sense of humor. I was indebted to her because she did everything in the world for me. It was my aunt who saw that I got up in the morning and had a good breakfast, who, along with my grandmother, sewed my clothes, and who tried and failed to teach me arithmetic. It didn't matter, I wouldn't have learned it anyway. She was ashamed that I did it so badly.

After my mother got over the first violent attacks of her mental disorder, she remained gentle, woozy, and continued to be my child. We did everything together we possibly could. When I got home from school, the rest of the family would be upstairs in the sewing room, and she'd sit with me or take a nap on the sofa or we would play little games, cards and so forth, jack straws, a low-grade sort of checkers. In the evenings, we took our walks together, went out together, went up to bed together.

My father was still very present in my emotional life and I think in hers as well. Sometimes as she sat on the porch, I would look at her through the front parlor window. She'd be sitting with her back to the street, talking to herself softly, gesticulating, smiling, and laughing in her way. I just knew she was remembering my father.

The bitterness against my father continued in the minds of my grandmother and my aunt, and even increased after he failed at his business in Providence. He'd apparently tried to patch it up as best he could and finally had to go to Florida on borrowed money.

My Taunton family believed it wasn't respectable to borrow money, nor was it respectable to get a divorce. My father continued to insist we deserted him and I think he tried several times to get us back. He never contributed any money to my upbringing. Despite the bitterness around her, my mother had no ill feelings towards him at all. She would tell me stories about when he was a little boy in Minnesota.

I'm sure I was born a very extroverted, happy-go-lucky child and not until the shock of my mother's mental illness and the shock to me was there a change in my temperament. In that category of extroverts and introverts we were using some time ago, I think the trauma of my young life changed me into a subjective extrovert, someone with an active outer life and an equally active and hidden inner life, secretive and imaginative, based on reading and daydreaming.

NEW ENGLAND SURROUNDINGS

Taunton was an old New England town. Downriver toward the mouth of Narragansett Bay was the great Dighton Rock, which had inscriptions and drawings on it, mostly crude representations, the way children would draw a man. The thought was that these scratches were from the Portuguese, who followed the herring up the river much earlier than the English showed up at Plymouth. Taunton was first settled by a woman by the name of Elizabeth Poole, who was supposed to have bought the land from the Indians with a pot of beans or something like that; the Poole Silverworks is still there. Because it was founded by a woman, the town had the Latin motto, *Dux Femina Facti*, which comes out of Virgil and was written about Dido. It says "a woman is the leader of the expedition."

The change of seasons in New England was both rigorous and fascinating. In our yard, the enormous apple tree bore five different kinds, from what you call scions or budded stock. We had the four pear trees and a great big cherry tree and in the spring all of them were lovely with the apple blossoms pink and white, the pear blossoms white and frothy and the cherry blossoms not quite so pink and not quite so white but beautiful nonetheless. There was the long grass with the fallen blossoms in it and the first of the bluebirds beginning to sing in the trees.

Years later, I saw the apple blossoms in Normandy. They were lovely but I never thought they were as lovely as the apple blossoms in New England. New England apple blossoms were much pinker than Normandy apple blossoms.

We had three elm trees on our lot and all the way down the street there were elm trees. The street was vaulted with them. Everyone had front porches. In the summer people would be sitting on their porches up and down the streets and the moonlight would be coming through the elm trees and the city fathers would very economically turn off the city lights. That was wonderful, people on porches enjoying the moonlight coming through the vaulting elms and my mother and aunt would bring out the guitar and banjo and sing the kind of sentimental songs they sang in those days, always ending with "Good Night Ladies." All the people on the porches would applaud, and you had a lovely sense of a community enjoying an evening. It was so lovely in itself you could never forget it.

We had a great many oak trees, some years they'd turn red and some years they'd turn russet. People rode out from Boston all along the Mohawk trail to see the colored leaves. We didn't have any sugar maples or pure golden leaves, those were farther north. Even so, the autumns were wonderfully colorful.

In the winters, snows were always exciting. They didn't always come before Christmas, sometimes they come before Thanksgiving. I remember high school football games when the first snow would begin to fall on the boys. Then other years, the snows wouldn't come until January and all the oldtimers would say "a green Christmas makes a full graveyard" — but I don't think people died any more when Christmas was green than when it was white. The first snow was beautiful in the backyard and on the trees. Often, it would change into a chilly rain and melt away. Everything would get grimy and muddy after that.

We all wore long winter underwear and heavy coats in the winter. I had terrible head colds. I was kept home from school a lot, sitting in the sewing room by the great steam radiator, wrapped in a blanket with grandfather's old linen handkerchiefs — drying one handkerchief on the radiator while I was using another — having a wonderful time reading the *Last Days of Pompeii*, *Ivanhoe*, or *The Talisman*.

The springs in Taunton were the superior season. All winter, you'd wait for the wonderful things that went on in the spring. In May, there was Decoration Day, the formal decoration of veterans' graves, and generally it was wet and cold and there were the last survivors of the Grand Army of the Republic who'd lived through the Civil War. They'd be taken in open cars to the cemetery and they'd all get pneumonia and die like flies.

Also in May, there was the custom of the May baskets. The twilights were getting longer, and in the early twilight after supper there would come a loud and hasty ring of the doorbell and you'd rush to open it, and there'd be a little basket made of paper with paper roses, filled with candy and things. You had to ignore the beauty of it and rush out and try to find the children who'd hung the May baskets on you. If you caught them, you brought them in and you all ate the candy and cakes in the basket. My mother made the most beautiful May baskets I ever saw.

That was a delightful experience, running around and chasing after people, laughing and joking in the early twilight, before the full dark when everybody had to go home. The ringing of bells and footsteps of the May baskets went on through high school –– we were never too big in those days.

Another Taunton spring ritual was completely unique to the town itself, the natural ritual of the running of the herring. The herring came up the Taunton River every spring in that pigheaded way of fish that are hellbent to spawn. They must have done it that way since the founding of the town, and even before that, back before the river was discovered by Portuguese explorers. As the town got bigger, the people built a big fish staircase to help the herring in their annual struggle upriver.

The biggest celebration for my family was on the Fourth of July, because Uncle Charlie was born on the Fourth. We always went out to his cottage at Field's Point on Narragansett Bay and had our first clam-bake of the year.

Taunton might be said to be a Victorian or mid-Victorian situation. Respectability was part of the morality of the times. It wasn't bigoted. It was the kind of respectability that paid its bills. People kept up appearances and put their best foot forward. It had its charm.

There was little crime — although every house was carefully locked.

I don't suppose we ever sat down to noon dinner that my grandmother didn't say, "Go see if the front door is locked, so nobody can crawl upstairs." I always wondered why somebody would crawl upstairs, but that was always the way it was said.

These were very cautious people who didn't stick their necks out for fear of being hurt. Long winter nights make people pretty cautious. They were petrified about many things. They were especially petrified about the first murder I remember, the famous Lizzy Borden case in Fall River. The rhyme was passed around:

> Lizzy Borden took an ax
> And hit her mother forty whacks
> And when she saw what she had done,
> She gave her father forty-one.

Lizzy Borden was arrested for murdering her parents and brought to Bristol County jail. Eventually she was acquitted, but everybody always believed she did it. My cousin Pauline refused to get off the train at Fall River because she was afraid of Lizzy Borden.

We weren't much of a religious community. Actually we were, in the sense that you'd never meet anybody who didn't go to church. What I mean is, people went to church because it was the accepted thing to do, but without any great fervor. We were a conformist society to an extent, and most of the moral and social constraints had to do not so much with pure theology but with business practices. The feeling of Taunton and of the wide middle class of which it was composed seemed to be devotion to respectability more than to religion even, respectability based on paying your bills and paying your taxes and not having a mortgage on your house. Religion itself was somewhat an embarrassing subject among literate people.

My father, as I've said, had converted to Episcopalianism after having been brought up a Quaker. My mother was also an Episcopalian. Her mother, that is my French grandmother, was not a member of any church until after she got married and had children. For some years, she and grandfather went to Methodist meetings on Wednesday nights. It was her little Walter's diphtheria that made her send my mother scurrying to the Episcopal rectory, and the rector came to baptize Uncle Walter before he died. After that, the whole family became Episcopalians.

I was baptized Episcopalian as a baby. I was confirmed in the church by Bishop Lawrence Barnes, presiding bishop of the diocese. The church was part of my background throughout my childhood, to the time I went to college. Aunt Fanny taught in Sunday School.

At the Sunday School I attended, St. Thomas Episcopal, we mostly learned the catechism. It began, "A member of Christ, a child of God and inheritor of the kingdom of heaven." And the next question was: "What did your sponsors then do for you?" Firstly, they renounced the devil and all his works — well, that was pretty good. I thought I was a little young to be involved directly with the devil.

The catechism really came down to two important issues: duty toward God and duty toward your neighbor. The duty toward neighbor part began: "My duty to my neighbor is to love him as myself and to do unto all men as they should do unto me, to love, honor, and succor my father and mother," or maybe it was "parents." The next bit always struck me as a little odd. It was: "to render myself lowly and reverently to all my betters." Frankly, I thought it quite out-of-character to render myself lowly and reverently. What, I wondered, could all this mean?

Then there was: "to learn and labor truly to get mine own living and to do my duty in that state of life which it has pleased God to call me." This one bothered me as well. In the United States we're not supposed to have fixed "states of life," or to stay in one class. If we don't like the state of life we're born into, we're supposed to be able to struggle out of it. Embedded right there in the Episcopal cathecism was something that began to seem to me more and more unAmerican. As a matter of fact, I began to suspect that the catechism was the basis for the whole British class system.

Though I later was confirmed and all that, the church never struck me as making good sense, or as something I could act on for the rest of my life. Maybe it was that same skeptical streak that I'd developed from my troubles, or maybe that innate skepticism I'd inherited from my Quaker father, my French grandmother, and my Bonapartist ancestors had affected me especially.

In Taunton at large there didn't seem to be much distinction between the Trinitarian, the Unitarian and the Catholic, though the Catholics were looked down on as foreigners. The Portuguese were beginning to come in and there were several Portuguese Catholic churches. On dull New England Sunday afternoons, down at the end of our long street, suddenly there'd be music in the air, and you'd see the brass band and the crimson banners of the Portuguese Catholics having a procession. I thought it was a great idea to have processions on dull Sunday afternoons.

The only real religious agitation I can remember was when the Christian Scientists arrived in Taunton from Boston. My family had a copy of *Science and Health* in the house and they looked it over, but it wasn't anything they could accept. The realities of life were too apparent to gloss them over with what we considered wishful thinking. I say "we" — I was on the outskirts of it.

Parents of a close friend of mine became Christian Scientists and later so did she. They were devoted to the mother church in Boston but still they died of hardening of the arteries. That convinced me, if I needed any convincing, that Christian Science wasn't completely reliable.

HIGH SCHOOL

The life of the house became sadder as everybody grew older. My aunt was overworked but she kept at it with a driving force, and my grandmother would sit in the sunny kitchen with the fire in the stove and the geraniums blossoming by the window and say: "Oh dear, I wish Fanny wouldn't run so. She just flits from one thing to another."

I remember going home at noon, almost praying that nothing bad had happened that day and never knowing what the atmosphere in the house was going to be like. We always had midday dinner together, grandfather would come back for it, and you never knew what sharp things had been said in the morning that were going to come up again. Grandfather I'm sure was glad to return to the foundry.

It was clear by now that Aunt Fanny was never going to get married. She was still very pretty and always dressed in style — grandmother saw to that — but she had fewer and fewer friends. Her best friend got married, which left her with only one acquaintance down the street. They played whist together. That was Aunt Fanny's social life.

She had the same kind of standoffishness that was also deep-seated in my grandfather. Darling man that he was, he also had no close friends, and to my astonishment insisted that you shouldn't make friends because they always cheated you. Aunt Fanny believed the same. She had resented it bitterly when her sister Alice got married and went to live in Wallingford, Connecticut. I don't know whether she had resented it when my mother married my father, but I wouldn't be surprised. Maybe that was the source of some of her bitterness about him.

My outer life was pleasant and complete. I had many friends and some I'd kept since the Cohannet Grammar School. There were five of us who played around together always.

One was Pauline Starrett, the prettiest one of the lot, the least — shall we say — intellectual. In fact, she wasn't intellectual at all and the boys were crazy about her. She was a comfortable and charming potential mother and wife.

Another was Margaret Blaine. She was tall and had small blue eyes, blond hair and a great sense of dignity. She wasn't very pretty, so she and I shared an unattractiveness to boys without saying much about it. Margaret lived in a large house on High Street. Her mother was from one of the oldest families in town with inherited money. Her father was the manager of the biggest grocery store.

Sometimes, Margaret's coachman would drive us to dancing class in a neat little covered carriage with a fat grey horse, Molly. That was before the Blaines got their car, the first one ever seen in Taunton. They lived a very well-to-do life but that didn't affect our friendship. It didn't make any difference to any of us which family was richer or poorer.

The first time I traveled by myself was during high school, when Margaret's family invited me to go with them to East Jaffrey, New Hampshire. They always went camping for the summer. Actually, they lived in tents but ate in a hotel, which was all extremely civilized. We drove up with their chauffeur.

On the way back they dropped me in Pittsfield and from Pittsfield I continued alone to Boston, took the train from North Station to South Station and another train back to Taunton. It made me feel very grown up.

There was Edith Siebel, whose family were Scottish Catholics. She was literary-minded, so the two of us were more bookish than the others. We read a lot of books together. Her father owned the trolley company, so she always had free passes. Since her father was a member of the yacht club, in the summer we'd go together on the trolley, eat lunch at the yacht club, then sit on the porch and read.

The fourth in our group was Madeline Beers. She was the most well-rounded of all my friends. Her father was German and had the second largest jewelry store in Taunton. Her mother was Scottish, quiet but impressively intelligent. I don't remember Mr. Beers much — I never knew the fathers of my friends as well as I knew the mothers.

Being with Madeline was especially important in the summers, because her family had a cottage on a lake. It was one of those summer colonies at a place called Nelson's Grove. Later in high school she and I would go out there alone, after her family had returned to Taunton. Luckily, this was considered safe. Three or four of us would stay for the weekend and do our own cooking. There were always boats, motorboats and sailboats, that we took across the lake for picnics.

I couldn't swim in those days, but I could bathe in the lake. Once we took Madeline's brother's sailboat out on the lake and the wind began to kick up. Madeline had the tiller, and she got confused. For some reason I felt very self-confident, took over the tiller, and triumphantly sailed the boat back to the pier. Neither of us knew how to furl the sail, so we just let it down and left it with the canvas drooping in the water. The next week, her brother discovered it and we got the dickens. Word got back to my grandfather. He gave me a lecture about my sailing without knowing how to swim.

For my confidence in a sailboat, I can thank my Uncle Charlie. He'd come back from Minnesota and married a lovely woman who hated her name: Antoinette Evangeline Winsor. I called her Aunt Nettie. They didn't have children and considered me the child they would have liked to have had.

Uncle Charlie was working as an inventor in Providence, and he and Aunt Nettie had a charming cottage at Field's Point down the Providence River where it joins the Narragansett Bay. As far as the eye could see, there was open water. A little river steamboat came down the river and took passengers to the various parks they had in those days. On the left-hand side of the bay was Crescent Park, where I ate my first ice cream cone. They had a contraption called Shoot the Shoots and we shot the shoots and went on the merry-go-rounds and all the rest of it.

Sometimes the entire family would go out to the cottage at Field's Point, and other times my mother and I would spend the weekend. Grandfather had bought Uncle Charlie a large rowboat and they'd stepped a mast on it. It sailed with just a spit and a sheet and of course a tiller. My uncle took it out every Sunday, and every other day he possibly could.

It was a great joy to go out with him and my grandfather. They were close companions who never said anything. Silent men the both of them. I was an unnecessary accessory. They didn't actually teach me to sail so much as they issued terse orders: "Trim the boat," "Keep your hands off the gunwale," "Dodge the sheet when she comes about," and "Keep still." Yet sailing with them in that boat was the happiest time of my childhood.

I must have learned to sail without thinking about it. Of course, grandfather's people came from Cornwall, and I think the sea was in my blood. From the beginning, I've had a constant interest in the sea. If I'd been a man, I would have been more seagoing than I've been able to be.

I was never seasick in small boats, but I could be seasick for a day or two on a large ship. Whenever I got seasick, I always thought about my great-great-grandfather, Captain Brown of Kittery, Maine. He was one of those brave men who made voyages to China that took two years. I thought of him in Valparaiso on the Pacific, where surely he'd put up after some terrible trip around the Horn. How beautiful that old and small harbor must have seemed to him and his crew. Eventually, he and his entire ship went down in a typhoon in the China Sea, but I tried not to imagine that.

My Uncle Charlie and my grandfather were the only men in my life all the way to high school. I knew little about males in general, and less about sex. I personally matured at the age of 12. I wasn't told much about that, either. It was a great surprise to me, and my own family — my mother and grandmother — looked completely concerned and rather frightened and embarrassed. They told me I had to be careful the rest of my life about getting my feet wet at certain times.

I didn't discuss it at all with the other girls, but Madeline Beer's mother had told Madeline directly and simply. Well, whatever she said was more about pregnancy and less about sex, but whatever she said Madeline passed along to me.

People can't imagine how ignorant we were about the whole process of maturing and sex and femaleness. It was a very taboo subject, particularly in a family like mine that was dominated by a grandmother. Though my grandmother had borne children herself, I doubt if she could have explained how it happened, theoretically.

In ninth grade, we had cotillion dances. That's when I began to experience the awful ordeal of being a wallflower. I was fat, my hair was greasy, I wore glasses, I giggled, I was completely self-conscious with boys, and I wondered why none of them wanted to dance with me. Like many fat girls I was a good dancer, but that didn't make any difference to the boys.

In high school we had dances for cadets, two or three companies of boys, a battalion of boys from the local armory. All the girls I knew went. Twice a year they had special dances, the Junior Prize Drill and Senior Prize Drill, when the boys could invite a date. I never got invited. No boy ever wanted to take me anywhere. Pauline Starrett, the beauty of our lot, always had boyfriends and her steady was Fred Nichols. They took me along to my first dance in high school.

At intermission my mother and aunt came down to pick me up and they asked me very pointedly — especially mother who had never lacked for beaux in her lifetime — how many dances I'd danced. I had to say I hadn't danced many. Poor old Fred Nichols had to dance with me once, but I don't think he liked it. He'd rather dance with Pauline. A boy named Herndon asked me to dance two dances, and for that I was pretty grateful. He was kind of unattractive, so we made a good couple.

I took it to heart more than I should have. What compensated for my being a wallflower was that I got along so well with the girls. As a matter of fact, I was always the one thinking up exciting things to do — Halloween parties, parties in somebody's cellar. Sometimes, about eight or ten of us girls would get together Friday afternoons and play a strenuous game of kick the can. That was our organized athletics for the time. In those days we wore heavy long skirts and heavy jackets and hats and all sorts of unnecessary impediments, so running and hiding were very strenuous exercise.

On other afternoons after it got dark, two or three of us would go to my grandfather's foundry to watch the latest pouring off. There was a big front office and then a room full of grinding machines, and in back the big fireplace where they heated scrap metal in crucibles. The process was exciting. The coremakers were making metal pipe. Two men worked the flaming metal with tongs. The crucible was filled with the great molten mass, which was then poured into a flask and finally cooled in a sand mold. After the metal had cooled, the flask was opened, the sand removed, and there was the finished pipe. They took it out to the front room, to grind off the ragged edges in the grinders.

During high school, I continued to benefit from wonderful teachers, some of them male. Mr. Walker was my math teacher. It wasn't his fault I couldn't do math. Then there was Ernest Heyward, the son of our family doctor, who'd gone to Harvard and returned to Taunton to teach Greek and Roman history. He taught both very well. Unfortunately, he also tried to teach me German. I didn't like German, especially the horrid sounds.

My English teachers were Blanch Grant and Florence Stone, both extremely well prepared. Miss Carey Perkins taught French. She was a friend of the family, and I was brought up to call her "Aunt Carey," but of course I couldn't do that in school.

The greatest teacher I ever had was Mary Hamer, who gave me four years of Latin. If I got any education at all I got it from her. She was a short, heavy-set woman with a magnificent head, a sharp Roman nose, sharp black eyes, and black hair drawn back in a bun. Her head looked more like a queen's than Victoria's did and she had Queen Victoria's body — kind of bunchy. Miss Hamer sat in a heap in her chair behind her desk. She had a sarcastic, stimulating mind and believed nothing was too hard to learn if the student took an interest in it.

Miss Hamer had written a textbook called "Easy Steps to Latin" that the school board adopted for use in her classes. It began with the conjugations, which we all had to learn. Then right away we went into Virgil. We read Virgil and memorized the first ten lines of the Aeneid. Miss Hamer introduced us to several hells, including the descent into Avernus, Dante's idea of hell and Milton's hell in *Paradise Lost.*

I still can quote Virgil. It's very hard for me to work it into the ordinary conversation, but I'm delighted to show it off.

In high school, I think I already had a writer's temperament. I learned very early that you don't have to know all the facts because you can always look them up. I wasn't a particularly good student, but I was a good researcher. I became what you'd call a hunter in libraries, first in the Taunton Public Library and later in the great Boston library. It gave me a great feeling of joy, knowing there was so much that I could put my hands on.

My high school graduation was held on June 12, 1908, in the Taunton Theatre. Several students read their own essays, which was the custom at the time. My friend Madeline's was called "The Story of Van Dyke's 'The Other Wise Men,'" and mine was called "Cap'n Thad." I was also privileged to write the "Parting Ode," which was printed in the program and set to music by Miss Clara L. Bowman. It was full of gray-green pines and roughened trails, crests, ridges, valleys and pigeons. The last stanza went as follows:

> We have climbed together in sunny weather,
> And in days when the clouds were black,
> So linger we here, with a smile and a tear,
> To send our farewells back.
> But the trail calls us on; let us turn and be gone,
> For heights are yet to be passed.
> With courage to strive and with purpose alive
> Let us climb bravely on to the last.

COLLEGE

However limited the family fortunes due to my grandfather's increasing difficulties at the foundry, my grandmother insisted very early that I must go to college. I think she understood me better than anybody else. I was a good deal like her. She still had hopes that I could make my own living, even though she'd given up on the idea that I'd do it through music.

Aunt Fanny had a special and very secret bank account, comprised of whatever money she had accumulated from giving music lessons at the house, plus doing part-time bookkeeping at a local bank and at the foundry. I don't think grandfather was supposed to know Aunt Fanny had this account and it was jealously guarded by my grandmother. I suspect that grandmother even took money out of the housekeeping budget from time to time and stashed it away in the secret account. It sent me to college. This was a sacrifice for which I could never thank them enough.

My aunt would have preferred it if I'd been willing to go to the Framingham Normal School: get up early every morning, take the trolley out, come back every evening. That's what she would have done. But she knew I wouldn't do it. I wanted to go to a good college, and my mind was set on Wellesley. Wellesley was the nearest good college in those days and I chose it even though my good friends were going elsewhere — Madeline to Mount Holyoke, Edith to Smith, and Margaret to Bryn Mawr. I could get to Wellesley by taking the train into Boston, then changing at South Station for another train to Wellesley. The whole trip took an hour and a half. With my mother's shaky condition I didn't want to stray too far from home.

My mother wanted me to go to college, but I now believe that when I left in the fall of 1908 for Wellesley that she began to die. Her whole life had been centered around me and without me in the house she had nothing left to live for, and thinking about this even now gives me deep sorrow. I can't express what I feel about it, but my grandmother saw very clearly what had to be done. She understood that even if my mother's life depended on my staying at home, my life depended on my getting away.

My aunt went with me to get me settled at Wellesley. It shocks me to remember how the two of us left the house, with my mother behind at home. Along with my terrible sorrow, I confess to a great feeling of freedom as well. It was as if some of the burden I'd carried since I was six years old was lifted. There was a new joy in life, in living, and in experience.

In those days, the freshman class lived in the village, and I took a place at 7 Cottage Street — naturally the cheapest room in the house, up in the attic. To me, it was also the nicest room in the house. It was a single room, papered with blue and white paper. It had a little iron stove. The owner of the house would come in early every morning and wake me by starting a fire in my stove, so by the time I reluctantly decided to get up the room would be warm. My window looked out over green gardens and into trees. I loved it.

After my aunt said goodbye, I was alone in the house, since none of the other girls had arrived. I'd already bought some of the books you had to have, including the important Brander Matthews' *English Composition*. That very first night, I sat up by the oil lamp — electricity wasn't extended to the attic rooms — and read it from cover to cover. I read until late into the night, and to me it was the most illuminating and exciting reading I'd ever done. It seemed I learned more that night than I'd learned in all of high school English. Everything Mr. Matthews said about topic sentences and outlines I accepted then and there.

Since I'd gotten practically straight A's in high school English, here I skipped the regular freshman English course and was enrolled directly in English 12, an accelerated course with a lot of special work for people who were going to major in English composition, as I did.

We had a large class in English 12, and the first thing we had to do was write a letter home. I wrote my letter home and the teacher, Miss Perry, said it wasn't the kind of writing you'd write home. Miss Perry was completely wrong — letter writing is entirely free. My particular letter described the beauty of the campus. That fall at Wellesley, the oak leaves were brilliant scarlet and the scarlet was mirrored in the lake and the lake was blue and the sky was beautiful and I talked about it in the letter. Miss Perry had me read it aloud to the class as an example of the something you shouldn't write, but I got a big round of applause from the class and at once was established as a writer. That reputation stayed with me the rest of my days at college.

Wellesley was not only a college for women students, it was also run almost entirely by women. Miss Pendleton was my ideal of a college president: a handsome woman who'd been a professor of mathematics, very dignified and haughty. We were scared to death of her.

The head of the English department was Sophie Shantel Hart, a perfect blue stocking. She was tall and not very pretty, but distinguished and cool. We called her "Sophie on the half-shell." She wore expensive green and blue silk dresses, and her standards for composition were very high. It was a great department overall, with Katherine Lee Bates, one of the foremost Shakespeare scholars in the country and famous for having written "America the Beautiful," the Wellesley college song that became our second national anthem; Florence Converse, whose poems were published in the *Atlantic Monthly*; and Vida Scudder, whose book *Social Consciousness in English Letters* was a revelation to me.

I had to take two sciences. Freshman year, I took Zoology One, which began with dissecting the left hind leg of a grasshopper and went on to dissecting earthworms and frogs. I don't think I would have liked to carry this any further. We also had a certain amount of marine biology, and I learned to use the microscope. Oh yes, in that first year I discarded my glasses. It wasn't until I got to college and had a physical exam and the doctor said I had perfect vision that I realized I didn't need glasses anymore. My wandering eye had been corrected, but I hadn't noticed.

There were seven of us in the house at 7 Cottage Street, two in each of the three rooms below me. All of us became friends.

Carolyn Percy was a cousin of my friend Pauline Starrett from Taunton. She must have made a big impression, because I remember exactly how she was dressed when I met her. She wore a gray squirrel neckpiece and a gray squirrel hat with a red poinsettia on it, very smart in a New York style. Carolyn came from somewhere in New York, and arrived in Boston with the aura of the big city clinging about her. She was younger than most of us, tall, heavyset, bright and precocious. She had a photographic memory and could repeat whole pages of trigonometry.

Sally Kaswell came from Norton, Mass., not far from Taunton. She was a small girl with regular features, conservative in a classic woman-student way. Her line was mathematics, chemistry and physics, and she made Phi Beta Kappa easily. She wasn't too good in English. She always claimed she didn't know what a style in writing meant, and I looked at her in amazement.

Dorothy Deemer came from the Midwest and after college she went on to become president of the National Federation of Women's Clubs and a friend of President Eisenhower. Her roommate was Louise Noble, a big girl with a creamy complexion who had a bad habit of snoring. Dorothy couldn't stand it and I didn't mind, so I let Dorothy sleep in my room and came down and slept in her bed in Louise's room.

There was Marian Johnson, who was as good as engaged when she got to college; and Bess Oldershaw, talented at Latin but enigmatic to me. All of us liked the idea of being in a women's college. I'm a keen advocate of women's colleges still. There aren't many of them left—for financial reasons some have been forced to admit boys and all that. Thank goodness it hasn't happened at Wellesley.

For my kind of person—undeveloped in many ways and perhaps too mature in others—a woman's college was the answer. It freed me of the pressure of the boys' presence, which made me very self-conscious. Since I was still unattractive to them, at least at Wellesley they weren't around to remind me of it. I could forget all that. I could be myself as an individual, as opposed to a young girl. There were no men to take over. And men do take over, bless their hearts, they've always had to take over, they're out there in front, in the cold as it were, sticking their necks out. When men are in an institution, they tend to dominate it. It's their nature. I don't object to it, it's just that they can't help it. From childhood, they are brought up to be competitive, always comparing themselves to one another. In the early 1900s, girls weren't brought up to be competitive, unless you consider their attractiveness to males, but that was a side issue as far as individuality was concerned.

We were more or less sheltered from everything, and especially from sex. I don't think anybody can imagine how ignorant, how innocent girls of my kind were in those days, in the winters of 1913 and 1914. We were an ignorant and an innocent generation. The word sex was not spoken in respectable families. I knew nothing whatsoever about reproduction. In junior and senior year, we had lectures behind locked doors. It was supposed to be sex hygiene but it wasn't about sex at all, it was about pregnancy. Nothing was said whatsoever about how you got pregnant, except that it was a secret process.

I'm sure that other young women in my class knew as little about sex as I did. One girl fainted when the lecturer showed a picture of a pregnant woman. Nobody explained, even in whispers. In zoology class we saw pictures of copulating earthworms and a good deal was said about frogs. But outside of the general idea that something had to happen between the male and female, we were completely vague. I had some dim idea it had something to do with the navel.

Need I mention that most of us were virgins? From 18 to 22, we were just as virginal as we had been when we began to mature. I continued to be unattractive, overweight, and had a kind of nervous giggle, which ensured that no boy would take me anywhere. During my entire four years at college, no man took me to a dance, or even to lunch. Secretly, of course, I was immensely attracted to them, and suffered a great deal.

Strangely enough, I made straight A's that first fall, including the solid geometry. I was the most surprised person in the world. Everybody looked at me with respect: "She made straight A's and never studied." Well, I never did study. I was too busy living.

I went home for Thanksgiving and Christmas, my mother seemed all right. I had not wanted to think about what had been going on at home, and I was reassured to discover that my mother was getting along without me. At least, I had to think so.

Aunt Fanny showed up once or twice, but neither my grandmother, my grandfather, nor my mother came to visit me in my years at college. Mostly, this was due to their not wanting to pay for the train ticket, which shows how strapped they were. Back home, they'd rented out the front bedroom and hung up a curtain so the renter could get to the bathroom without bothering the people in the middle bedroom. This helped pay my tuition.

We kept in touch through the mail. My grandmother, who thought of so many intelligent little things, had the bright idea of supplying me with a whole pack of postcards, so from my first day I wrote a postcard to my mother every single day and continued all my college years. If I got the postcard in by 3 o'clock she'd get it by the 11 o'clock mail the next morning. At that I never failed.

I did fail trigonometry in the second semester. My idea of the worst possible thing you could do is have to get up early and go up to college in a sleet storm for an 8:30 class in trigonometry. When I got my grade I was shocked but not surprised.

The second year in college, Carolyn and Sally and I moved up to a dormitory on the edge of the campus, called Fisk. That's when we became devoted to each other.

Fisk was an old public school made over as living quarters for the girls who needed help with their school expenses. At Fisk we all had to work but the work wasn't strenuous. I wiped the dishes and the silver; Carolyn would sweep the corridors with a wide broom, singing at the top of her lungs. Sally did heavy work and helped cook the dinners. Far from being embarrassed by the fact we were earning some of our keep, we were exhilarated and happy. We'd made a game and a party of it.

I took trigonometry over again, and the instructor gave me a passing grade just to get me through. By that time, I was known as one of the best students in English, and no disgrace to the college. I always fought against the idea that was fashionable in those days, something called mental discipline. You were supposed to be able to exert your will power and learn one thing as well as another. It's a mistake to force that theory on people like me — people who are good enough on things they like but blank-minded and pigheaded against the things they have no interest in understanding.

I was interested in English. I was interested in my friends. I was interested in the surroundings, the country, all kinds of organizations. We were conscious of ourselves as the Class of 1912. Given the kind of restrictive home that I'd had, the freedom granted us here was a great advance. We weren't hemmed in that much, or at least we didn't feel hemmed in. We could go into Boston on Saturdays, as long as we returned on the 5:10 train. I imagine if anybody was caught smoking, she'd have been expelled, but smoking was out of the question. It wasn't even an issue. I knew a couple of girls who smoked on their vacations — they felt very sophisticated and daring.

Sophomore and junior year we had required Bible, although Wellesley was nonsectarian and chapel was not required. One year, we studied the history of the writing of the old Testament. This was dull stuff. The new year it was the New Testament and that was more interesting to me. This wasn't religion, really, so much as straight Biblical history. We called it the "higher criticism," which was looked on with some distress by the churches.

Once in a while I went to Episcopal Church in the village or attended Congregational services at the college chapel. But without my grandmother to ensure my attendance, I lapsed. I was a late sleeper and usually didn't get up in time.

Junior year I was lucky enough to get one of the single rooms. I liked having a single room. That year I really started to write on my own. I wrote an essay that was read aloud in class and was taken by the Wellesley magazine.

I also took a geography course which has made a difference to the rest of my life. The professor was Miss Elizabeth Fisher, a woman of the world. When she was young she was taken to Vienna and learned to ride a horse, so when we had a big procession it was Miss Fisher who rode the horse, and every now and then the horse would raise up on its hind legs and Miss Fisher, who rode sidesaddle with a flowing skirt, would sit there unperturbed. I understand that she was the first woman to graduate from the Massachusetts Institute of Technology. She was one of the country's important oil geologists.

Apparently, she'd gone out to Oklahoma and was one of the first to discover a great oil field there. This was very hush-hush, and when she landed back in Boston, the reporters all gathered around and asked about the oil field. To change the subject, she announced that the beaches in Cape Cod were eroding. It made local headlines: "Professor at Wellesley says Cape Cod will disappear." Everybody who had taken summer cottages wired in and cancelled their leases.

During this uproar, Miss Fisher was called into the president's office. The president, Miss Pendleton, was sitting upright at her desk, looking stern and cold, with her cold blue eyes and her white, frizzy hair. "Miss Fisher," she said, "what's this I hear about Cape Cod being washed away in a few years?" "Oh," said Miss Fisher, "I meant geologic years." That was always one of our favorite stories about Miss Fisher.

In those days the department was called the Department of Geology and Geography. We had some of both — the shape of the earth, the mountains, and the glaciation and so forth, with a dash of anthropology and archaeology thrown in. Since I took that course, I've always thought of geography as a basic science. It led me to understand what I now like to call environmental geography. I think that's a phrase of my own coinage.

One of the negatives of junior year was that the gymnasium opened up and everybody had to do push-ups, or whatever the female equivalent of push-ups is. I was already troubled with rather strange pains in my legs as I tried to climb stairs. The pains were no more than twinges, but I'd have claimed anything to get out of gymnasium. Gymnasium was my idea of nothing to do.

I went to the head of the Mary Hemenway Gymnasium Department and said I couldn't do the gymnastics because I had rheumatism. This wasn't completely a lie. I've since found out that technically I do have a form of rheumatism, a reaction to my strong allergy against wheat.

I had to elect some kind of exercise, and there was a little golf course across one of the main highways in Wellesley. I could whack around at a golf ball, and it was lovely walking out in the country air. I wrote an essay called "Lost Balls" about how losing the balls was a good excuse for taking a walk. It was published in the literary magazine. I was beginning to feel more and more like a writer.

Three other professors may have greatly influenced my future thinking, although one wasn't aware of such influences until many years later.

The first was Emily Greene Balch, the head of the economics department who'd won the Nobel Prize in her field. Miss Balch had inherited a lot of money and lived modestly, which was a kind of economics lesson in itself. From her, we learned the fallacy of bimetalism and we all became ardent free-traders overnight. Although the Russians had just had their revolution, there was no hint of intellectual communism in Miss Balch's class. Communism would later sweep away the good sense of many otherwise intelligent members of the faculty, but not Miss Balch. She was too practical and skeptical for that.

Miss Balch also took it upon herself to give the girls a tour of the slums, welfare agencies, and saloons of Boston, as an introduction to the real world. We made maps and took notes on everything, except the houses of prostitution that Miss Balch pointed out. Although most of us could not have described exactly what a prostitute did with a man, we knew it was pretty scandalous.

It was very funny to watch this sophisticated, upper-class lady guiding her students around the slums. With a beautiful English accent, she would say: "Oh my dear girls, I'm sure your parents would be surprised at my taking you through these places but I'm also sure you will be very safe. My experience has been if someone comes up to you and says 'Hello girlie, where are you going?' you need not reply to him." Of all the people who might be approached by a man on the streets of Boston, Miss Balch was about the last.

We took philosophy from Miss Mary Whiton Calkins. We got some psychology in there, too, but psychology wasn't much more than a discussion of the inner ear and the rods and cones in the eye. I don't think the ladies at Wellesley had learned about Freud yet, or if they had they weren't talking about it. At any rate, Miss Calkins was primarily a philosopher.

She'd been president of the American Philosophical Association and was a friend of William James and other great philosophers of the time. I once asked an acquaintance who taught philosophy, whether Miss Calkins was much influenced by William James, and he said William James was much influenced by Miss Calkins.

She was small, dumpy and a tremendous force. She taught neo-idealism, which was the school of James, as well as modern philosophy beginning with Descartes. Neo-idealism, as I remember it, insisted that the only reality is the idea. I wasn't at all convinced about this. I felt when I sat in a chair, I was sitting in a chair. Later, I was happily reinforced in this belief by the pragmatists who also contended that a chair is something you sit on, while an idea is an idea. I was very much of that opinion and still am.

I was more interested in the monism of Josiah Royce of Harvard than in the neo-idealists. Anyway, philosophy was just something we learned that wasn't supposed to affect our religious beliefs. That's what it means, I guess, for knowledge to be academic.

I was influenced in a different way in a course called expression. This was the old elocution I'd had in high school, but fancier and more fun. The head of the Department of Expression was Malvina Bennett, and she wasn't young anymore. She still had a booming voice that could do all sorts of things and her mission in life was to smooth off the edges of the various dialects and accents of students from all parts of the country.

She attacked everything from the nasal tones of New England to the habit of saying "idee-er" for "idea" to the Western overemphasis on the r's. I got corrected for the broad "a" I'd inherited from my mother and my grandfather. Grandfather would have had a hard time with Miss Bennett since he had a thick Maine accent and never pronounced his final r's.

Some of my friends made fun of expression and didn't realize how important it was. I always thought it was important for women to have voice work. Even now, it seems to me I hear many sharp and uncomfortable voices for which there is little excuse. The sharpness of the woman's voice can be very distressing, particularly when you hear several of them together in a small room. If Miss Bennett had had a chance at some of the women I know, it would have done them all a great deal of good.

She insisted on articulation. Articulation was her major contribution to anybody who came under her influence, and she showed how our American speech has gotten slovenly and sloppy. "Pronounce your consonants," she'd always say. She fretted when people prounced "error" as if it were "era."

Miss Bennett had written a book of exercises, from which we recited up and down the alphabet. I don't remember the a's, but I still remember the b's: "Balmy breezes bore my bark beneath balconies and bridges and Bill the boatman bumped the barge against the breastwork of the breakwater." You couldn't slide over a b in her class. You couldn't slide over anything.

On the page with the m's, we practiced: "The moan of doves and memorial elms and the murmuring of innumerable bees." Not only did we have to read these things, we had to throw our voices out, holler so loud we could hit the back of the auditorium. Then we had to be whispery and still be heard across the room. It was all valuable to me. It prepared me for all my later public speaking.

As Wellesley developed our skills, we also became more convinced of a woman's right to use them. Myra Morgan, one of my classmates, founded the original Suffrage Club. Six of us from my class were members. Suffrage was scorned by many people, but I was always for it. My grandmother was for it as well. Miss Hamer, the wonderful high school Latin teacher, had said it was intolerable that some stupid little boy in her class who couldn't learn the first conjugation would soon grow up and have the vote while she did not. She was so right.

At home that Christmas of my junior year, my mother showed me a lump as big as a hen's egg on her beautiful left breast. She hadn't told anybody about it. I thought it was a swollen gland. I got her something to rub on it and went back to college and forgot about it. Then that spring, during one of our sex hygiene lectures, a doctor from Boston introduced the subject of breast cancer. I knew at once it must be what my mother had. I wrote home immediately and my family got a doctor. The doctor said my mother had to be operated on at once.

She became numb and even more childlike. I was with her every minute in the hospital — they gave me a room next to hers. Aunt Fanny would bring me a jar of soup and a sandwich for lunch, and at midnight the nurses let me come up and have supper with them. The night before the operation, my mother got into bed with me and I held her in my arms all night, except when I left to get her some hot milk so she could sleep. In the morning, they took her to the operating room in a wheelchair. I could hear her screaming for me as she came out of the ether. They let me give her cracked ice to keep down her fever.

During spring vacation, I stayed with my mother at home. She was cheerful and making a good recovery, but still stunned. The rest of the spring term I worried about her and visited her every chance I could. I thought about staying home all summer, but instead I took a job at a girl's camp in Maine. As much as I felt guilty about abandoning her, I also felt I had to get away. Also, I kept thinking we needed the money. Aunt Fanny had had to pay for the operation.

The owners of the camp offered me expenses and about $50 a month. That was the good part. The troublesome part was that I had to teach swimming. That was one of my jobs, and I didn't know how to swim myself. Once, they'd tried to show me the breast stroke but I thought it was stupid.

On the ride to camp I happened to read in a newspaper that people can learn to swim by doing the dead man's float and then splashing around with their arms. The first morning, when we were all supposed to jump in the water, I sneaked around the side of a pier in desperation and tried to do the float. It worked. The additional layer of fat that most women have on their bodies makes it easier for us to float. I was so bouyant in particular that I found I couldn't sink. I could practically stand up in the water and float vertically without moving a finger.

In twenty minutes I was swimming, and soon I was teaching the other girls. At the camp, I was a recognized expert in swimming.

Besides floating, sitting around, and reading, I accomplished a couple of other useful things. A friend from Wellesley who'd come to the camp was at loose ends and said she wasn't going back to college. I talked her into finishing her senior year. At many of our reunions, she told me how grateful she was that I did that.

Then there was the strange little girl whose father was hypnotizing her. He'd crouch in back of her and whisper something and she'd fall over flat in his arms. I told him he was a nice man and a good father, but that hypnotism would destroy the development of his daughter's will power. I don't know if I was right about it but I said what I thought. He agreed with me and stopped doing it.

I thought more and more about my mother and how bad I felt leaving her, and I left camp early to return home. In my absence, something wonderful had happened. My mother had turned against my grandmother years before the cancer was diagnosed, but now she'd let go of some of her antagonism. They became close friends again, as they had been in my youth. It was a joy to my grandmother that she and my mother had begun to take walks together and that their relationship revived. There was a time when my mother had been my grandmother's favorite child.

Senior year was exciting. There was a dramatic awareness that after June everything would be different and life in the world would begin. Actually, things already were different. Carolyn, Sally and I had moved up to College Hall.

College Hall was the center of Wellesley College life, the oldest building on campus, a Victorian redbrick structure at least a quarter-mile long. It was located on a slight hill overlooking the lake, the meadows, and the campus trees. In the middle was the great rotunda, four stories open to the high roof with balconies on the various upper corridors. There were palm trees and flowering shrubs that rustled in the wind when the huge rotunda doors were opened. Corridors, offices, and classrooms stretched out on two sides.

It was a great privilege to move up from Fisk to College Hall. I got a scholarship that enabled me to do it. Carolyn and Sally had a beautiful room and bath on the lake side; I had a delightful single room on the upper side of the balcony, also overlooking the lake. I loved leaving the window a crack open in the bitter winter with all the cold air coming in. I loved the freshness of the air from the lake and the snow extending over the frozen water. In the spring, you could hear the long, moaning boom of the ice breaking up. My room seemed more in touch with the outside world than any other that I'd occupied.

A few times I got up early with the bird study group to watch the flight of the myrtle warblers. I'd never been too keen on birds, and these were the first migratory ones that got my attention.

I can't remember a lot of things I had in class that year except the seminar with Miss Hart, the culmination of everything I'd done in English composition. I think I wrote a very stupid farce, which didn't please Miss Hart, but the other girls laughed their heads off. I wrote some other essays as well.

Carolyn and I became even closer friends, a friendship that lasted me the rest of her life. She understood me better than anyone else ever has. She wanted to be a schoolteacher and became a devoted one, first in St. Louis and later in that famous high school, Washington Irving in New York. We were close always, whether she was in St. Louis or New York and I was in Florida or wherever.

There was another wonderful gal we called D.Q. Applegate, though her name was Dorothy Quimby. Her father was a doctor and she was brought up in an old house in Brooklyn Heights long before Brooklyn became overcrowded. She was tall and heavy-set, with beautiful blonde hair and all the energy that fat people paradoxically seem to have. D.Q. was always chairman of this committee or that committee, and later became head of the committee that built the alumni building.

Senior year I got very involved in extracurricular activities. I was given my first real publishing job, editor of the college annual, *Legenda*. The same printing house in Boston always printed the annual — the owner knew all about it and guided me in all sorts of ways. Mostly, I did what he said, which wasn't too difficult.

The senior play was Anderson's *Sherwood Forest*, and I had the distinction of playing Friar Tuck. It was an outdoor affair, with alternate dates if it rained. The audience sat on the ground, along a little slope. Below the audience was the stage. A hill behind the stage created good natural acoustics. The trees along both sides served as our backdrops and curtains.

Friar Tuck was quite a big part as I recall. I wore a red ball wig and red whiskers and a pillow under my stomach and a priest's robe. I had to go to Boston and study with a woman director who did all the Wellesley plays. What I practiced most was getting my voice down.

When I read out my proclamation, the husband of the director apparently turned to her and said: "I didn't realize you had boys in the cast," so she must have brought my voice down to convincing depths. It was always low-pitched but I think I really hit bottom that time.

I also was elected Class Orator, which was very flattering, but I couldn't hold the office since only two major outside activities were allowed.

Most of my friends knew exactly where they were going after college: Carolyn knew she wanted to be a schoolteacher, Sally was heading to Vassar for an M.A. in chemistry and after that a good married life. My grandmother had sent me to college so I could make a living by teaching, but teaching was the last thing I wanted to do. I hated the idea. I didn't want to be sent off to some private prep school because that would remove me from my mother. If I stayed in Taunton, I'd have to teach in a small country school, an unexciting prospect. Towards the end of the year it became a big worry.

Commencement was lovely, with a tree day and processions, special events and parades. I was happy that my Aunt Fanny and my cousin Pauline Hopson from Connecticut had come to see me graduate. Pauline was a daughter of my mother's sister Aunt Alice. None of my family except Aunt Fanny had visited me at college in four years.

After the ceremonies, they told me something they'd deliberately waited to tell, that my mother's breast cancer had metastasized and she was dying of cancer of the spine. She was going through frightful pain and then through periods of coma. I got back home as quickly as I could.

Hours after graduation, I found myself at my mother's bedside. It was terrible to see her suffer.

Meanwhile, I'd enrolled in a training program that D.Q. Applegate dug up in Boston. Women who passed this course could then find jobs in department stores teaching salesgirls and doing personnel work. I'd hoped to take the course and travel back and forth to Taunton to see my mother. The week my friends and I were about to rent an apartment in Boston, my mother went into her last merciful coma and then died.

My father was notified in some way, I think. It had been years since anybody from our side of the family had had any direct contact with him. I'd been told he was living in Florida.

I was the one who made the funeral arrangements for my mother, took care of the details, looked after this and that. A strange and gruesome twist to an already terrible time was that Aunt Alice, who'd come to pay her last respects from Wallingford, Connecticut, died suddenly three days later. It was a very sad summer.

After the funeral, D.Q. Applegate arranged for me to borrow some money to pay my part of the rent in Boston and to pay our fees. I regret to say I gave my family the impression that I had a scholarship. I took the course, but I was numb all that summer. I couldn't feel, I was moving around in a state of mind that was completely different from anything I had ever known before. My family was glad that I was doing something that seemed to be pointing in a useful direction. I was glad to have escaped the house.

My closest friend, Carolyn Percy, had gotten a teaching job at a private school in St. Louis. Sometime that fall I managed to get hired at a department store there called Nugent's, so I could live with Carolyn at her school. My job was to make out sales slips and to teach the cash girls some grammar. If a cashier got into trouble, I was supposed to straighten her out. One girl stole something, and I managed to get her a job in another store by telling the manager there that she wouldn't do it again.

For this I was paid $15 a week, which took care of room and board and gave me a little left over to buy clothes. I began to thin down, and I was dressing better. These were external improvements. Actually, I was completely upset at my life, didn't know what I was doing, didn't like what I was doing. I felt like a misfit, a misfit with a job. Plus the summer in St. Louis was the hottest I'd ever experienced. I gather it has been greatly improved since they got air-conditioning.

I stuck it out in St. Louis for a year. Carolyn went back to her family in New York, which made me even more unhappy and dislocated. All I wanted to do was read.

Finally, I found a job at Bamberger's in Newark, New Jersey. I was offered the position of educational director at the department store — why department stores had educational directors I never really understood. Here I was teaching, the one thing I hadn't wanted to do. And instead of it being in a school, where at least I would have been teaching English or literature, it was at Bamberger's, where I taught basic skills to salesgirls.

But at least it was an escape from St. Louis, and my pay was raised to $20 a week. I moved to Newark as quickly as I could, and got a room near the store. I lived by myself. Luckily, there was a library just across the street.

It was the first time of my life when I was completely lonely. I knew nobody in Newark. I didn't go out much, and didn't get much exercise. It was a peculiar existence, just on the edge of things, it wasn't life, it was just making a living. It was a kind of vacuum and nature abhors a vacuum, and then of course life rushes in.

MARRIAGE

I'd gotten to know a few people through the social relations director at Bamberger's, Mrs. Henry. She took me under her wing, introduced me to her friend Paula Laddie, and invited me to Laddie family gatherings. The mother, sister, and brother were very kind to me. I don't remember if there was a father or not.

One day I met Paula Laddie on the street outside the store, as she was coming back from lunch. She was with a man named Kenneth Douglas, and obviously impressed with herself. Mr. Douglas was about six feet tall, thin and intelligent-looking, an ordinary dresser with good manners, and at least 30 years older than me. He was the church and social service editor of the Newark *Evening News.* I gathered he'd been working on the newspaper a year or two and had many connections in the welfare departments, the churches, and the city in general.

I ran into him occasionally, before we had our fateful meeting in the library. I came up to the desk to check out a book, and Mr. Douglas was standing there talking to the librarian. We exchanged pleasantries, and as I started to walk away he spoke to me again. No man had ever spoken to me again. I turned and looked at him, and realized he was staring at me with intense personal interest. It was startling, something I'd never experienced. After that he began calling me up, coming to the store, asking me to lunch. This was unheard of, bizarre, completely unlikely, and also spectacular. In about three months we were married.

Here was a mature man with standing in the community, paying attention to me. He proposed in the lobby of my apartment house just inside the front door. I didn't accept him right away but it didn't take long — about five minutes, I'd guess. I said "Yes," and turned and started up the stairs, and then thought, "Oh, no, I can't do this, I can't do this at all." I stopped and he noticed and asked: "What is it?" I was going to say, "I can't marry you," but I couldn't do it. Instead I said, "No, nothing, goodnight," and that was it.

On my part it wasn't love exactly. It was sheer delight. I didn't know Mr. Douglas well enough to have loved him. In fact, I couldn't have told you anything about him at all. It was all so overwhelming that I can't remember whether it was days or weeks before we got the marriage license. I do remember this part: My old friend D.Q. Applegate came into town for a visit. She'd been living outside of Newark, in a big house her parents had built. She invited me to lunch. I told her to forget the lunch and invited her to come along to the rectory and be a witness. Somebody from my apartment building was the other witness. Suddenly I was married.

I hadn't told my family. I hadn't told them I was engaged. I hadn't even told them I was interested. I'll never cease to regret the shock and pain to them. But these are excuses and I should never try to excuse myself. I simply had no power of judgment over anything.

Mr. Douglas and I left at once for the Hotel Belmont in New York. That was the whole wedding trip and it was great. I discovered sex. I came to the experience not so much with love or even passion, but with a wild, eager curiosity. There must have been a good deal of latent passion in me. At last, I'd found out about men.

I thought sex was a little crazy, really. It almost made me laugh. My husband had excellent manners always, and no less excellent manners in bed. He was kind and instructive and the whole thing was very successful. I became a ready partner and sexual activity almost began to seem normal as time went on. I'm sure it played a necessary part in my maturity. Without the experience of marriage, brief though it turned out to be, I wouldn't have been able to meet the rest of my life with the balance which I seem to have been able to attain. In other words, I got sex out of the way.

After a few days we came back from the Hotel Belmont and found our own apartment in Newark. There'd been a fire in my old apartment house while we were on our honeymoon. I lost a few things, but not much. Everybody said if I hadn't gone off with Kenneth, I might have been engulfed in flames in my little room in the back, which is where the fire started. Actually, I'd been engulfed in flames as it was. Anyway, the news of the real fire made my family feel better about the marriage.

By now I'd had to tell them, which I did through the mail. It was inexcusable that I hadn't prepared them beforehand, and yet there was a certain amount of self defense in it. I'm sure that my aunt would have thrown all sorts of fits. The whole thing was so impossible, so out of the picture completely, it was a terrible shock to them. Eventually, they were reconciled. They were too nice to have cut me off, or to have refused to speak.

A few weeks after the honeymoon, Kenneth and I made a visit to

Uncle Charlie and Aunt Nettie at their cottage in Field's Point. My grandfather and grandmother were unable to come down, but Aunt Fanny met us there as the family emissary. I think Kenneth's good manners partially won them all over.

Back in Newark, Kenneth was still employed at the Newark *Evening News*. We furnished a pleasant two-room with bath and kitchenette and I kept my cooking things on a sideboard in the sitting room. I'd given up my job at Bamberger's and like a proper matron I'd begun reading to the blind. It was a seemingly reasonable beginning for a married life until Kenneth was arrested.

He'd been working with a ministerial group on a vice survey of Newark. There was plenty of vice to uncover, and he'd penetrated farther than the paper would have liked. The powers behind the scenes got nervous, and put pressure on the paper to discontinue the series. There was some sort of campaign to discredit my husband.

I'm still very confused about what actually happened. Mr. Douglas had turned out to be an enigmatic figure, which partly accounts for the confusion. Certainly he was enigmatic to me. I knew as little about his background, his personal affairs, as I had the first day he saw me in the library. In the nuptial trance in which I'd placed myself, such details as where he was from and what he had done seemed irrelevant.

One afternoon, as I was reading to one of the blind people, a policeman came to the door. He asked me where my husband was. I told him I supposed he was at work. The policeman informed me that Kenneth might have fled town. There was a warrant out for his arrest on a charge of passing a bad check.

My husband didn't appear that night and I took refuge at the home of our friends the Doughertys. I found out later that Kenneth had sneaked back into town, returned to our apartment, seen that I'd gone, and concluded I'd heard the news and run away to Taunton. He went up to Massachusetts to try to find me. The minute he set foot in Newark again he was arrested. The next thing I heard was that he was in jail.

When I saw him there, he explained that he'd bounced a check at a friend's store, a trivial mistake the police were using as a frame-up. I believed him but there was little I could do to help. He was fired from his job and we had no money to make bail, so he had to stay in jail awaiting his trial. I got my job back at Bamberger's, thanks to the kindness of a man named Felix Fuld.

We owed a large bill on our furniture, so some of it was repossessed. I took a cheap room in a funny little boarding house. Every Sunday, I visited the jail. I wish I could say I understood all the complications, but I didn't. Even though my husband said he was innocent, and I was certain of his innocence, he decided to plead guilty. He told me he'd worked out some sort of deal with the prosecution.

They gave him six months in the Caldwell Penitentiary. All that summer, I went out to Caldwell in the afternoons and sat on the little seat outside a little cage where I could talk to Kenneth. Often I stayed after hours and was allowed to meet with him in the library. It seemed a little strange: Kenneth sort of accepted his fate and didn't seem much disturbed by it. The warden took him on as a secretary and Kenneth appeared to be satisfied with that. I think he was happy to be free of the hurly-burly of making a living, and may have preferred the prison.

My family was horrified, as usual, and wanted me to quit Kenneth at once. I couldn't do that. He was my husband and I wanted to stick by him. I had no feeling of shame or embarrassment and I felt he'd been unjustly treated. Later, when the situation changed and I finally left him, he wrote in one of his last letters to me: "I always thought you supported me out of nobility, now I realize you did it because it was an adventure." He was right.

I had a vacation coming to me that summer. Instead of going to Taunton I went to Hoosick Falls, New York, with Carolyn Percy. My family was just as glad not to have to see me. During our travels together, Carolyn said she could transfer from St. Louis to a private school in Newark so she and I could live together. That fall, she did.

I knew that one of Carolyn's reasons for moving to Newark was to persuade me to give up my husband. Just about every weekend, she'd say, "Oh, you're not going out to Caldwell again, are you?" Since I knew her efforts would be useless, it didn't bother me. Everybody tried to persuade me to give up my husband. They went on as if he were a murderer or a rapist.

Kenneth's prison term was up in the early months of 1915. As the release date approached, my family begged me to give up my job in Newark and return home. They didn't want me to be in Newark when Kenneth came out. Because of their relentless pressure, I gave in to their wishes.

Being back in Taunton put me in a kind of suspended animation. I didn't have any money and I didn't want to take a job because I had every intention of returning to Kenneth. My family didn't know what to do with me. The only person I could talk to was Mary Bird, an old friend from Wellesley.

Finally I heard from my husband that he'd borrowed some money and was in New York looking for a job. He said if I didn't join him he'd come to Taunton to get me. He sent some money. I tried to hide the letter, but Aunt Fanny saw it in my handbag. She had this terrible habit of reading other people's mail. After she read this one, she went off on a wild tantrum. My grandmother was brought into it, too. I insisted I had to return to Kenneth.

My aunt cried but she took me to the trolley in Taunton to catch the train for New York. Again, I regretted all the sorrow and worry I caused, but I also realized that if this was a bad marriage *prima facie*, for me it was a very good one — a release from old things and a discovery of new things of the greatest possible importance.

Some odd times followed. They began with our living in a nice, not too expensive family hotel up the west side of New York about a block from Central Park. There was a pleasant room and bath and we ate out and were comfortable. What's most curious is that I didn't do anything. I sat around without lifting a finger. I made no attempt to find a job, on the pretext that I couldn't have gotten good references because nobody approved of my reunion with Kenneth. I talked about working in a store, but that was as far as it got.

We were near a branch library, so I read a great deal. I sat in the hotel in New York and read Conrad in earnest. I walked through Central Park to the Metropolitan Museum and looked at the pictures. I was a perfectly useless person in a perfectly false, artificial setting. My husband was allegedly trying to find a job himself but he didn't succeed. We had nothing to live on at all.

He rented a typewriter, wrote a story and sold it to *McClure's* or one of those magazines. Then he wrote another story, but the agent supposedly had cheated him out of the money. I went and asked the agent for it, but the agent threatened to tell people my husband had been in jail.

We had to move away from the hotel because the rent wasn't paid, though I thought it had been. We left in a hurry, leaving my suitcase and walking out on the bill. Later I paid it back myself.

In a funny way it was also a passionless time. I had no interest in sex. We were two stumbling companions, drifting along. We wandered and stumbled together, occasionally trying to finish a short story. Kenneth would leave me in a room somewhere and wouldn't turn up until the next day. He said he'd gone to the Turkish Bath. I was so stupid I accepted it. I didn't even remember the time clearly. Once, I remember it was getting dark and we were still looking for a room outside of New York in one of the suburbs.

It was as if I'd given up all my mental processes to a person who wasn't capable of thinking at all. Later I realized that the tendency to give over everything to another person — usually a man — is something of a female characteristic. Certainly it was a characteristic of mine. It alarmed me.

There are many women, even in these so-called emancipated days, who easily succumb to a man's domination. It's easy to do. A man says something so positively and with such authority, that unless and until a woman looks at it carefully, she takes it for granted that he's right. Even now a woman has to be two or three times better than the men around her to have the same amount of influence on committees and so forth. At the time, I had no influence on my husband.

In my marriage I was completely dominated. Since then I've never wanted to give myself over to the control or even the slightest possible domination of anybody, particularly a man. I know I'm one of those women who's susceptible to giving up. It's antithetical: I'm so independent a person, basically, but I drifted through this queer limbo of life in Kenneth's tow. I wasn't in touch with my family and they must have been worried sick. Though I gave letters to my husband to mail, I don't think he ever mailed them.

Soon he asked me to sign a paper and I did it. I couldn't have been stupider. He was trying to get money from my father. I hadn't heard directly from my father for 15 years but somehow Kenneth had put us back together through some bank drafts! What an odd beginning for a reunion. There was some sort of draft you could sign on behalf of somebody else and then they'd have to pay it. First Kenneth had filled out one and then there were others. I didn't know my father was involved at the other end. Kenneth was a convincing talker, and this bank draft thing was on the edge of illegality. It didn't seem to get us anywhere, either.

Eventually, Kenneth left me at the house of a retired minister whom he'd known as an reporter in Newark, while he went off somewhere supposedly to look for a job. I was at the minister's house for several days and I guess they began to feel they were stuck with a crazy woman who didn't know what she was doing. Once I went out for a walk with evening setting in, and I returned and opened the front door to find the minister sitting with a man I didn't know. They both got up and the minister said: "I'd like you to meet your uncle, Dr. Edward Stoneman."

I was completely surprised. Dr. Stoneman was my father's brother, Uncle Ned, who'd been lost for years in the schism of the two families. I knew he lived in Springfield, Mass., but we'd had no contact since I was a little girl. Here he was in front of me, a tall man with thick glasses. Behind the glasses I saw extraordinary bright eyes. He seemed easy and relaxed as if he had just dropped in for an idle social visit after a decade and a half. "So glad to see you," he said. Actually he was here on a secret diagnostic mission. Any idiot might have realized this, but in my perturbed state I didn't.

Uncle Ned said he'd like to meet my husband and get acquainted with him as well. Kenneth phoned a lot and kept in irregular contact, so setting up a meeting wasn't hard. In fact, the three of us met at a park the next day. Uncle Ned told Kenneth he remembered me from when I was a baby, and would be delighted if the two of us could visit him at his house in Springfield. "I'd like to see the two of you separately if you don't mind," he said. "I'll get reacquainted with Marjory first and you can come up a few days later."

I moved immediately into Uncle Ned's house and got to know his family. Uncle Ned's son, Lloyd, was a wonderful pianist and practiced four hours a day. I was completely removed from my problems and lost in a world that was more compelling than my problems possibly could have been. I listened to Lloyd play Schoenberg and I read Balzac. Uncle Ned gave me news of my father who'd lived in Orlando and then moved to Miami to start a daily newspaper. I was hardly curious about why Uncle Ned had dropped in on me so suddenly, how he'd found me, what sort of communication he'd had with my father. What really happened, of course, is that my father had learned of the bank drafts and realized I was in some trouble. He'd sent Uncle Ned to investigate.

In a few days Kenneth arrived, and after having a couple of talks with my husband Uncle Ned invited me into his office. He laid the situation before me as it had never been laid before. Uncle Ned said that although Kenneth was a very nice man, he'd now had the chance to study him, and could give me a true picture of what my husband was like. He called him a "threshold case" and said that drinking is what put him over the threshold. He said Kenneth drank more than I might realize.

When one or two drinks put him over the threshold, Uncle Ned continued, my husband was capable of doing things like forging my name on my father's bank drafts. My father knew about all this and was alarmed and upset. I told Uncle Ned that I hadn't really understood the situation.

"Well," he answered, "I want you to understand it clearly. The man has a great many abilities but he is a threshold case and you will have to face that if you continue living with him." This was Uncle Ned's wonderful technique, treating me as a rational being, which was quite optimistic at the time. He gave the following speech:

"If you continue living with him, he is doing some very illegal things about these forged drafts and these things will increase. If you're not careful, you will be implicated as an accessory after the fact.

"Your father has recently married again to a lady he's known a good many years, and I am anxious that you leave your husband and go down to Florida. It's time you knew your father — you've been separated a very long time. I must say your father was reluctant to offer this invitation, until he talked it over with his wife.

"The new Mrs. Stoneman has said that you should come to Florida. She feels your place is with your father and she would be happy to have you."

I was touched by this speech, moved by it, flabbergasted by it, though there was a little twinge, a hint of bitterness that my father had given me up for so long. Then I realized he'd had to really, because the Taunton family had been so bitter. I was curious about his life, what he'd become, and about the new Mrs. Stoneman of whom I was entirely ignorant. Most of all I was touched by Uncle Ned's fair and under-standing presentation of the whole dilemma. I knew I couldn't go on the way I'd been living.

So I told Uncle Ned that I thought it would be better if I returned to my father, but I'd have to tell my husband. He called Kenneth into the office, went over the legal ramifications, and asked Kenneth what he intended to do. Kenneth acted bemused, almost indifferent. He'd been bemused for so long, I guess nothing seemed to matter. Off-handedly, he said, "Oh, perhaps I'll go to Columbus, Ohio, and get a job on a newspaper."

I accompanied him to the trolley, and we sat on a stone wall at the edge of the line and talked. When the trolley was ready to move out I said goodbye, and that was the end of it. I went back to Uncle Ned's house, back to Balzac, back to listening to his son play Schoenberg on the piano. My father sent me the money to come to live with him. In the next few days, I was on my way to Florida where I could also get a divorce.

II

A New
Life

FLORIDA

I left my marriage and all my past history in New England without a single regret. I didn't regret my marriage, and I didn't regret leaving it, either. It was an education but now it was over, and I was heading south with a sense of release, excitement, and anticipation. I was seeing my father again for the first time since I was six years old.

It was a long train trip from New York to Florida in those days, something like two nights and a day or two days and a night. It was September, 1915, and in New York there was cool, fall weather. I managed to collect enough money to buy a new dress: blue serge with blue taffeta and trimming. I didn't own much of anything else except a coat, a skirt and blouse or two I'd been wearing in the strange odyssey of my married life.

The train was nearly empty, and the ride from Jacksonville to Miami seemed interminable. I kept looking out and seeing pine trees go by. Pine trees for hour after hour, an infinity of pine trees. There was a man somewhere up ahead who came down looking for somebody to talk to. We talked.

The train was scheduled to get into Miami at 7 a.m. I'd been told my father would come for me at 9. I was still asleep when the train stopped. I awoke, dressed hurriedly in my blue serge outfit and went to the Pullman door. Outside was a brilliant sunshine, a funny little yellow-white depot and a beautiful sky. I had to get out to see what was what. I knew the water was East, and I could pick out East from the sun. By this bit of celestial navigation, I left the station and headed through the town.

My dress turned out to be much too warm. I was hot and sticky, but I liked the heat. I passed a residential street with small wooden buildings, two or three boarding houses with such names as Minnesota and Indiana, plus a few odd trees that looked as if they were made of cement. There was no particular vegetation, nothing interesting to speak of, and then suddenly this marvelous bay. It was cool, blue and green, with the wind coming off the sea in the slanting early morning sunlight. It was a wonderful setting at the edge of a second-rate town.

I returned to the train and sat back down in the Pullman car and heard a couple of men speaking. One said to the other, "Morning, Judge," and the "Judge" was my father. He came down the aisle of the Pullman car and I stood up. He came towards me and suddenly he stopped. Unconsciously he took a little step back as if he were surprised. I knew exactly what was going through his mind. As a small child, I'd had straight hair but mother always kept it in curler paper so afternoons and evenings I had a lot of curls on my head. Now its droopy nature was revealed. As a small child, I'd worn glasses but now I didn't. The way I'd developed, the way my face had developed, was a great shock to my father. He expected a pretty girl, but now I wasn't. My face was always a bit crooked, and if anything, it had become crookeder. That's why he took a good look at me and then started to back up — a slight and almost imperceptible jerk backward. He couldn't help it. My mother was beautiful.

Then he said, "Hello, Sweetheart," and I said, "Hello, Father," and he kissed me and there we were reunited with no fuss and feathers. I was calmed by his courtly manner, his fundamental sense of ease and quiet confidence.

I don't know that I would have recognized him as my father if I hadn't been told. I had only the distant memories of a six-year-old. He was tall and broad-shouldered and carried himself well. He had a handsome head which had grown handsomer as he grew older. He had the same eyes as mine — a kind of indeterminate hazel. His mouth was changed in shape as he now had false teeth. It was an intelligent and kindly face. He still had his large Roman nose. There was a lock of greying hair over his forehead that he constantly pushed back with his first two fingers. I could see he had a good deal of the Quaker in him still, even though he'd long ago converted to the Episcopal Church. For instance, I noticed that he took his hat off to women.

We walked out of the train and he carried my bag. We got into the car he'd rented and went out toward Riverside across the river in Miami, the first subdivision beyond the bridge. We drove quite a way out in a district where all the trees were cut off. There were lawns and maybe a couple of bushes. It wasn't what I'd expected Florida to look like but that didn't matter.

We stopped at the curb in front of the plain wooden house, and instantly my new stepmother came dashing out and down the steps, approached me with arms outspread, her dear affectionate face all lighted up as if she'd known me forever. I was deeply affected by her welcome. She said she and my father had been friends for years after he'd met her in Orlando. Later, I learned they'd waited to get married until two years after my mother's death.

Her name was Lillius — very strange, since my mother's name was Lillian. Lillius Eleanor Shine. We called her Lilla. She was born in North Florida, a baby in the Civil War. She remained my first and best friend all my life in Florida.

Theirs was a funny house, all open inside, the living room open to the dining room, father's books all around on the walls. Upstairs were two full-sized bedrooms, a bath and a small sort of hall bedroom. It was a totally unpretentious house and the furniture wasn't anything much, except for the magnificent dining room table that had been Thomas Jefferson's. It was an enormous thing with reeded legs and a huge mahogany drop leaf that could be stretched out to accomodate about 25 people, right in the middle of the plain little house.

The table was a symbol of my stepmother's background. Her grandfather, Frances Eppes, was Thomas Jefferson's oldest grandson. At 18, he was sent to manage some of Jefferson's plantations in Virginia. When Jefferson died bankrupt, Francis Eppes left Virginia with his furniture, his cattle, and his slaves in wagons and came down to Florida, where Jefferson had another tract of land near Tallahassee. In 1841, Eppes became one of the earliest mayors of Tallahassee. An intendent, he was called. They should name the mayor that now. It would be so historic. Nobody listens to me but I still have hopes.

Along with Jefferson's table, my stepmother had a beautiful silver pitcher about a foot tall, hand engraved in New York, presented by the citizens of Tallahassee to Frances Eppes for starting the police force that brought law and order to that riotous town.

After the Civil War, Francis Eppes moved from Tallahassee to Orlando where he homesteaded a tract of land under the Homestead Act of 1862. One of his three daughters, Virginia, married Tom Shine, a captain in the Confederate army. These were Lilla's parents.

Tom Shine later became tax assessor of Orlando. He headed the committee that planted all those oak trees. They were all Episcopalians. They lived next door to the cathedral and sang in the choir and Virginia ran a boarding house — the only thing ladies in the South could do to make a living. In Florida, it was a very profitable thing, because all those nice damn Yankees came down and stayed. My father had been one of them.

He caught me up on his own life: how he'd studied law, passed his bar exams, migrated to Orlando in 1896 to practice law there, boarded in that boarding house and met Lilla. He fell in love with her very early but my mother was still alive and he never would have divorced her or anything like that. We talked about how my Northern family was always bitter because he'd refused to contribute any money to me. He confirmed that he'd refused because he thought my mother had deserted him. He didn't have any money, anyway. After ten years of struggling as an attorney, he took an old flatbed press as a bad debt, put it on the railroad, came to Miami and started the first morning paper called the *News Record*. That was 1906. After he moved to Miami, he sent Lilla some copies of his first newspaper. Later, she came to Miami to join him.

He wanted to fight the Florida East Coast Railroad out of politics and he wanted to stop Governor Napoleon Bonaparte Broward from draining the Everglades. Father had very strong opinions about draining the Everglades even then, though there wasn't much scientific information to back up those opinions. In fact, my earliest notions about the Everglades came directly from him.

His editorials made Governor Broward so furious that when father ran for circuit judge and won the election the governor refused to sign his papers. Father never became a circuit judge — though he'd been a magistrate of the police court, which is why people called him "Judge." He was saved from a life of shame, because he didn't have to submit to an election every two years and go around and ask people for votes. He was happy being the editor of a newspaper in a frontier community. He said he'd never lived in a finished town in his life.

After father incurred the enmity of the governor, the newspaper almost went into bankruptcy. But then Frank Shutts came along and rescued it. Shutts had set up a leading law firm in Miami, and then got interested in the newspaper. He put some money into it and became the publisher, and he and my father reorganized it as the Miami *Herald* in 1910.

My father didn't want to hear much about my early life, even about my going to college, which somehow he resented. We had a good relationship from the first, with the exception of this blind spot.

My second night in Miami, a Sunday, my father, stepmother and I went to the movies. I'd been to the movies in Boston but in Boston it hadn't seemed quite right to go on Sunday. Here the movie house was an open-air place with seats in sawdust, and it had a canvas top that was pulled back in good weather. These were silent movies, of course.

After the movies we came down Flagler Street. There weren't many people outdoors. The moonlight was over everything and it was beautiful and somewhere there was a night-blooming jasmine, because you could smell it all over the city.

We returned home on foot. The moonlight lay on the white dust of the streets because the streets in Riverside hadn't been asphalted or paved; it was like moonlight on snow, only warm snow. There was an empty lot in front of my father's house, one dead pine tree was all that was left, it didn't have any needles and it was a silvery color. It was a Caribbean pine, much scantier than the Southern long-leaf, it had an almost Japanese way of growth that was riveting in the moonlight and the dust of the road. Above us was the enormous Florida sky. This was all a Florida that I'd had no idea about. I was fascinated with the strange landscape that surrounded my new home.

The little house in Riverside — distinguished by Jefferson's dining room table — didn't really matter. I saw at once that houses in general didn't really matter. You didn't live in the house, you lived on the porch, you lived in the outdoors with the lovely air blowing in all the windows. The houses were not impressive and the town was not impressive, but the people were impressive. Many of them were adventurers who'd worked in South America or Europe and liked Miami's position on the map, liked the climate and the tropic air and the sea. There were ex-missionaries and engineers, particularly from the Spanish-speaking countries. Miami had a Latin connection even then.

I had the front bedroom in the house, Lilla and my father occupied the other. On my bureau was my favorite picture of my mother. That was all that had to be said. I never entertained the nonsense about being a stepchild — Lilla and I simply became friends.

I was grateful to her for how she'd taken care of my father. He'd been down here in Florida all those years, living in boarding houses and keeping to himself in his way. Father later confessed to me: "You know, if anything ever happened to Lilla, you and I would be out of luck."

I don't think he had the slightest idea what to do with a grown daughter. Theoretically, he was opposed to divorce, but approved of my getting one. I had to stay in Florida two years before that would be possible, and he expected me to make my own money. After all, I was an able-bodied woman of 25.

He had that Quaker sense about women which is different from the usual Protestant attitude. Quakers made no distinction between men's and women's minds; they didn't think that minds had any particular sex to them. My father never had doubted my intellectual ability. In fact, he got over his disappointment in my looks very quickly, because he discovered we had similar minds. We had an instant rapport over books, although we always had a literary quarrel going. He distrusted most novels, and pronounced them unhealthy to read. I couldn't read enough novels, of course. He preferred Thackeray to Dickens and I preferred Dickens to Thackeray.

He held out for the idea that somebody else wrote Shakespeare. I defended Shakespeare against all comers. I accused him of saying Francis Bacon wrote Shakespeare because Bacon was a Mason and so was my

father. He said he doubted that Bacon was a Mason. That was the kind
of friendly argument we had.

The two of us were companions in this Miami frontier where most
people had no interest in books. Both of us would rather read or think
than to buy and sell real estate or to do other commercial things in
which the new city was so feverishly engaged. His friends were the
lawyers and the lawyers were the only people who read books. There
wasn't even a public library in Miami. The only library was run by the
women's club.

I suppose that religion might have divided us, since my father was still
a practicing Episcopalian and I had pretty much lapsed. Once I said to
him: "You know, I'm more interested in the Quaker thing than in the
Episcopal thing." He answered: "You don't think the Quakers would
take you in either, you old heathen, you? At least we got you baptized."
Of course he was joking. He really felt that religion was my own business.
Everything was my own business, really. From the day I arrived in
Miami, I never felt my father tried to dominate me. Though we were
from different generations, we met on even terms.

THE MIAMI HERALD

Soon enough, I became a part of my father's newspaper. This solved
the job problem and in a way it was inevitable. I'd been in Miami a short
while when father called up from the office to say that the society editor's
mother was sick and that she had to go home to Georgia. He asked me
to fill in for a while. Since this was a temporary assignment, I worked
from the house on the telephone. I'd call up two or three women from
the women's club to get the news, and the *Herald* would send a boy on
a motorcycle to get my copy.

I was delighted to be working on the *Herald*. It was as if everything else that I had been doing since college had been all wrong and suddenly I found what I was meant to do — even if it was as simple as writing society blurbs in a small city newspaper. I didn't care what I was writing about as long as it was writing. It was a great leap forward in my individuality.

After this short period of filling-in, I took over the society editor's job full-time. Some of the former editor's friends felt my father got rid of her in order to give me a position. That was an insult to his sense of justice. He would never in a thousand years have done anything like that. He was a scrupulous gentleman and the rumor was something I've always resented.

My father taught me many things about the newspaper business, especially the part about getting the facts right. He'd stop doing almost anything to look up a fact in a reference book. He insisted that the facts in his newspaper be correct. He insisted on the correct middle initial of people's names. He was always checking about dates, places, statements. He kept the scholarship of the paper, and especially of the editorial page, unsurpassed.

Eventually I was given a desk at the office. It was a two-story building located on a corner of Miami Avenue, two or three blocks from a bridge that went over to the south side of the river. The downstairs lobby was devoted to circulation and the classified department. Back of that was the pressroom where the big press ran. At the classified ad desk stood Joe Cotten, the boy who did so well in the civic theater and later went to New York and Hollywood and made a name for himself in the movies. Besides being one of the most handsome young men I'd ever seen, he was awfully nice. He exemplified the ad department for me.

Next to the advertising department, the steep stairs led up to the city room. You had to walk through the city room to get to my father's office at the end of the building. He had an oblong table for a desk, and his view was a plumbing shop and the traffic on Miami Avenue.

Two or three reporters is all we had. I was the only woman. There was a charming city editor, a good deal like a small family terrier. I wish I could remember his name. There was a large and impressive presence named William Stuart Hill. He'd been a judge of the juvenile courts so we always called him "Judge," just as my father was called the same thing. Judge Hill moved slowly and ponderously and wrote slowly and ponderously, but at least he was dependable. My father might gripe at me — "I sent you out to do a story and you come back with three sunsets and an editorial" — but he never had to criticize Judge Hill.

Judge Hill's most important literary effort was naming the Tamiami Trail. The Dade County part of it was being built in those days, and he came up with the "Tamiami." Everybody always thinks it had to do with Indians, but it's simply a shortened version of "Tampa to Miami." I don't think Judge Hill ever got enough credit for that.

There wasn't much Miami society to cover, especially in the summers. To me, this was something of a blessing. I don't know if I was meant to be a society reporter full-time. I was happier to share general assignment duties with the regulars. That's the way I got to know the city.

On one of my first regular assignments, I was sent out in a car with Judge Hill. We went to the edge of town to meet the first motorcade that had ever come down from Jacksonville. The roads in those days were spotty, in some counties they were terrible. At New Smyrna, the original washboard road of logs was still there. It took days for the motorcade to reach us.

On the running board of the lead car, I saw a tall young man who became very important to my life for many years hence. His name was Andy and he was a reporter on the rival afternoon paper, the *Metropolis*. The *Metropolis* was the original newspaper in Miami, run for Mr. Flagler's railroad.

Miami began as Henry Morrison Flagler's town. When I arrived, it didn't have 5,000 people. As I got to know it better, my original impression was confirmed. I didn't think it was very attractive, nor worthy of its site. The city was designed by the railroad engineers in 1896. Streets were narrow and laid out at right angles. Buildings were uninteresting and arranged in predictable gridiron fashion. Miami was no more than a glorified railroad terminal. Mr. Flagler himself never thought much of it. He was more interested in Key West, and as soon as he got as far south as Miami, he was busy planning his overseas railroad through the Keys. Miami grew up in spite of Mr. Flagler.

It's a pity that early Spaniards hadn't stayed here longer, because the Spaniards knew how to build beautiful cities. They would have put a great plaza on Biscayne Bay. My original impression of the bay was confirmed as well. It was magnificent. There was turtle grass on the bottom, and the water changed its color from blue to green. There were schools of mullet jumping in the sunlight and flocks of birds turning and wheeling so their white wings would catch that light. You could see them far in the distance, shining as they turned, the egret and the ibis and all those wading birds we don't see now.

Unfortunately, they'd dynamited the rapids of the Miami River near its mouth, which caused a lot of silt and muck to pile up in the bay. My father always felt the dynamiting of the river was the beginning of growth in Miami. It was also the beginning of the end for a pristine bay.

There'd been an important Indian mound on the north point of the Miami River left by the earliest inhabitants. These weren't Seminoles but the Tequestans, or some such name that the Spaniards could pronounce. The site along the Miami River must have been the focus of Indian life along this wonderful bay. The shocking thing is that when the railroad came in, old Mr. John Sewell, who was working for Mr. Flagler, had the whole mound torn down.

It must have been a burial mound, because old Mr. Sewell reportedly found some skeletons. He threw them away, probably. Once the mound was leveled, his men began building the hotel that was there when I arrived. It was the Royal Palm. It was not more than four or five stories high, a long yellow and white building, mansard roof and breezy verandahs, surrounded with beautiful tropical gardens right on the river. In front of it, on the land side, was a big park, surrounded in turn with fancy houses called "cottages." The first occupants, the original settlers as it were, lived in comfort and ease. Living in Miami was never a hardship.

In addition to destroying the Indian mound, Mr. Sewell's crews cut down the beautiful hammock of live oaks that extended north of the river quite a way. The live oaks that made this the greatest tropical jungle on the mainland of North America were destroyed as the city advanced. With the exception of the hotel and its landscaped park, Miami proper was barren and uninteresting. There was a Presbyterian church on the corner of the park and Flagler Street — Mr. Flagler gave land to several churches. Behind the church and opposite the cottages was the Woman's Club.

Kitty-cornered to the Woman's Club was the Halcyon Hotel, an elaborate and picturesque structure made of cut oolitic limestone with towers and pillars and porticoes. You walked to it up a slope, which must have been a part of the Indian mound they'd forgotten to level. The

Halcyon was Miami's second best hotel.

Both hotels opened up on New Year's for dinner, and that marked the beginning of the Miami social season. A table was always reserved for my father but he never went. He told me that when he married Lilla, he warned her: "I know you are very socially-minded and accustomed to a good deal of social life in Orlando, but you're going to have to accept the fact that I'm a working newspaperman."

As society editor I generally got invited to the openings. There was dancing for the out-of-town guests as well as for the Miami notables who attended. This was my first real taste of the high life in its relaxed Miami version. People who came to these hotels complained about the formality of Palm Beach, where they had to dress three times a day. Here they could be informal. There were many dinners and parties through January and February, and after that the cosmopolitan evenings declined into strictly local affairs.

That first winter in Miami, I became thoroughly habituated to working. It became my life and I was absorbed in it. It was writing and writing was what I was trained to do. Besides, any idiot ought to be able to write for a newspaper.

The quality of writing on the *Herald* editorial page was as good as I'd read anywhere. Because of it, father enjoyed the friendship of newspapermen all over the country and they'd come to see him. Ed Howe of Kansas was a friend. Mr. Cyrus H.K. Curtis who visited Miami on his yacht every winter, would drive over to the *Herald* and send up his chauffeur to ask if Mr. Stoneman could come down. Mr. Curtis couldn't climb stairs. Clarence Darrow once made a special call on my father and later he called on me. That kind of visitor inspired us to keep up the paper's standards. We felt the eyes of the world were upon us.

The most famous people I met were the Bryans. Mr. and Mrs. William Jennings Bryan, I mean. After he'd resigned as Secretary of State under Woodrow Wilson, the Bryans came to Miami and built a beautiful mansion, Villa Serena, toward the end of Brickell Avenue on a bluff overlooking the bay. It bordered on the impressive Vizcaya estate, which was still being built.

My father and I couldn't agree with some of Mr. Bryan's ideas. Anybody who'd taken a course under Emily Greene Balch couldn't have supported his bimetallism, for one thing. For another thing, it was hard for us to believe that God sat down and wrote the whole Bible and that

God invented every creature on earth. To us, this evangelical religion and literal interpretation of the Bible was very odd. To me, what was even odder was that Mr. Bryan was a Democrat. After all those years of growing up among Abolitionists and Republicans, I'd only recently met my first Democrats. One of them was my father.

On the other hand, some of what Mr. Bryan advocated seemed both daring and quite correct. He supported the direct election of senators and a graduated income tax. He was a magnetic personality and Mrs. Bryan was magnetic in her own right. They would laugh together about absurdities in politics. Very early when Villa Serena was finished, Mrs. Bryan invited me to visit her. She was in good physical shape — though not for long — and asked me and two or three other women to help serve tea on Wednesday afternoons to people who'd come to see Mr. Bryan. I'd stand around with the tea, and overhear all these admirers troop in and say, "Oh, Mr. Bryan, I've voted for you three times, and I'd vote for you again." I realized what an influence he'd been.

Two of Mr. Bryan's favorite pastimes were hunting and eating radishes. He ate one radish after another, and he liked them as much as he liked shooting ducks out on the bay. One time, he dashed across the tile floor in the living room with a loaded gun in his hand because he'd just seen some ducks through the window.

It's a pity that this intelligent man got involved in the Scopes trial and took the side he did, because Clarence Darrow made so much fun of Mr. Bryan that it killed him. He died soon after, in fact. His wife later told me it wouldn't have happened if she hadn't had arthritis, because she got too weak to talk her husband out of his stupid, half-baked argument. Actually, Mr. Bryan was the last of a certain kind of Midwestern intellectual, brilliant in many areas but a witless backwoodsman when it came to religion.

Mrs. Bryan was a devoted suffragist, and I got to work with her on that count. The women's suffrage amendment had been passed in some states, but hadn't gotten too far in Florida. In the spring of 1916, Mrs. Bryan enlisted me and Mrs. Frank Stranahan of Ft. Lauderdale, plus the widow of old Governor Napoleon Bonaparte Broward and the widow of another ex-governor, W.S. Jennings, to speak to the state legislature about ratifying the suffrage amendment. Mrs. Jennings I'd met before. In fact, the Jenningses of Jacksonville were the Jenningses of Bryan's middle name. There was some direct relation.

We went to Tallahassee by Pullman train. I remember the red dust of those red hills beyond the Suwannee seeping in around the joints of the Pullman car. In Tallahassee we stayed in the old Leon Hotel, which was full of lobbyists where you'd expect to see them, down in the lobby discussing politics all night long. Mrs. Broward was sick and had to stay in bed, but she'd go over and speak to the legislators and return to bed as soon as she got back. We'd sit on her bed and she'd tell about the days when her husband was governor and when he was running guns to Cuba in the Spanish-American War. Mr. Broward was a canny old pirate, and he'd smuggled guns down the Florida coast. I liked Mrs. Broward and her stories even though my father was her husband's greatest enemy in the dredging of the Everglades.

Mrs. Jennings was younger than Mrs. Broward, and Mrs. Stranahan and I were younger still. All four of us spoke to a joint committee, wearing our best hats. It was a large room with men sitting around on two sides with their backs propped up against the walls and large brass spittoons between every other one of them. Talking to them was like talking to graven images. They never paid attention to us at all. They weren't even listening. This was my first taste of the politics of north Florida.

These were the so-called "wool-hat boys in the red hills beyond the Suwannee" and they ran the state. Because of them, Florida was the last state in the union to ratify the suffrage amendment. Even though our testimony was ignored, it was valuable for me to work with women who'd struggled in this political arena. It was a long time before you began to feel that the legislators from north Florida even knew there was a south Florida. That was also a thing I had to learn.

I also got to know some of the local Miami politicians, and especially the big developers. Carl Fisher was one I met. He had this big idea of filling in Miami Beach. He was the first to realize you could create land by pumping it up from the bay bottom. He knew my work from the newspaper, and he wanted to hire somebody to help him with publicity. I made an appointment to see him in his office, and he kept me waiting two hours. I got mad and left just as he was coming in. Later, I told my father I couldn't put up with Mr. Fisher. He was too pretentious and wanted everything his way, and I could never have worked with him. My father sympathized with me on that.

His wife Jane I knew better. She was proud of being Carl Fisher's wife, but otherwise she was very plain. She tried to be a little snobbish but didn't succeed very well. There was nothing remarkable about her except her husband, who in fact was quite an exciting person.

My favorite developer was George Merrick. We became close friends. Mr. Merrick planned and built Coral Gables. He and his brother, Richard, had come down to Miami as boys. Their father, the Reverend Solomon Merrick, set up a church when Coral Gables was a grapefruit grove. George had the brilliant idea of buying up the land and making something of it.

Later, at the height of the Boom, he paid me $100 a week to write publicity for him. This easy money didn't last very long, because the Boom soon busted, and Merrick lost all his money. The citizens of Miami finally got him elected postmaster, which saved his life in his final years.

Like Carl Fisher, Merrick had sunk everything into his great idea. The difference was that he was nice about it.

My father said he had never lived in a finished country. His kind of people were not particularly of one state or another, they'd always been traveling, always going somewhere else. I shared in his delight of discovery but I also felt cut off from my Massachusetts family, just as I had felt cut off from my father all the years I'd lived up there. Both sides were still bitter and didn't communicate. When I was in Florida I couldn't talk about Massachusetts, and when I visited my aunt and my grandparents I couldn't talk about Florida. I was cut apart, disjointed. I continued to live a double life but it wasn't intolerable. A positive way of looking at it is that both sides gave me a lot.

At least I got caught up on some of my father's relatives. Forrest Rundell, the promoter who'd caused so much trouble, apparently had moved to Florida himself, as so many promoters seemed to do. Uncle Forrest thought Miami wouldn't amount to anything so he didn't buy land here. Instead, he bought land 10 miles from the coast near Melbourne and created a town called Feldsmere. He built a sugar mill up there and then he found out that sugar couldn't be grown in the area. The sugar mill promptly failed. They took my cousin, young Forrest, out of college and had him running a bulldozer. He never finished college and always felt inadequate as a consequence.

I continued writing the society column, plus the occasional general assignment piece, through the winter and spring of my first year in Miami. That summer, father and Lilla took a month's vacation out West, to California and to Denver. He lightly tossed me the editorial page. Basically it was sink or swim. I was terrified, but challenged. I soon got the hang of clipping good editorials from the wire services and putting the credits at the bottom so the readers wouldn't notice they came from elsewhere. Through such sleights of hand that my father would never have approved, I managed to produce enough copy to fill the page every day.

During this ordeal, I lived at my father's house in Riverside. There was no problem in my staying there alone. Even in those days, women worked long hours with the men. I kept going until far into the night. I'd get to work around noon, pick up lunch in town, then return to the office and work some more. I traveled back and forth on a little trolley car that ran across the bridge. There also were jitneys, old broken-down cars that picked up passengers for 10 cents a ride each way.

My work on the editorial page sparked a rivalry with Miss Hattie Carpenter, editor of that dreaded other paper — the *Metropolis*. The *Metropolis* was the older paper and the afternoon paper in an afternoon-paper town, but the *Herald* was gaining ground in circulation and advertising. The two papers had different points of view but I don't remember about what. My chief objection to Miss Carpenter's work was that she put quotation marks around everything. Her editorial page bristled with quotation marks, which I knew wasn't correct, and so I felt superior to that extent.

My problem was with content. I knew my quotation marks, but Miss Carpenter knew her local history. She delighted in pointing out my errors in her columns. Every time she did it our city editor would have a tantrum and call me in to say I'd disgraced the *Herald* and my father. When my father came home and I confessed the mistakes, he laughed heartily and dismissed the whole business with "That'll teach you to check the facts."

In spite of our spirited rivalry, I got to know several reporters on the *Metropolis*, starting with Myrtle Ashworth. Her husband was an engineer surveying in the Everglades. It was through Frank Ashworth that I began to get some idea of the extent and the strange nature of that country behind us, about which I was largely unaware.

I also met a charming man who remained my friend always and whose death I still regret. It was Simon Pierre Robineau, whom we called Pete. He was born in France and raised in Chicago, but still as French as anyone you'd meet in Paris. It was his Frenchness that I particularly loved, being the Francophile that I am. He was slender when I met him. He had a long French nose, dark eyes, a little moustache, and a humorous mouth. He was witty, charming, and well-read. He walked with not quite a limp, but an easing of the left side. The limp resulted from the wound he got while fighting the Germans, and for me it was the first sign of the World War. I never actually saw the wound, but I was told it was a dreadful bayonet scar.

There was a clear-cut understanding from the first that Pete was engaged and about to be married, or else I might have been interested. He made up for it by getting me together with the man I'd seen earlier on the running board of the first motorcade to Miami. This is the man I'll call Andy.

Andy worked for the *Metropolis*, along with Myrtle Ashworth and some other friends, the Keenes. The summer I was struggling with the editorial page, all of us rented a house over on the beach for a week. Carl Fisher had just finished filling it in. You got there over the Collins Bridge that went rattle-rattle across the bay. Or you could take the funny little tin-pot ferry boat that left from the pier at the foot of what is now Flagler Street. On the other side, you'd cross over a mangrove swamp on a boardwalk to get to the beach itself.

Most of Miami Beach was a blank layer of sand with streets laid out — no houses, just markers. The trees that were planted were no more than sticks. There were a few buildings along the beachfront, mostly the bathhouses that were called "casinos." There was Smith's Casino and next to that was Hardie's. The only house I remember had a sign in front saying: "Salubrity, the Home of J.N. Lummus." It stuck out like a sore thumb.

During the time we rented the beach house, somebody would drive me over every night after work. I never drove a car myself, and never wanted to learn. We lived in bathing suits and ran up and down the beach — there was nobody around but us. We spent our evenings in the moonlight — there was seagrape and sea lavender on the ridge, untouched and really enchanting. We'd swim and light fires, cook on the beach, then get up early the next morning to swim again. The water was full of phosphorous.

The beach opened up what I've always felt was the true Florida world. I realized then I was a saltwater person who would never be happy living inland. Of course it was the perfect setting in which to fall in love, and I fell in love with Andy. Andy seemed to fall in love with me. We were overtaken by the moonlight and the ocean and it was romantic and a natural thing to be paired off, to feel more and more drawn to each other.

I was twenty-six by then, technically not yet divorced. I didn't know until later that Andy was four years younger than I — he'd let on that there was only a year between us. It might have made a difference, because I was attracted to older men. It may have been a father complex or something. But Andy was playful, he was fun, we did silly things, played silly games. We didn't care about past or future. It wasn't a very deep involvement at first. We were having a happy time almost without noticing it.

After the one week we took the house for another, and I continued to shuttle over from the office. Soon Andy got more serious, and both of us were emotionally involved. Once, he said to me: "Look, I don't understand about your marriage. What is it, are you married, or divorced?" I told him I was here to get a divorce, but it would be some time before it came through. We were holding hands and kissing by that time.

I don't like extramarital sex. I think it's too difficult. My father would have been absolutely shocked, hurt, and disgusted, and so would I. I was a respectable woman, and I liked being respectable. I told Andy I didn't want to be a wild woman, and he accepted it. He would have liked an affair, I guess, but it wasn't in the cards.

We had something of an engagement, but it wasn't definite. We couldn't have gotten married for a year at least, and times were changing. It was the summer of 1916 and the war in Europe was in full gear. I thought of it as a vast whirlpool drawing in single men from all over the world. They all began to feel the extraordinary pull of war that men always feel and Andy was feeling it, too. Finally, he said to me: "I can't stand this any longer, I've got to get into it somehow." He signed on with the American Ambulance Service to go to France.

I took it hard. I'd had a broken marriage and before that my husband was in the penitentiary, and here I was faced with another period of longing and waiting. I resented it, but what could I do? There was no way

I could hold Andy and I wouldn't have. His life would be extraordinarily enriched by service abroad.

The night he left we'd had dinner together. The train went out at midnight. Some other friends were joining him in another restaurant for one last last-night snack. I walked him to the restaurant and we parted on the street corner outside. He didn't kiss me, we just shook hands. He went into the restaurant and I walked away. I spent the night at a friend's house nearby, lying awake and feeling miserable. I could hear when the train started — it always hooted — and I knew Andy was on it and I might never see him again. I was plunged into another period of unhappiness and longing, the sort of thing that women have had to endure, especially in wartime.

A romantic love that stirs the imagination is the worst kind because you live in the imagination. I waited for Andy's first letter from Paris, but for a long time nothing arrived. Then I finally heard from him. He'd been picking up the wounded in the battlefield, in the Ardennes. He got so interested in the whole thing he'd decided to enlist in the Lafayette Esquadrille, Americans who'd become French aviators. He was very proud of his uniform.

That made me worry more, because he'd be flying. The war was escalating and my father had seen it coming. He said if they bombed our ships we'd have to get in, we had no choice. Some stupid so-and-so wrote an article about how the *Herald* was a jingo newspaper, meaning that we were clashing swords and itching for a fight and so forth. That wasn't true at all. Some people don't realize there are inevitable wars that just have to be fought. Pacifism isn't always noble, and it isn't always intelligent. You have to stand up for some things in this world.

Soon I was standing up for something myself — though it was a bit of an accident. So much of what had happened from my marriage to my divorce seemed to result from outside forces, and from spontaneous or unexpected events. This time, the Navy had sent a ship from Key West to Miami to enlist men and women into the Naval Reserve. I was supposed to do a story for the *Herald* on the first woman to enlist in the state of Florida. We'd been told that the wife of the plumber from the plumbing shop across the street from the newspaper was going to sign up.

I arrived at the ship and the next thing I knew I was sticking up my hand, swearing to protect and defend the United States of America from all enemies whatsoever. I guess they talked me into it. I called my father at the paper and said: "Look, I got the story on the first woman to enlist. It turned out to be me." He said, "I admire your patriotism but it leaves us a little short-handed."

Luckily I wasn't called up for a while, so my father had enough time to find another society editor. He made a great discovery: Miss Jefferson Bell, an unreconstructed Southern damsel from Ocala. This was an improvement over me. Miss Jeffy turned out to be a wonderful cook as well as a good editor, and the *Herald* cooking page became famous everywhere. Her recipes were copied all over the place.

The Navy made me a yeoman first class. I was employed in the reserve headquarters down at Elser's Pier at the foot of Flagler Street and the bay. Mostly we gave out boat licenses. Of course I was bored and that made me rebellious. They couldn't put me in the brig if I turned up late, which I frequently did. They couldn't do anything to me because there were no penalties for women in the Navy. When they scolded me I just looked at them, because it all seemed so farcical.

A year in the Navy was probably the worst I'd spent, the most wasted year of my life. Though I was proud of the association, given my seagoing ancestry, I was no kind of yeoman. I couldn't take shorthand and had to write all the letters in longhand. My typing was newspaper typing, which is very different from secretary typing. My biggest trouble was that I could write better letters than many of my commanding officers. When I rewrote what they'd given me, improving their grammar and so forth, it made them furious. They'd say, "That's not what I said," and I'd have to do everything over again. It didn't endear me to them, nor them to me.

To be fair, I must mention my best time in the Navy was when I was loaned to Lt. Commander Albert Cushing Read. To me, he was the real Navy and a pleasure to work with because he dictated letters in excellent English and said exactly what he meant. He was an aviator who flew one of the early crossings to Europe, and I was proud of having worked for him. Eventually, he made the rank of admiral. After he retired, he and his wife — a Miami girl, Bess Burdine — became my friends and neighbors in Coconut Grove.

Another good thing about being in the Navy was that it inspired me go overseas. In fact, I began to work hard to improve my French. My French grandmother once had said I'd regret that I didn't speak better French, and of course she was right. I knew a Madame Faudel, who spoke with the soft, lovely accent of the south of France, and I started going to her house on the trolley car almost every evening.

She insisted on giving what they called *une petite dicte*, the way the French liked to teach. The teacher dictates, and you have to write everything down. It sharpens your ear but you're paying so much attention to spelling and accents that you get into the habit of speaking French by typing the words in your mind and then reading them back to yourself, which slows you up. But at least Madame Faudel got me going, and encouraged me to speak freely even if I didn't get it right.

Meanwhile, I managed to convince the commandant in Key West, Captain Johnston, to help me put in for an official discharge. The Navy was as glad to get rid of me as I was to leave. In my place they got some trained secretaries, girls who were cute and more useful in that sort of job. It's always important to get the right person for the right task.

I joined the American Red Cross and got an assignment overseas in a department called Civilian Relief. Overseas meant France, and Andy was my biggest motivation. I wasn't certain I'd get to see him, but I thought I'd have a lot better chance in Paris than in Miami.

OVERSEAS

I left Miami in the summer of 1918, first for New York. In New York I stayed with Carolyn in her apartment and both of us got the flu. It took a month to get over it, so I didn't sail for Europe until September. A convoy of Red Cross women was leaving from Quebec.

I'd packed so much in my suitcase that when I picked it up at Carolyn's apartment, I discovered it was too heavy to lift. A boy on a bicycle volunteered to carry it to the elevated train. He turned the corner with the suitcase and I never saw it again. Fortunately, my steamer trunk had already been sent along with the unit.

As these things often turn out, the stolen suitcase became an advantage. Because of my small misfortune, I got a lot of concessions on the ship, including a separate stateroom. The contents I never really missed.

We crossed the Atlantic in rough weather, our convoy of ships all camouflaged, everything blacked out. The first day or two I was seasick but as we got into a real storm I got my sea legs and all my seagoing proclivities came out. You've never seen the sea until you've seen it from a blacked-out ship. I was so thrilled to walk the decks, I forgot all about how we were vulnerable to submarines.

The passage took almost a week and we landed at Avonmouth, which is downriver from Bristol, England. A Canadian officer took several of us to tea at a Bristol hotel, and we took the evening train to London. The city was completely blacked out, with no lights at all except the blue lights of the underground shelters.

We proceeded to France via channel boat. I started to get seasick again, threw on my clothes and went up on deck. There I was all right. We landed at Le Havre and took the train to Paris. Red Cross headquarters was at the old Regina Hotel near the Place Jeanne d'Arc, right on the Rue de Rivoli, which I think of still as the center of Paris. I slept upstairs in a little room and hung around the headquarters for several weeks.

The Paris we know and are supposed to love on sight is not the crowded, filthy old medieval city that grew up on the Seine from the time of Julius Caesar. The Paris we know was planned by Baron Haussmann under the direction of Louis Napoleon. He must have had tremendous feeling for beauty and harmony. He opened Paris up with those wonderful circular boulevards.

I first saw Paris in a kind of blue-gray light, with all its buildings so harmonious with their mansard roofs and their elegant proportions, everywhere the grace of trees and little green spaces and parks, parks of gravel instead of grass because people used them so much that grass wouldn't grow there. All Americans are supposed to feel the charm of Paris, and I, for one, did.

It's a city that can hardly be improved, and with all the obvious excitement of settling down in it, there was my secret excitement of knowing

that Andy was in France. My old friend Pete Robineau, who'd introduced me to Andy, was back in Paris with some intelligence agency and
he came to see me at once. I had news about his wife and their new baby,
born in Miami after he'd left. I told Pete about the lovely little girl he'd
never seen, and he told me about Andy. Andy had been transferred
from the French air corps to the American air corps and was stationed
at some airbase out in the countryside. Pete said he'd let Andy know I'd
arrived.

There wasn't much civilian relief work to do at the Red Cross headquarters, but I pitched in as best I could. I went out with a doctor to see
some of the war refugees and she taught me something I've never forgotten: A refugee is a person in a state of shock. I saw families where the
mother sat in a kind of trance while the children swirled around,
ignored. These images stayed with me, and helped me understand the
plight of refugees in Miami sixty years later. They, too, were in shock and
they, too, had fled difficult circumstances, especially those who came
from Haiti and the West Indies. It's difficult for refugees to adjust until
they've had a rest from fatigue, and that can take time. This traumatic
condition needs to be recognized much more than it is.

In the lobby of the Red Cross headquarters, I bumped into Ethel
Sullivan, who'd been an instructor at Wellesley. I complained that I
didn't have enough to do. She put me to work at what I could do best:
writing reports. She'd been doing publicity for the children's bureau of
the Red Cross and was about to be sent home. I became her unexpected
replacement.

The idea was to send dispatches back to the States about the good
work the Red Cross had been doing in France. I was supposed to travel
all over the countryside, mostly to ceremonies at children's hospitals and
clinics that the American Red Cross had started and that the French
were about to take over. There was a sense that the war would soon end.

One day I was working at headquarters, scribbling around at a desk
in a little office, when through the door behind me I heard my name
spoken. I knew it was Andy. The moment of seeing him, I'll never
forget. He couldn't wait to tell me he'd gotten the *Croix de Guerre*
with two palms. He was wearing the decorations and he looked wonderful in his uniform.

He took me out to dinner that night and at first I was ecstatic. As the
evening went on I realized there was a great deal of stiffness between us.

We were not as free with each other as we had been, there were all kinds of differences now, a lot of water under the bridge. He told me about a girl with whom he'd had an affair. I didn't regret that at all because he'd been fighting and could have been killed at any time. I couldn't regret anything he'd wanted and the affair was over and he said he was coming back to me. We walked around Paris and I was happy, in a constrained sort of way.

During our walk, he told me the war was ending and he was going straight back to Miami. It was so funny. I had just gotten to France, and the most exciting thing about France in the first place was that Andy was here, and now he was going home to get a job.

After he left I had that familiar sense of loss, of his always leaving for somewhere, but I consoled myself with his promise that he'd still be in Miami when I returned. In the meantime, I loved Paris so much I could hardly be distracted from it by any personal troubles of my own.

I left the room at the Regina and took up lodging in an inexpensive sort of student dormitory, on a sweet little street called the Rue de Grande Chaumiere. I was on the second floor with a window looking down into a garden. It was a bare room but it had a comfortable bed, and the best part of all was the fireplace. It meant a great deal to me because I was always chilly. In the French style, a man would come up to the room and fill the fire box with kindling and with *boulets* — little round balls of coal dust.

There was a closet with a bowl with cold running water, and the toilet was down the corridor. I could heat water in a tea kettle. For two francs fifty I could take a bath in a great old French tub in the box room downstairs. For another 50 centimes, a linen sheet was put in the bathtub before the water was poured in.

The Red Cross paid us something like $100 a month for expenses, so we couldn't afford many lined baths. Since the Regine had a beautiful bathroom with plenty of hot water, we usually took our baths there.

We discovered the Queen of Hearts, an odd one-room restaurant on a side street off the Montmartre. A group of us in the Red Cross who played around together used the Queen of Hearts as our base of operations. Americans had more or less taken the place over, we got to know each other and sat together. You rented your napkin by the week, and stored it in a napkin ring left on a rack. I thought it was a sensible way to handle napkins. I don't remember that the food was remarkable but the food wasn't remarkable anywhere in those days. The only dessert was something called Riz a la Confiture, a boiled rice with jam, and when we could afford that, we felt pretty luxurious. We paid with food stamps.

At the Queen of Hearts I met a tall man with a pointed van Dyke beard. His name was Sidney and he'd been with the American ambulance corps in Italy during the retreat from Caporetto. Sidney had run into two interesting people he liked to talk about, a man named John Dos Passos and a man named Hemingway. He told me about their new kind of writing, stripped of its superfluous words down to bare bones. The young writers were staying in Paris, but I didn't suspect they were going to create great literature in America. I met Dos Passos just to say "How do you do?" but I never met Hemingway.

Later I wondered if the retreat from Caporetto, a long and bloody ordeal, didn't affect the psychology of these writers and in a way bring about their new kind of writing. Hemingway seemed to have the cynical point of view that all human nature was undependable, and the war had proved that. There didn't seem to be much good in anything. His terse, epigrammatic style fit that terse, bare conclusion.

One of my closest new friends was a man in my department at the Red Cross named Frederick. Then there was Bertha from the YMCA. We'd all do things together. Carolyn Percy later came over with the Red Cross canteen service. An American salmon manufacturer must have sold the Army on canned salmon, because the canteen girls served the troops endless trays of it, along with peas. Carolyn and I were both out of town a great deal, but I saw her in Paris.

I was only in the city for a month or so when the rumors began to fly that the war was really over. It had been a terrible war, a war of the trenches that had killed off a generation of young Frenchmen and Englishmen, to say nothing of Germans, though I can't be sorry about the Germans because they were the ones who invaded.

For me, who hadn't seen the war firsthand, it was a time of excitement, a feeling that history was being remade. On the morning when the peace treaty finally was going to be signed, a hush fell all across Paris. We were in the office on the balcony, and I stood looking down the Rue de Rivoli, amazed at the silence. One woman was running along the street crying and it was so quiet I could hear her sobs.

Suddenly, the silence was broken as the guns went off from up and down the river, they boomed out from both banks, and sounded 20 to 25 times. All the pigeons in the Place de la Concorde rose up and flew to all the roofs. The war was over, it was extraordinary, everyone was gasping for breath, everyone was crying with grief and with joy — grief for the men who were dead and would never see such a day as this. Thousands of people rushed into the streets, down the Place de la Concorde and the Rue de Rivoli; the city was jam-packed with people. I'd never seen anything like it.

I rushed out of the building but couldn't shove my way through the crowds. There was a great procession and I was carried along in it, happy to go wherever it went. Everyone was kissing and shouting and crying, as Paris had erupted. You could almost understand the French Revolution when you saw how they came out for this amazing moment.

General Jack Pershing was stuck in his automobile in the middle of the crowd. I saw him and yelled and he waved back. We ran around, we hollered, we shouted, we danced and sang the Marseillaise in the streets, the excitement lasted far into the night. Finally, I found an elevated perch on the coping on one of the fountains in the plaza — I think it was dry. From there, I watched the crowds empty out and circle around — first there would be nobody and then a multitude. A French woman with two darling children came up to me and said, "Madame, would you kiss the children? I want them never to forget this night." They've grown up now and had their own children and suffered another war, but at the moment I kissed them, another war seemed inconceivable. Everybody was kissing everybody.

The war was officially ended but I stayed on with the American Red Cross. I was expected to travel from place to place and write stories about the turning over of Red Cross clinics to the local authorities. My department tried to produce five stories a day that could be submitted to the AP wire service — whether they took them or not was another question. I think they took some of mine, though there was no byline so it was hard to tell. My family in Taunton wrote and said they'd seen some articles in the Boston paper about events I'd been covering.

I traveled French railroads on an *ordre de mission*, a sort of free pass so I didn't need a ticket. I saw a great deal of France that was beyond the normal tourist boundaries. I wore a uniform, an oxford grey skirt that came down to my ankles plus a heavy tunic modeled after the British officers' tunics with huge unnecessary pockets. Red Cross uniforms were so heavy and baggy that I could even sleep in them and nobody would notice any extra wrinkles.

At the various banquets given in honor of the clinics there were long speeches and wonderful food. I tasted wines that I've never tasted before or since. Just one glass from any of the five varieties we'd be given at a dinner, and I'd hear the flowers and smell the birds. This was delightful work.

After the fighting stopped, I was sent to Italy. My assignment was to chaperone five carloads of corrugated iron barracks for people who'd lost their houses in an earthquake outside of Florence. During the crossing of the mountains from France, the five carloads somehow disappeared. I never found out what happened to them. I had to report the loss to Colonel Bartlett, the head of the American Red Cross in Italy, whose office was in Rome. On my way to see him, my wallet and all my money disappeared.

We made a stop in Turin, where I learned that Colonel Bartlett had left Rome and gone to Florence. I changed trains at Pisa and headed for Florence, reduced to mumbling "No speak Italian, no speak Italian" to conductors who asked for my ticket. The British Army was in charge in Florence, and the officers I met were very helpful. As Red Cross workers we were supposedly helping them, but generally it worked the other way.

I finally caught up with Col. Bartlett in the mountain town of Montecatino. I was the only English-speaking woman within miles. Col. Bartlett had a room at one end of the enormous hotel and very judiciously got me a room way at the other end so there would be no scandal. We drove back together in his car to Florence where I stayed with a lovely Italian family who lived in the earthquake country outside the city. They told me stories in French and in English about the recent quakes.

A couple of Red Cross friends and I went to Venice for the weekend and also had a week in Rome but I missed Paris. To my mind, Paris was the center of the world.

Then in the fall of 1919 I was sent with a cameraman, Captain Edwardt, into the Balkans. The Balkans were largely Mohammedan and no male doctor was allowed to see a woman, so the Red Cross had collected all the women doctors they could find and installed them in crude baby clinics way up in the mountains. They taught the local women to bathe their babies in big wooden bread troughs. A lot of left-over war supplies, powdered milk and tongue depressors, etc., were being diverted to these clinics.

We went down through Italy to Trieste: my cameraman, his trunk of movie film, and me. We went from Trieste on a broken-down Austrian railway carriage to Zagreb, in Croatia. Those days there was Croatia, and Serbia, Montenegro, Albania, and Macedonia, all separate countries in very bad condition. Now it's all Yugoslavia. From Zagreb we took a narrow-gauge railroad to Ragusa — now Dubrovnik — right on the shores of the Adriatic. Every time we arrived in the newest strange place, I'd sit down on the trunk of film and wait for Edwardt to find the Red Cross headquarters.

From Dubrovnik we boarded an Italian gunboat with some American nurses. Most of us were below decks, and when the boat started to pitch and roll everybody got seasick. I put on my clothes and went up on deck but it didn't help. A company of Italian soldiers and I lay on the decks and vomited into the scuppers, their boots were in my face and my boots were in their faces. I had a very useful heavy cape, and somebody picked me up and put me on a bench and covered me with it. I finally slept and they woke me up at Durazzo (now called Durres) farther down the coast.

We left a lovely hotel there, piled into a truck and headed into the mountains. I was amazed we didn't fall over the edge as we moved through Montenegro, Cetinje, and Podgorica (now Titograd), visiting the clinics in each successive place, carrying powdered milk and bales of pajamas in our truck.

There were Serbian refugees living in caves along the river. We entered one cave to see how the people were getting along, and a very silly man from the Red Cross began to toss out boxes of milk and the pajamas. The Serbians rioted, screamed, and mobbed us for these things. I never thought we'd get out of the cave alive.

Next, we went to Sarajevo in Bosnia where the war began. We stayed there for a day or two. I stood on the street corner where the archduke was assassinated, which prompted Austria's invasion of Serbia and changed the whole history of this century.

Then it was on to Albania, where there were few roads, let alone any transportation. We had to go up and down the mountains on little horses that plodded patiently as we sat on them and watched the scenery. The women were provided with gray sateen knickers underneath our skirts, so we could ride in decency.

Albania still was run by various tribes, a few of which had made their peace with the British. They didn't exactly understand what the American Red Cross was doing. At a place called Elbasan, where neither the British nor the Americans had heard from local authorities, I carried a letter from a British general to present to the head man of the tribe. That was Hassan Bey Elbasanni. He was dressed and ready for me in a frock coat and a white fez. He had the idea I was an important government official.

I met with him and with his council, all men of course, in their chambers. A Red Cross nurse went with me because I couldn't be unchaperoned. Through a French interpreter, Hassan Bey Elbasanni asked me if the United States would be willing to take over Albania. I said I was only traveling through and couldn't make such decisions on my own, but the United States did not take over other countries. We'd be happy, though, to help the women and children in the clinics.

As I was giving this speech, a barefooted servant came in and stood beside me with a great silver tray, on which he balanced a few glasses of water, a glass full of spoons, a glass of jam, and an empty glass. I didn't know what to do with these. The interpreter told me the ladies in the harem took a spoonful of jam, ate it, and put the used spoon into the empty glass. This was a local concession to females.

At night, we put up in what was called a Turkish Han, a low masonry structure like a barn. It enclosed everything, horses, people, etc. The men slept on a platform around a fire, but they didn't know what to do with me. I was too odd to be taken to the women's quarters. Finally, I was allowed to lie down next to them, my feet to the fire with theirs.

Soon we arrived at the waters of Lake Ohrid, on the border of Albania and Macedonia. From there, we were taken by jeep across the mountains into Serbia, where Dr. Rosemary Slaughter ran a famous clinic. After I got the story of that, we went on to Salonika at the head of the Aegean Sea. My cameraman wanted to stay and get more photographs but I was fed up with horseback and rain and wanted to get down to Athens to a decent hotel.

I went ahead on the first train I'd seen for months. There was pink-shaded electric light in the dining car. A nice English gentleman whom I'd met at Red Cross headquarters invited me to dinner. As we tunneled down through the Vale of Tempe, a great low hump of mountains, I asked the waiter, "What mountain is that?" and he said, "Madam, that is Olympus." I never thought of Olympus as anything but a towering Olympian, and here was this glorified hill. I saw no gods.

In Athens, the Britisher took me up to the Acropolis by moonlight. It was like coming back to Florida, the same warm and easy climate, the pepper trees and the blue sky and the view of the blue Aegean beyond.

Still it wasn't Paris, which I was more anxious than ever to see. I took the first ship out of Athens, which turned out to be a ponderous Amazon River steamer that had carried troops to Constantinople and was now going to Marseilles. It had an enormous general cabin where about twenty passengers ate. I was put in a small stateroom with three other women: a schoolgirl going to France from Athens, an old French governess going back home for the first time after the war, and a very jolly woman, loud-voiced and singing, who was going to start a sailor's boarding house in Marseille. She spent most of her time down in the hole with the sailors.

The food was awful. They cooked a great deal in rancid olive oil, everything tasted of it. I haven't been able to touch olive oil since. I lived mostly on tea and crackers, and arrived in Marseilles with the best figure I'd had for a long time.

At the head of the table sat a romantic figure, smoking a cigarette in a long holder just like in the movies. Her name was Madame Rosnopolous. She had her eye on a Canadian naval captain who had been stationed on one of the Greek islands. He and I and two Greeks, one who spoke French and this Canadian who spoke no French, tried to play bridge. It was a little difficult. The only book in English, a report on Shackleton's trip to the South Pole, this Canadian insisted on reading aloud to me. It was very boring.

As we came out the end of the Corinth canal, somebody told me of the great battle called Lepanto. Two giant fleets, one belonging to the Pope and Don Juan of Austria, the other to Turkey, clashed in the last campaign in which oared vessels were used. I thought how terrible it must have been on the oars: If you lost you died and if you won you didn't have anything to do but keep on rowing.

We stopped in Naples harbor. There was a storm and smoke from Vesuvius was mixing with the rain and people came out under umbrellas to sing "Funiculi Funicula" to us and tried to sell us things. The storm was so bad we had to put back a couple of times, and the volcano of Stromboli was acting up. Finally we sneaked out and eventually got to Marseilles. By that time, Madame Rosnopolous, who still had her eye on this British officer, said to me: "Does he belong to you?" I said, "No, he's nothing to me. If you want him you can get him."

When we got to Marseilles the British officer took me up to a very fine hotel and gave me a wonderful luncheon. Just as we finished, in walked Madame Rosnopolous. Such a coincidence. The three of us went to Paris together on the afternoon train, and the Britisher put me in my compartment, shook hands, and left for another compartment. In the morning, I looked out and there were the Britisher and Madame Rosnopolous going off in tandem. They had no language in common, but seemed to get along very well.

The Red Cross was closing down in Paris, and they'd moved their headquarters from the Hotel Regina to an old American woman's club on the Rue de Chevreuse. I took a room at another hotel, the Lutetia, where I lived for the rest of my stay. I hung on as long as I could. Meanwhile, my father cabled that he could offer me the job of assistant editor of the Miami *Herald*.

Oh yes, another thing. I forgot to mention I was engaged to be married. Or at least I think I got engaged. It was to Frederick, one of my pals from my sojourn in Paris. He and I had been having a good time intermittently, and when I returned to Paris he'd decided he was in love and asked me to marry him. My first reaction was: "No, Frederick, dear." I was still carrying a torch for Andy, so I had no thoughts of other men and couldn't entertain them. But Frederick came on very strong — like the Navy recruiters had, I suppose. I didn't realize he felt all that. Then he began to mourn around. Finally I said, "Oh, Frederick, all right," if only to make him happy. I don't suppose I really meant it.

COMING HOME

Frederick and I came back on the same ship. That made me nervous, but it was nothing compared to having to go to his hometown in Pennsylvania to meet his mother. He'd been married before and had a little girl and there I was all mixed up with it. The family owned the local newspaper, which made our marriage very sensible theoretically — if only I could have been happy living with Frederick. I realized by then I couldn't, but I didn't tell Frederick that. I told him I didn't think I'd be happy in Pennsylvania. Then he said he'd come to Florida, which only got things more confused.

To escape the whole dilemma, I went to New York to visit Carolyn, who by then was teaching at Washington Irving High School and had an apartment in Greenwich Village. I found out Carolyn had organized a dance for me, in honor of guess who. Frederick couldn't get there for some reason, which was all for the best. It also turned out well for Carolyn, because somebody brought a delightful older man named Kelley Cole. He was an opera singer with a wealthy mother, who had his suits made in London. Even his underwear was specially tailored. The two of them fell in love and got married almost immediately.

After the party for Frederick without Frederick I went back to Taunton to visit my grandparents and my aunt. My grandfather was quite old by then. This was the last time I saw him, since after I returned to Florida he died at 94. He'd always been afraid of being buried alive, so his casket was laid in a sort of marble cave he'd had built at the cemetery on Mayflower Hill — placed beside the caskets of my mother and little Uncle Walter.

My grandmother and aunt were bitterly disappointed I planned to go back to Florida. They still harbored the deep antipathy towards my father, after all those years.

On my way south, I made the rounds of other relatives. I saw my cousins, the daughters of my mother's oldest sister Alice, at their big farm outside of Wallingford, Connecticut. Of the three of them, Margaret, Mabel, and Pauline, I was closest to Margaret. I always think of her as a long-legged dark-eyed child with the wonderful sweep of long glassy chestnut hair, running around with her hair blowing in the wind.

I stopped over in Washington to see my father's sister, Aunt Stella. I looked like Aunt Stella. She wore thick glasses. The Stoneman women were not pretty. They were not even handsome, but they were so intelligent it didn't matter. I got to know my aunt's adopted child, Margaret. This cousin Margaret was the head of Red Cross workers at St. Elizabeth's Hospital for the Insane. Years later, she knew Ezra Pound when he was brought back from Europe after World War II, accused of broadcasting against the United States and put in St. Elizabeth's. She didn't like him particularly. Margaret told me that stories of his being mistreated at St. Elizabeth's weren't true at all. It was a lot of hooey about him — in any other country and at any other time he'd have been shot for a traitor. Margaret liked Mrs. Pound, whom she got to know after Mrs. Pound came over and was sort of dumped at the airport. Mrs. Pound called Traveller's Aid and was put in touch with Margaret. Margaret went straight to Eleanor Roosevelt, who was a friend of hers, and Mrs. Roosevelt arranged to have Mrs. Pound taken care of.

I arrived in Florida sometime in January, 1920. As I rode the train from Washington, I realized how thrilled I was to be getting back. Andy was in Miami, but Miami itself was enough of an attraction. Again I felt that sense of discovery, or in this case, rediscovery. My roots had gone down well in the three years before I went abroad.

By this time my father and stepmother were living in a small apartment. He was building the house that he would occupy the rest of his life in a development called Spring Garden, a kind of an island upriver a bit from the Seybold Canal. Mr. Seybold had given him two lots for the price of one, in return for his putting up one of the earliest houses.

The small apartment had no room for me in it, so I was taken in by Philip and Mary Clarkson, old friends from my earlier time in Miami who lived in Riverside. Andy and I resumed our involvement with a glad cry. By now, my divorce was final and there was nothing standing between us. All bets with Frederick were off as well. Poor Frederick — whom I'd been avoiding anyway — was promptly forgotten. It didn't surprise him much. I don't think he was ever convinced I meant it when I got engaged to him. I don't even think he was very sad about me. He stayed in Pennsylvania and we corresponded. We stayed friends.

The trouble with Andy was that he was a returned veteran, and returned veterans are often battered men. He was exhausted from fighting in the war, and also progressively unhappy. He tried to get a newspaper job but ended up in real estate, which is what half the city seemed to be doing. He struggled along, made enough money to buy a car, then lost the money and had to give up the car.

I had a steady position, assistant editor, that paid $30 a week, which was quite decent in those days. My father insisted there be no discrimination in salaries between men and women on the *Herald*. I worked on the editorial page and had a column of my own, called "The Galley." The title didn't make much sense, but it gave me a voice. "The Galley" was a string of short items, sayings, and musings on local and national affairs. I commented on the plight of women ("the more you read books about women written by men, the less surprised you are that men don't believe that women are people"); and about the spirit of south Florida ("Is it any wonder that south Florida, this new Florida, is young and hopeful and confident? The tired ways of the old countries and of the north have no meaning for us, who are conscious of the banner of a great new belief").

I wrote poetry at the head of every column. Most of it wasn't any good, but who can write good poetry every day?

Generally, I felt I was moving ahead while Andy was flopping around. Slowly, I began to see less of him. It wasn't that I had another boyfriend. Since I expected to be married again I couldn't have had another boyfriend and surreptitious affairs were out of the question. I never saw any use to them. It was simpler to live out in the open.

Though Andy and I were engaged, that meant nothing in the way of immediate marriage. His work continued to be unprofitable and he wouldn't have married a woman who had a better job than he did. He couldn't face it and I didn't blame him. It was just too much. Finally he was offered a job by a friend in a Northern city. He said he thought he should go and I agreed. That's the last I saw of him for many years. He left me with the familiar sense of misery.

In time, I heard Andy was married and had children and a happy life. It was inevitable. I was beginning to realize that I was not the marrying kind. In my secret heart, I didn't want to get married again. I never wanted children. I wanted books. I couldn't see why every woman had to have children. It wasn't necesssary. I didn't want a normal family life, I wanted my own life in my own way. I was too interested in writing editorials and in writing my column. It was in the column that I started to talk about Florida as landscape and as geography, to investigate it and to explore it. To me, this was more important than getting tied up with a man.

I discovered in myself — as many women, even if they outwardly reject the idea are inwardly aware — that when you're in love with a man, you are unconsciously dependent on him. You're dominated by the force of masculinity. I couldn't have been more in love with Andy, but I couldn't let him dominate me. Possibly because I was four years older, I would have tended to try to dominate him. That wouldn't have worked, either.

At the same time I was also in love with him in the imaginative way. He was fixed in my mind as a source of affection long after he'd gone and had children and lived happily ever after. It was a protection for me to have him in the back of my mind. There were plenty of men to frolic with in Miami in those days, and I had fun going out to dinner and to dances at Felzer's Pier, and a group of us revived the business of swimming over at the beaches in the morning. But there wasn't any man in whom I was remotely interested as I had been in Andy. He was my great safeguard. I recognized that and was grateful for it, because it enabled me to go on as an individual and as a writer. After Andy, I was completely free of marriage, even in my unconscious.

It's not difficult to talk about my sex life — it can be dealt with in one sentence. I didn't have any sex life. Sex ended with my marriage. Marriage taught me that sex can be a good and healthy thing, and I enjoyed it while it lasted. I wasn't one to have sex outside of marriage, and I would have been ashamed in my father's eyes because he himself had lived in Florida alone for many years before marrying Lilla. In fact, he'd waited for two years after my mother's death before he remarried. Especially because he'd become a good Episcopalian, my father wouldn't have tolerated a daughter who was running around being stupid and promiscuous. It seemed stupid to me, too. And since I wasn't going to get married again that was it for the sex.

So I haven't had any sex since before 1915 and I've done very well without it, thank you. It hasn't been any great loss. People don't seem to realize that the energy that goes into sex, all the emotion that surrounds it, can be well employed in other ways.

Miami in 1920 was completely different from the Miami I had left four years before. The small town I'd known on the Miami River and the bay was teeming with people, men who'd come back from the war, men who remembered how delightful it was down here in training camps. Miami had doubled in size, and that was just the beginning of the energy that would culminate in the great Boom of 1922-26.

When I had left for France, there were the two casinos, one house, and no trees on Miami Beach. When I returned, there were dozens of buildings and great clumps of imported landscaping, and the art deco hotels had begun to appear. The beach itself was getting crowded. The Roney Plaza was built, and Carl Fisher had created the Roman Pools. In the fall and the winter, we swam in the Roman Pools and danced upstairs in the ballroom. In the spring and the summer, we danced on the dance floor outside the hotel, danced under the moonlight and electric light, danced to a good band with the wind blowing in from the sea.

During Prohibition, the hotels had tea dances. After a tea dance, we'd go someplace to eat, then go back to the beach for some swimming. "We" included numerous old friends with whom I'd been reunited: Frank Ashworth, the engineer and his wife, Myrtle, the reporter on the rival paper who scooped me constantly. The Ashworths had poker parties. I never played cards of any kind because I had no card sense, but I enjoyed sitting around the table and reading a book and listening to the funny things they said. People are witty and amusing when they play poker.

I got to know lovable Franklin Harris. He was a pianist who'd toured the country playing for musical comedies before he came to Miami in the real estate boom. He stayed on after the bust and the hurricane of 1926, and volunteered to help Dr. Bowman F. Ashe rescue the University of Miami. Dr. Ashe had sacrificed everything he had — up to and including his own life insurance — to build the campus, and developer George Merrick gave the land. The war interrupted the project, and the administration building stood there unfinished for several years, with Dr. Ashe in all kinds of financial trouble. Franklin Harris arrived as a delightful, piano-playing reinforcement.

Harris's wife Alice was always amused when I called her a bluestocking. With her French and her literary background, she was proud to be an intellectual snob. The Harrises were great friends of the Fairchilds of Coconut Grove. David Fairchild was the plant explorer who traveled the world to collect tropical plants, many of which he brought to his plant introduction gardens in Miami. The Fairchilds bought a beautiful bayfront estate in Coral Gables, and I was delighted to make their acquaintance. David Fairchild was one of the people who stimulated my interest in local flora and fauna, which in turn stimulated my interest in the Everglades.

David Fairchild would never have become a botanist if it hadn't been for a wealthy and eccentric benefactor named Barbour Lathrop. At Natalie Newell's bookshop, sort of a gathering place in town, I first ran into Uncle Barbour, as I was soon privileged to call him. He was an elderly gentleman of the old school who had stuffy relatives who'd raised hounds in England, etc., and he'd inherited a lot of money. Every winter, he came to Miami to be near the Fairchilds.

On his frequent trips around the world, Uncle Barbour kept seeing plants and trees that he thought should be in the U.S. He met David Fairchild on a boat going to Naples. Fairchild was an entomologist at the time and was on his way to study Italian termites until Uncle Barbour talked him into becoming a botanist and gave him enough money to study in Bonn for several years. After that, the two of them went around the world looking for plants. Uncle Barbour was a hoity toity gentleman and traveling with him must have been a pain in the neck for David Fairchild.

Then Uncle Barbour gave the U.S. government the money to start a bureau of plant introduction and David Fairchild was hired as chief explorer. After Fairchild married Marian Bell, the daughter of Alexander Graham Bell, they came to Miami to start their tropical garden and bought their beautiful estate. They had a plain brownboard house with airy, high ceilings, like the ones the British built in the West Indies. It was built on a ridge, overlooking Biscayne Bay.

The year I returned to Miami, the Fairchilds were off traveling around the world again, and my friends the Harrises were house-sitting for them. The Harrises invited me over for dinner many times, and on weekends, I stayed in the guest cottage. Franklin Harris would play the piano and we'd go swimming in the swimming pool and cook supper outdoors. That's when I began to realize I belonged in Coconut Grove. It was connected to Miami but had its own character, a town in its own right before Miami was ever conceived.

That same year, I had dinner once a week with Uncle Barbour. He'd send a car and chauffeur for me, and we had a special table at the McAllister Hotel. He was a delightful companion, but you had to watch your step with him. He kept you on pins and needles, and you never knew when your head would be shouted off about some little thing.

Eventually, Uncle Barbour was paralyzed with some illness and it was dreadful. You couldn't understand a word he said. Thank goodness he finally died.

I saw many other old friends, including Mrs. Bryan and her daughter, Ruth Bryan Owen. William Jennings Bryan had died by now, but Mrs. Bryan still lived in Miami. Ruth had been overseas in the war, sent to Egypt as a nurse with the British. There she had met a retired major, Reginald Owen, who had some kind of service-induced malady called Bright's Disease and was told to live in a warm climate. The two of them got married and came back to Coconut Grove and bought a big house called Chota-Khoti — which in Burmese means "little house." The little house behind it was called Burra-Khoti, which means "big house." Reginald's family had had tea plantations in Burma.

Ruth Bryan Owen lectured, ran the women's clubs, and eventually ran for the legislature. She was the first woman to represent Florida in congress. She was tall and beautiful, and blessed with the oratorical ability of her father though she never agreed with his ideas on bi-metallism and religion.

One of the great local projects of the early 1920s was the completion of the formal gardens at Vizcaya, the Italian estate along the bay built before World War I by James Deering. I got to know the Deering family through Marian (Mrs. Charles) Deering, the widow of the brother of James Deering. The Deerings were from Chicago. All of them were very rich, thanks to the agricultural machinery business.

I met Mrs. Charles Deering through a local French club. We were supposed to speak French all the time, but usually we broke down and spoke English. She was a brilliant woman who spoke good French already and didn't really need the practice. Since James Deering never married, Mrs. Charles Deering's daughters, Mrs. Chauncey McCormick and Mrs. Danielson, were the heirs to Vizcaya.

The Charles Deering place was in an undeveloped part of Dade County, south of Miami, between Old Cutler Road and the bay. There was a beautiful frame house and next to that a newer, uglier structure made of limestone and concrete. On the estate was an enormous Indian mound which Charles Deering kept intact. Later, when its tremendous archaeological value became known, it was bought by the state.

When you went to Mrs. Deering's place for dinner, you'd have cocktails in the drawing room of the rock house, then go out across a boardwalk to the old frame house, where there was a parlor and a big dining room. They had a butler from Spain, named Eusebio, and an upstairs maid named Catherine, who were married.

Mrs. Deering was hospitable, amusing, and very frank. One time we were supposed to play bridge, and I refused. She said to me: "You'll never be a social success if you don't learn how to play bridge." I retorted: "Mrs. Deering I don't really want to be a social success. I'd have to spend all my time playing bridge, and I don't like bridge." She was the kind of woman who'd accept comments like that. It didn't matter to her.

There were a lot of stories about Mrs. Deering's penny-pinching, and I think most of them were true. For dinner, she would serve fish that were caught right off her own pier so they hadn't cost anything. Her specialty was cheese souffles, I suspect because the ingredients were inexpensive. We'd have vegetables from her garden. There was always a meat course, but the meat was terrible. You could hardly cut it, because she'd have bought the cheapest kind.

The first time I sat next to her son-in-law, Chauncey McCormick, he murmured: "Don't drink the champagne — she's had it around for years and it's flat." Another time, Mrs. Deering herself told the story about having asked the butler why people didn't smoke the cigarettes that were offered them, and the butler had said: "It's because the cigarettes are full of worms." She ordered the cook to bake the cigarettes and put them back in the boxes on the table. She was surprised when her guests didn't smoke the cigarettes with baked worms, either.

When Mrs. Deering went to Paris, she'd stay in her brother-in-law's place — boarded up and with sheets over all the furniture — so she wouldn't have to pay a hotel. Once, she sent her son to Switzerland, and had him going around and around on the same train because the ticket was good for the whole summer.

I think she was rather proud of her reputation as a tightwad. When the Spanish Republic was taken over by Franco, she was truly overjoyed. To her, Franco was the tightwad who could bring Spain to its senses and keep it frugal!

But it didn't matter what we ate at the Deerings, we always had a good time. And they were smart to have kept the Indian mound and to have resisted digging into it. It's been very important to Florida history.

Though James Deering built Vizcaya and gained a national reputation as an intellectual and a lover of art, he hardly ever read a book and knew nothing about art. It was his brother Charles and Mrs. Deering who had the art books and studied all the art. Eventually, the art in the Charles Deering house went to the Art Institute of Chicago, but I convinced the Deering heirs to give the art books to the University of Miami Library. It's a terrific collection.

DISCOVERING THE EVERGLADES

The *Herald* was a becoming a bigger and more important paper. I spent three years as assistant editor, plus writing my column every day. There was more pressure in this than I realized. There were all kinds of pressures. People wanted to know me, people wanted me to do things for them, to use my column to advertise things they believed in. I became a bit of a Miami celebrity.

Once in a while, my column would make a difference to somebody. A story came out in the paper that a North Dakota boy came walking into Florida and was arrested and put in a labor camp as a vagrant. They did that in those days. They made the vagrants work very hard and they beat them when they didn't. This boy was named Martin Tabert. He was beaten to death in the labor camp.

The news of his death shocked me so much I wrote a simple ballad titled "Martin Tabert of North Dakota Is Walking Florida Now." It went as follows:

Martin Tabert of North Dakota is walking Florida now.
O children, hark to his footsteps coming, for he's walking soft and slow.
Through the piney woods and the cypress hollows,

A wind creeps up and it's him it follows.
Martin Tabert of North Dakota is walking Florida now.
They took him out to the convict camp, and he's walking Florida now.
O children, the tall pines stood and heard him when he was
moaning low.
The other convicts, they stood around him,
When the length of the black strap cracked and found him.
Martin Tabert of North Dakota. And he's walking Florida now.
They nailed his coffin boards together and he's walking Florida now.
O children, the dark night saw where they buried him, buried him,
buried him low.
And the tall pines heard where they went to hide him.
And the wind crept up to moan beside him.
Martin Tabert of North Dakota. And he's walking Florida now.
The whip is still in the convict camps, for Florida's stirring now.
Children, from Key West to Pensacola you can hear the great wind go.
The wind that he roused when he lay dying,
The angry voice of Florida crying,
"Martin Tabert of North Dakota,
Martin Tabert of North Dakota,
Martin Tabert of North Dakota,
You can rest from your walking now."

When this poem was published it received enormous attention. It was read in Tallahassee, read in the legislature, and as a result they abolished beating in the labor camps forever. What they substituted was a kind of sweat box, which may not have been much more humane, but at least they abolished the beatings. I think that's the single most important thing I was ever able to accomplish as a result of something I've written.

One important influence on my column was Mrs. Robert Morris Seymour, a distinguished lady who was involved in the Irish Revival, a rediscovery of Irishness for people who'd forgotten about it that resulted in a rediscovery of such writers as Lady Gregory and Synge. Mrs. Seymour had elaborate theories about regionalism, and noticed that I was writing things about a region but I wasn't calling it that. She gave me the idea of a region as the basis for what I was doing which was very useful. On the other hand, she was very dictatorial and wanted to direct everything I said along those lines. I wasn't ready to be directed. My instinct was to protect my life and my writing from all encroachments whatsoever.

But I have to thank Mrs. Seymour for steering me toward the Everglades, which changed my life much later on. One project I supported in print, partly out of my interest in regionalism, was the Everglades National Park. This idea really started with Ernest F. Coe. He was a landscape architect who'd come with his wife to Miami and, like so many others, lost his money in real estate speculation during the boom and the bust. In the meantime, he'd discovered the Everglades and decided it should be a national park.

Mr. Coe could be recognized by his seersucker suit frayed around the sleeves. He was always imperturbable and always talking about his park. Even people who were convinced there should be a park would have to hear Mr. Coe tell about it over and over again. My father was completely in favor of the park, but every time Mr. Coe came into the office his heart would sink, because he knew Mr. Coe would read him all the letters he'd gotten and all the letters he'd written.

A committee was formed with David Fairchild, John Oliver LaGorce of *National Geographic* magazine and other notables, but really it was Mr. Coe's project and it was Mr. Coe who persevered. He never got enough recognition. There ought to be a memorial to him out there. I'd love to see a life-sized bronze replica of a catamount like the one that stands in the monument avenue of old Bennington, Vermont. The catamount is the same as the Florida panther, *Felis concolor*. How we could afford such a statue I don't know, but it would be a fitting way to remember Mr. Coe.

I was also put on the park committee, and had begun to know the Everglades myself. Let me say right away that knowing the Everglades does not necessarily mean spending long periods of time walking around out there. Unlike other wilderness areas, where the naturalist is a hiker, camper, and explorer, the naturalist in the Everglades must usually appreciate it from a distance.

Most of the Everglades is under several inches of water, of course, but in the early 1920s the Tamiami Trail was being cut right through the heart of it. When I first visited the Everglades, the two-lane road was finished out as far as the Dade County line. A group of us would get up before daybreak and drive to the end, build a fire in the middle of the road, cook our breakfast, and watch the sun rise. There was the

Everglades beyond us, completely untouched. The grass and the islands of hardwoods stood alone in the light and the beautiful air. Sometimes, we fished in the canals and caught gar.

Once, I went out there with an Englishman. It was a cold morning, we were all frozen, and I guess we were being dull about the whole business because we'd been there before. We had our breakfast. We didn't see any birds, probably it was too cold for them to rise. Only the Englishman was bright and gay. Coming back on the Tamiami Trail he saw something, and yelled, "What's that?" We looked out at a great wheel of white birds slowly drifting over the land. It was an extraordinary sight. Birds seemed to leap into the air and then swing around in a huge circle. As soon as one group landed on the ground, another would lift off and fly.

Back in Miami, we asked around and discovered we'd witnessed the nuptial flight of the white ibis. That's the way they begin the breeding season. I saw it myself that dull, cold morning.

Far south of the Tamiami Trail was the Royal Palm Park, a raised crescent of limestone originally called Paradise Key. This little park got its start due to the pushing and prodding of Mrs. Mary Mann Jennings, wife of the ex-governor. The state built the road and so forth, and the Jenningses owned a lot of land nearby. I cast no aspersions, but there is something inevitable in thinking the Jenningses wanted to develop the land and that having the road built with public funds didn't hurt.

Anyway, the Jenningses donated the Royal Palm Park to the Federation of Women's Clubs, and this began the public purchases and other donations that led to the founding of the national park much later. I used to go down to Royal Palm Park and watch birds. In those days, birds were around everywhere. You could stand on the old roadway and look back toward a little bridge and see white ibis and wood stork sitting on the railings. You could walk over very quietly and watch the heron fishing. Owls in the trees would ask: "Who cooks for yoou?" Way off in the distance, others would answer: "I cooks for myself."

In the Ten Thousand islands at the edge of the Everglades, I saw great flocks of birds, amazing flights of 30,000 to 40,000 in one swoop, either coming from the sandy coasts to their rookeries or going from the rookeries to the sandy coasts where there weren't any predators.

There was another road into the Everglades, south to Flamingo at the eastern edge. Driving on it was like sledding across a plowed field. You'd go from higher land down to a long watery plain, and there was the little town of Flamingo. Once, a flight of bald eagles stayed over our heads almost all the way there. We always saw herons and egrets.

The houses in Flamingo were built up on stilts. There were the remains of an old hotel. People tried to make something of it, but it was just too remote. On one of my trips, I saw what looked like an old barn and next to that a still. As I was looking around a man came over the ridge with a rifle on his arm. I backed away and said something like: "Nice place you've got here, and what lovely weather." It one of the Robertses. There was a clan of them.

Another time I came across one of the Robertses on one of the rare bits of high ground, digging a hole. He was trying to plant a garden in what could hardly be called soil. "What are you doing for fertilizer?" I yelled. "I reaches out and gets a handful of mosquitoes," he answered.

Mosquitoes were thick in the Everglades, but they never bothered me much. They seemed to come and go in predictable fashion. The seasons of the Everglades are the mosquito season and the non-mosquito season. During the worst part of the mosquito season, people would move their cows up to Florida City where the cows wouldn't be killed by the bugs. People sent hives of bees down from Pensacola on flatboats to get the mangrove honey, but in the mosquito season, they'd take the bees away so the mosquitoes wouldn't kill them, either.

Photographs

My family on the porch of the Taunton house in 1893. Standing in the back (from left to right): Uncle Forrest Rundell and Aunt Katie, Aunt Alice and Uncle George Hopson, my grandfather Daniel Trefethen, and my mother Lillian (sitting on the railing). My father, Frank Stoneman, is holding me in his arms. Seated at left is my father's mother Aletha White Stoneman. Seated in the center is my Aunt Fanny, and on the right is my French grandmother Florence. On the steps are three cousins, Forrest Rundell, and Mabel and Pauline Hopson.

My mother Lillian.

My French grandmother
Florence.

My other grandmother, Aletha
White Stoneman.

I am one and a half here.

My senior class picture at Wellesley. I had a blank look. But if you look in the yearbook, all of us seemed to have blank looks. *Photograph courtesy of the Florida State Archives.*

The Fools' Club at Wellesley. A group of us dressed up and acted silly. Kneeling in the foreground, I am April's Fool. *Photograph courtesy of the Florida State Archives.*

With friends on Miami Beach in 1921. We called ourselves "The Sons and Daughters of I Will Arise." We cooked breakfast on the fire. That's me to the right wearing a bathing cap and with my stockings showing.

My house in Coconut Grove soon after it was built in 1926.

A group of us from a Miami women's club plant trees in South Miami. The man did most of the digging, and we did most of the standing around.

My father, Frank Bryant Stoneman, in front of his new house in a Miami development called Spring Garden.

In front of my house with one of my many cats.

In front of a friend's house, Coconut Grove, 1920s.

At Mt. Pélee, Martinique, 1930s.

Me, taken sometime in the 1940s.

Bookmobile, 1940s.

Signing copies of the first edition of *The Everglades: River of Grass*, Burdine's department store, 1947. *Photograph courtesy of the Miami Herald.*

At a lighthouse on North Carolina's Outer Banks. I was researching my book on hurricanes. My pointing out that the Carolinas had attracted a great number of hurricanes infuriated local boosters. *Photograph courtesy of the Florida State Archives.*

On the porch of the house next door to mine. The man in the chair is my Uncle
Charlie, not long before he died. The woman at my left is Marion Manley.
Photograph courtesy of the Florida State Archives.

Another edition of the Everglades book, 1965.

With a Miccosukee Indian in the Everglades, 1965. Actually, we're a few feet from the Indian headquarters and the water is so shallow the canoe ran aground. *Photograph courtesy of the Miami* Herald.

Stumping for the Friends of the Everglades, 1972-73. Man to my left is the great conservationist Art Marshall. To his left is Marjorie Carr, another noted conservationist. *Photograph courtesy of the Miami Herald.*

Tallahassee, April 4, 1985. On my 95th birthday, the state named the new Department of Natural Resources building after me. *Photograph courtesy of the Florida State Archives.*

At my desk in my house in Coconut Grove, 1985. I've lived here continuously since 1926. *Photograph courtesy of the Miami Herald, Albert Coya, photographer.*

III

On My
Own

One of the aspects of life in South Florida that I detested was the condition of the blacks. I had no sympathy with the old white Southern attitude. To me, slavery was the greatest crime ever committed, which we are still suffering to expiate. If my father taught me anything it was that. As a magistrate in Miami when he started the newspapers he had a reputation for absolute fairness between black and white.

I was particularly shocked in the auditorium of the high school where the American flag was on one side and the Confederate flag on the other. Now that I think of it maybe it wasn't the Confederate flag, maybe it was the state flag of Florida, which looked Confederate. Anyway, my stepmother was a Southern lady and as I often joked, she made the mistake of marrying a damn Yankee and got corrupted. Actually, she thought the Southern obsession with the Civil War, the Daughters of the Confederacy and so forth, was silly. She could think for herself.

Miami was not a typical old-fashioned Southern city. There were many Yankees here, so the feelings were complex. Still, the early settlers had set the civic tone, one of complete disregard for blacks. The men who built the city installed the usual Colored Town around Fifth Street. Blacks were servants but otherwise kept out of public life. Meanwhile, the best white families made a lot of money putting up shacks they rented to blacks at high prices.

There were neither toilets nor running water in the shacks. The inhabitants got their water from a standpipe stuck out in the street. When blacks didn't pay their rent, the doors of their houses were removed so they had to leave.

Every summer my father had the dengue fever, which the locals called breakbone fever. We learned it was carried by mosquitoes from Colored Town. I had it once, and it was very uncomfortable. You got sick and went to bed and perspired. It was totally unnecessary, and resulted from the fact that people in Colored Town had no running water and no toilets, and the whole arrangement was filthy. There were outdoor privies next to the public well and soon the well water was completely polluted. Residents of Colored Town washed their own laundry — and also the laundry they took in for white people — in the polluted water.

You can only keep a person in the gutter by getting into the gutter yourself, and that was exactly what happened in this business of the white people not caring what conditions in Colored Town really were like.

One thing I did on the *Herald*, at my father's suggestion, was start a Baby Milk Fund. It was the first charity in Miami not run by a church. Many families couldn't afford milk for their babies, and we raised the milk money through the newspaper. We also went out to find the families that needed the most assistance. Florence Coleman helped me in this effort. We had good success, but I began to realize that a milk fund wasn't enough. Next we needed family counselling, legal aid, job training, low-cost loans, and all the other services the black community lacked.

My father wouldn't hear of it, and said it was too much for the newspaper to handle. It was an important point on which we were divided. It was hard to tell people of his generation, the men who'd founded the city, that a helping hand was necessary, or that improving the lives of the disadvantaged would improve the lives of everyone else. To them, it was all a matter of making money and getting rich, then worrying about the rest later. Even my father, who didn't care about making money for himself, was in general agreement with this frontier mentality.

There was even more friction between me and the publisher, Mr. Shutts. He never liked me and I never liked him. He resented the criticisms in my column as if they were personal criticisms of him and of the men who had built the town. When it comes right down to it, I guess he was right. The friction between us was quite a problem for my father, and he tried as best he could to mediate.

Toward the end of 1923, I'd begun to get tired. Every day I had to do stories, had to do a column. The pressure had mounted more than I was aware. In 1924, I began to have a case of nervous fatigue. It worried me and I couldn't sleep at night. This led to my first real nervous breakdown.

I think I may have had minor breakdowns before. Maybe I inherited some flaw that my mother had. Or maybe the early trauma in my life, all the bitterness, had to have some long-term effect. It began to show up during the time of my marriage. I'd be talking to one of my friends and there'd be a blackout, only not black. I'd sit rigid with arrested thoughts, a blank space that lasted for a minute or two, as if a shutter had been drawn down over my mind.

I didn't consider this important, and I didn't think much about it. Then there was the disappointment of breaking up with Andy, plus the rancor between me and the publisher and the disagreement between me and my father. All this upset me deeply. I was living at my father's house up the river at Spring Garden when everything seemed to come to a head. I left the house late one night and walked up and down the empty streets until morning. I was dressed and I just walked around. I was unhinged a little, not quite aware of what I was doing.

After daylight I returned to find that my father discovered I hadn't slept in my bed and was worried all night. He insisted that the family doctor come to see me. The doctor said I had nerve fatigue, which is the first time I'd heard that term. He said the *Herald* was too much pressure for me, and I needed to get away from it.

This was difficult for my father, who hoped I'd go on to be the editor after he retired. We were still very close, in spite of our professional differences. The only ongoing tension between us had to do with his not wanting to hear about my early life, about my going to college which somehow he still resented. He took it for granted that I'd continue to work on the *Herald*, not anticipating that the paper later would be sold to the Knight family, or that the Knights would have wanted their own people to run it. Besides, I didn't really want to keep on with the *Herald*, and the doctor was on my side. I took his advice and got off the paper.

I was living at my father's new house, the one he'd built at Spring Garden. It was airy and comfortable and pleasant with the live oaks. From my corner room I could look out and see the boats going down the Miami River. Sometimes, I'd see a manatee. My stepmother was very considerate and I could work in my room and write all day and nobody bothered me. I recovered by being quiet, sleeping late, and by beginning to write short stories.

STORIES

After the First World War, there was a boom in the magazine business such as we've never seen before or since. All kinds of magazines. While I still worked on the *Herald*, I'd begun to contribute to some of them. First I made a little extra money by sending in one-line aphorisms to *Smart Set*. I'd take some of Oscar Wilde's sayings and twist them around: "Love is one thing but marriage is something else" — that sort of thing. I got in touch with an agent in New York, Robert Thomas Hardy. Maybe I'd seen his ad somewhere.

Whenever I needed $100, I'd cook up a one-liner and mail it off to Bob Hardy and he'd sell it for me. As I got more confident with the one-liners, I decided to try some short stories. They weren't very good. One was called "The Queen's Amber," and even I don't remember what it was about. To my great astonishment, Hardy sold that, too.

After a few short stories came my wild novella, called *White Midnight*, of all things. It was about sunken treasure in the West Indies, a place I'd

never been. It featured a villainous character by the name of Zam. Zam
was based on somebody I'd seen in Miami, a tall blind man who played
guitar, sang through his nostrils, and knocked his feet against walls to
figure out where he was going. I sold *White Midnight* to a magazine called
Black Mask and got $600 for it. I've since learned that *Black Mask*
bought and printed stories from several unknown writers who later
became famous, most notably Dashiell Hammett.

That summer after my breakdown, the summer of 1924, I took
whatever money I'd saved up and went to Taunton to visit my aunt and
my grandmother. My dear grandfather had died by then, as I've said. I
stopped over in New York to meet Bob Hardy. He must have been six
feet four, the tallest man I'd ever seen. He was a good agent, and an
honorable man. You always knew you'd get your money from him.

Mr. Hardy suggested I write for the *Saturday Evening Post*, and that was
the beginning of my true independence from the newspaper. From then
on I decided to try to freelance full time, and the *Post* was the place to
do it. In those days, it dominated the magazine field. The editor was
George Harris Lorimer, who developed the theme of what he called the
"romance of American business." He was the typical exponent of the
average American mind. Among other things, Mr. Lorimer said he
would never have cigarette ads because the boys who delivered the
magazine would read the ads and smoke the cigarettes.

The *Post* had plenty of advertising without cigarettes. In fact, the
advertising was tremendous. It also had good writing. Just about all the
great writers of the time from Fitzgerald to Hemingway appeared in the
Post, though many people looked down on it as a formula magazine, and
too commercial.

That summer in Taunton I sat down and deliberately studied the kind
of story I thought Mr. Lorimer liked. I decided he generally liked a
success story with a noble main character, tangled up with a little sex and
a few cuss words thrown in. A perfect opening for a Lorimer story was
something like: "Hell," said the Duchess, "Take your hand off my knee."
I concocted a story about a beauty parlor owned by an old gal named
Augusta who'd been a stewardess on a ship. She ran her beauty parlor
in nautical language.

I hesitate to admit this, but I might as well make a clean breast of it
— the story was called "At Home on the Marseilles Waves." I sent it to
Mr. Hardy and he sent it to Mr. Lorimer and Mr. Lorimer took it. The

only thing he didn't like was how it ended. I worked out a more melodramatic end, but that wasn't any good, either. Finally I did something that Mr. Hardy called "more natural" and whatever it was, Mr. Lorimer accepted it. It was a great moment in my life.

My Aunt Fanny was flabbergasted. Years before, when I'd told my grandmother I wanted to write and not teach, she drew herself up to her full five feet and said, "Then you will die in a garret." Though she was a great reader, she was convinced that writers always die in garrets. The short story sale put everything in a different light for my family and for me. They looked at me with new eyes. I returned to Miami and wrote more stories in earnest.

I continued to aim for the *Post*. There were no contracts so every story had to sell on its own merits. As time went on, I didn't try to conform so blatantly to formula, and wrote more things I wanted to write. If the *Post* didn't buy something, my agent could always sell it to the *Ladies' Home Journal*, or the Chicago *Tribune* Sunday magazine.

Many of my stories were about Florida, which is one of the reasons Mr. Lorimer sought out my work in the first place. Florida was a new field in those days. Though I did some nonfiction articles, I began to dislike the research, the digging up of facts. It was easier to write fiction. For me, it was a perfect job. I hadn't been a good employee. I hadn't liked regular hours. I hadn't liked being told what to do, or working for other people. In a way I was a loner at work, the same way I was a loner at home. I wanted to be an individual rather than an employee or a female. I mean, I didn't mind being an employee or a female, but I'd rather be an individual.

A HOUSE OF MY OWN

I was still living at my father's new house, the one he'd built at Spring Garden on a island between the Seybold Canal and the river. At night we often played checkers. He took it for granted that I'd always want to live with him, but from this, too, I sought a bit of independence. Though he and my stepmother couldn't have been more considerate, they were getting older and I wanted to be able to have parties without feeling I was disturbing them. I needed my own place. After all, I was 34 years old.

It's curious how one thing leads to another. It was my brief engagement to Frederick that got me my house in Coconut Grove. This happened as follows. At Frederick's mother's house back in Pennsylvania I'd met a friend of theirs named Henry Schulz. In 1924, several years later, I was making a speech at a women's club in Miami and Henry and Bertha Schulz were in the audience. They came up afterwards to say hello. Henry Schulz told me he'd just bought a large piece of land on Stewart Avenue in Coconut Grove.

I'd always loved Coconut Grove. It wasn't a large area, but it had its own character, separate from Miami. Coconut Grove was settled earlier than Miami, as I've said. It had beautiful foliage. People built their houses on a ridge of rock running north and south, with the land sloping downhill towards the bay. The houses on the ridge were backed by long gardens and driveways that extended to the main road. When I first saw the road, it was no more than a glorified cowpath.

To me, Coconut Grove was a kind of half garden, half community. It was full of exotic fruit trees. The people whom I liked best seemed to gravitate here. To start with, there were the Fairchilds and the Harrises, plus other like-minded people who enjoyed their neighbors but didn't want to live too close to them. They came from everywhere and had experienced many things. There were writers and painters, but it wasn't a colony, just a collection of sympathetic individuals.

Anyway, I mentioned to the Schulzes that I might like to live in Coconut Grove and we got together right away. Henry said I could build a house on a slice of his property, a funny-shaped lot with a 50-foot frontage and 160 feet deep. He offered the lot next to mine to my good friends the Franklin Harrises. Then he offered the lot next to that to our friend Natalie Newell who ran a bookstore. The Schulzes lived nearby.

From me they took a second mortgage, so I could get a first mortgage to build a little house. It couldn't have been nicer.

I didn't need much of a house, just a workshop, a place of my own. All I wanted was one big room with living quarters tacked on. I knew an architect, George Hyde, who drew up some plans. He mostly built factories, which was fortunate, because I hoped my little house would be as stout and as sparse as a factory, with not much to worry about.

I had to borrow the money. My first contractor defaulted with most of it. I was rescued by Willard Hubbell, the son of Henry Salem Hubbell, the portrait painter. Bill had gone into the contracting business. He built my house carefully and took plenty of time — which was imperative since I'd used up the mortgage loan and had to rely on magazine money. He'd build a little bit and stop, and every Saturday I'd tell him either to go ahead or to wait for the next bit of cash to come in from a short story or an article.

The house was finished in the fall of 1926. The big room, which comprised most of it, was beautifully proportioned due to George Hyde's excellent design. I hadn't moved in any furniture, because I didn't have any furniture. That was fortunate, because that fall I went back up to Taunton and the great hurricane of 1926 struck Miami. I read about the hurricane in the newspapers but I didn't really believe it until I got word from friends that it actually happened, and that the town was badly damaged.

Nobody knew how strong the winds were when the hurricane's center hit Miami. In those days, the anemometers blew away at 120 miles per hour. The peripheral winds drove the water from the bay up the shore, along with the rain and a very high tide. My little house was built on the Coconut Grove slope, six and a half feet above sea level at its lowest point but the tide reportedly had risen to 12 feet. My father was also out of town, in Jacksonville, but he quickly returned home, saw that his house was in good shape, and managed to get over to Coconut Grove to investigate mine. I called him from Taunton and he said there was a lot of seaweed and stuff inside, but the house itself wasn't damaged, and had held up like a factory. He'd found water marks along the outside walls but not the inside walls, so maybe no water had seeped in. The windows were blown out and all the glass was broken, and some shingles were missing off the roof.

The hurricane insurance people appraised the damage and wired me in Taunton that they'd offer $250 cash. That was great, because $50 put the shingles back and the other $200 gave me the finished floor I'd been unable to afford in the first place. To me, the hurricane of '26 had done more good than harm.

After I returned to Miami and the repairs were made, I began to acquire some furniture. I got a yellow marble coffee table from Carolyn. It was a high library table. She saw it while inspecting a house for sale in Saratoga, New York, bought it, and sent it down as a surprise. I had it cut down just below the top so the lower legs and spreaders were intact. They took the middle off the legs. I got a little dressing table with a beautiful gilt mirror that was broken. I managed to tape the frame together and put some plaster to replace the curlicues at the top. I had a long bookcase built on the inside wall. Somebody else gave me a big Philippine chair, called a bilibid, one of the originals made in the Philippine penitentiary. An interior decorator friend named Florence sold me an Italian desk, called a duelling desk, with a long secret drawer for hiding the swords. My kitchen was so small I couldn't get a conventional refrigerator into it, so I had to have a little ice box. I didn't plan to do much cooking or housekeeping, anyway.

I salvaged a round table from a failed restaurant and put it in the kitchen. My stepmother was throwing out a black walnut cabinet made originally by J.P. Coates for thread. I scraped and refinished it and used it as a chest in my dressing room. The rest of the place I finished sparsely, only with essentials — which meant books. When I came to Florida, I'd brought the first Dickens I read in my grandmother's house when I was eight years old. It must have dated from the 1870s. From there, I went on to build a nice collection. I've always had more books than I knew what to do with. Gradually, I put up more and more shelves to accommodate them.

The house was a great influence on my life, and so important that I often think of it more than the other things I was doing in those years.

FRIENDS

My social life in Coconut Grove centered around the houses that belonged to Arthur and Helen Gulliver on St. Gauden's Road. They had several little clapboard cottages built for the tropics, cool and comfortable, and they lived in one and rented out the others. Later, they turned some of their cottages into the Gulliver School.

Marion Manley, the architect whom we called Archie, lived in one of the Gulliver houses. She became one of my best friends. She'd hung out her shingle in the 1920s, and became the first architect for the University of Miami, for which she's never been given enough credit. The reason is that she brought in a big-time collaborator, Robert Law Weed, who proceeded to elbow her out. To hear him talk — and he talked a great deal — you'd think he was the primordial architect of the university. It wasn't true.

We were all mad, and Archie herself felt bitter, but she never said a word to protect herself. She wouldn't do a thing. I would have been in there fighting him tooth and nail all the way, but not Archie. To her, it wasn't skittles. She had a keen sense of pride and discretion and all that. That's not a weakness, in her it was a strength. She could take it, you see.

It was at the Gulliver houses that I also met Elizabeth Virrick. Her husband Vladimir was a Russian whose father had been architect for the czars. We called him Bobo. Bobo was sent to America as the youngest man in the czar's commission to buy munitions for the czar's army just before the revolution. He was still in New York when the revolution began, and his family wired him to stay there. Elizabeth met him in New York and married him. Then they moved to Coconut Grove.

Bobo was an extremely good architect in his own right, and set up a practice down here. They had an apartment house in Grove Center right next to the black area. At first, Elizabeth was annoyed by the noise, then she got to know the black people and found out they had no running water. She sounded the alarm that there were no sewers or water mains in the Colored Town, and then formed her own organization, the bi-racial Coconut Grove Slum Clearance Committee. I was put on the board.

The first thing we did was to draw up a petition for a referendum

requiring that all houses in Dade County should have indoor plumbing. We installed card tables outside of grocery stores all over the city
to get the required signatures. This took two years to pass. I suggested
we set up a loan fund to enable black people to borrow the money to
build the bathrooms for themselves. We lent thousands of dollars this
way, and every cent was paid back. Not one single person defaulted
on those loans.

Finally, we got the water mains and sewer lines, and the name of the
committee was changed to Coconut Grove Cares. Elizabeth set up an
office and continued to work as a volunteer, attacking all sorts of
problems from housing to education to drugs. She devoted her life to
fighting for black people, and to helping black people fight for
themselves. Speaking of fighting, Elizabeth Virrick also started a famous
gym, and became a sort of Mother Teresa of boxing. Participants in her
amateur boxing program often enter the national Golden Gloves
contest. Many professional boxers, including Muhammad Ali, have
made it a point to visit Elizabeth's gym.

Later, I got the Miami mayor, Maurice Ferre, to pay Elizabeth a salary
for what she was already doing.

We solved the water and sewer problem around the end of the Florida
land boom and the beginning of the Great Depression. The Depression
didn't depress me so much since I wasn't involved in real estate — but
it affected my friends. Marion Manley, who at one point was employing
eight draftsmen, was left practically without a cent. The Bust left her
high and dry. I had a little extra room off my kitchen, a tiny little room
not much more than a closet, where maybe you could stick a cot and
a bureau. I told her if she could put up with it, she could share the house.
She did.

She stayed with me during the Depression for at least three years,
maybe more. She had an old sewing machine truck that we drove
around in, which was great for me since I had no car. Also, she designed
a grocery store for an old friend of hers, for which Archie took out her
fee in groceries. Those groceries also fed me, and together we managed
to get along comfortably. Little by little she was able to pay off her debts.
After that she went on with her successful career.

I had other friends and acquaintances who kept me in touch with the
flora and fauna, and contributed to my growing awareness of the natural
world that later became my primary interest. Early in the 1930s, a

Colonel Robert Montgomery, who'd been a member of a distinguished New York accounting firm, came to Miami and bought some land on the old Cutler Road. The Montgomery tract had several exotic trees. There was a sausage tree near an old filling station that we all thought was quite remarkable. Colonel Montgomery decided to start a botanical garden there for David Fairchild, who became its director. He hired me to write a pamphlet about the garden.

I went to New York and did research in the New York Botanical Library and also at Colonel Montgomery's house in Greenwich, Connecticut. The pamphlet was called "An Argument for the Establishment of a Tropical Botanical Garden in South Florida." After I wrote it, I was in great demand for speeches at the local garden clubs. I was delighted to support the Fairchild Garden, and I served as the first secretary of the board until they replaced me with Alice Wainwright, whose knowledge of the law was of crucial importance. The garden was a wonderful idea, one of the greatest achievements for the entire area. To this day, it is the only tropical botanical garden on the continent of North America.

For years I also served on Ernest Coe's committee for the Everglades National Park. We also got a lot of help from Ruth Bryan Owen, daughter of William Jennings Bryan, whom I'd come to know very well. She was the first woman elected to the U.S. House of Representatives from Florida, and the first American woman to be named ambassador to a foreign country, Denmark. She was defeated in her bid for a second term in Congress.

I felt sorry for her, that she didn't fulfill all her hopes for herself. She was very bitter. It's the kind of reaction I've seen more than once in women who seem to have everything — intelligence, beauty, personality, wonderful speaking voice, etc. — and then are devastated when one thing goes against them. I often felt that Ruth Bryan Owen wasn't quite sure where her looks ended and her mind began, and she depended on her looks more than she realized. She expected everybody to follow her for herself and not for the policies she advocated. She didn't want to make the mistakes of her father, advocating certain silly things, so instead she never came out definitely for anything.

That's where she missed out. She was defeated for her second term because her opponent took the popular stand against Prohibition and Ruth refused to commit herself on the issue. She would never say whether she was for it or against it. And instead of realizing that her defeat resulted from this miscalculation, she chose to take it personally. It's almost as if she didn't know there was anything more important than herself. Her bitterness ruined the rest of her life.

I had another beautiful friend named Prunella Wood who was bitter about her understandable defeats. She was six feet two, and gorgeous. She'd come into a room and men would fall on their faces. Her parents started a tearoom in Miami, and her father worked part-time as a piano tuner. Prunella went to New York, got a job on a Hearst paper, became the ally of the managing editor and soon was the head of the women's pages for all Hearst publications. She was a smart woman and a distinguished figure in the newsroom. But when she lost her job after the boss died, she couldn't accept it. She, too, died an unhappy woman.

It's better to be plain and unnoticeable, really. You get by with a lot more. I can speak from experience about that.

Another close friend during this period was Natalie Grimes. One summer she and I met in New York and we took the Canadian Lady Boat, a steamship company line, to the West Indies. That was in the days before cruise ships. There were about 14 round-trip passengers including a group of five men from Princeton. It was a happy trip for Natalie, an attractive girl who'd never had any beaus and was as academic as I was. These Princeton men made a great fuss over us — principally over Natalie — and she just blossomed. After that trip I went to New England to visit my aunt (I think my grandmother had died by this time) and when I got back Natalie told me she was engaged to be married. She tried to write short stories and didn't succeed for some reason, and I suggested she go into teaching. She was one of the bright stars in the English Department at the University of Miami.

Most important was my continuing friendship with Carolyn Percy, now Carolyn Percy Cole. It always makes me mad when men seem to think that they are the only sex that can have friendships. Men sometimes like to dismiss women's friendships as emotional crutches, or no telling what else, when actually the modern woman is as capable of genuine friendships as the man. My friendship with Carolyn was a great force in my life.

As I've said, I'd met her in high school and had known her well since college. She was a tall fat girl and I was a short fat girl, she was brought up on cream and maple sugar and I was brought up on cream and butter. The results were much the same. We were at Wellesley together and lived in the same dorm. I took a job in St. Louis to be near her, she took a job in New York to be near me. She came to Newark, and was with me when my husband went to jail. When I went overseas, she got up her courage and went overseas. She gave me the dance in honor of Frederick, which resulted in her marriage to Kelley Cole.

In Florida, they visited me often, putting up with my funny little house and cramped quarters. Then Kelley got sick in Washington and I went up to be with the two of them and suddenly he died. I returned with Carolyn to Bennington, Vermont, where she opened up Kelley's old family house and almost had a nervous breakdown. I stayed with her all through one spring and didn't return back to Miami until she was in better shape. That was sometime between 1926 and 1929.

Then with the Crash, her great wealth in stocks and bonds diminished to almost nothing. She moved to New York and got another job teaching in the public schools. She was determined to stick with teaching until she got her pension, no matter what happened to the stocks and bonds later.

By the time I got established in Coconut Grove, the beach at Miami Beach was getting more and more built up, so we couldn't go swimming there in isolation. I was delighted to discover a little beach a few blocks south of my house in a section of Coral Gables where the land opens up to the bay. It was an artificial beach put in years earlier by George Merrick, the developer. He'd left a simple little beach house there — just four bare poles that held up a palmetto-thatch roof.

A group of old bachelors, plus several husbands of wives who didn't like to swim, came down to this beach almost every day. It was called Tahiti. Several of us women showed up there three times a week, always at 11 o'clock. I swam year-round, except on the coldest days. After Tahiti was closed, we moved south to Matheson Hammock and swam in a big lagoon down there. For decades, I kept up my swimming. I didn't give it up until I was well into my 70s, when my eyes had gone bad and I couldn't go outside without wearing my dark glasses and my hat.

My other favorite exercise was dancing. I wish I had a dollar for every mile I danced, especially in the summers on the beach or at the Roney Plaza outdoors, or at the tea dances during Prohibition times.

I wasn't really interested in sports like golf or tennis. I could never play tennis. I used to whack around a golf ball occasionally, but I was no golfer. I could manage to keep up with badminton, a gentle sort of game.

I think it's a big mistake to goad yourself into doing a lot of things that aren't really in your nature. You see these poor people jogging around, panting and looking horrible, and then you learn that some of them even die jogging. Too much exercise is bad. You've got to know yourself pretty well, as I hope I have.

My system wasn't well organized enough that I ever felt comfortable driving a car. I always used the bus service, which was quite adequate, or else my friends drove me around. Shopping was easy enough. You go out to dinner with somebody and ask them to stop by a grocery store on the way home. Or else you have things delivered. I've never regretted not driving a car.

Some people confuse a car with independence, and wonder how a self-reliant person like myself could have missed the freedom behind the wheel. Actually, my independence has had more to do with my owning a house, where I could hide out and come and go as I pleased. A car is just a nuisance, plus the big expense.

While we're on the subject of health and exercise, I can't say it's been all smooth sailing since 1925. There was the continuing problem of the nervous breakdowns. During this period we've been discussing, sometime in the late 1920s, I had a second one. I remember not being able to sleep one night, then getting up and running around outside again in my dressing gown. My friends next door got worried and called my father. He brought down the first doctor he could get his hands on, and it turned out to be a gynecologist. I didn't happen to be pregnant — it would have been quite amazing if I were. In fact, it would have been an immaculate conception.

I was wild and screaming, and the doctor used a hypodermic to fill me full of drugs. I woke up in a hospital, languid and sleepy and not knowing what had happened to me. The doctor continued with the drugs, and I was getting worse and worse. They kept me in a drugged, woozy condition.

Somebody had the sense to realize I wasn't getting the right care, and a second doctor, Dr. P.L. Dodge was brought in. God bless Dr. P.L. Dodge. He'd been a doctor in Boston before he got arthritis and moved to this warm climate. He came into my room to look at me and that very night the nurse called him and said: "The patient is dying. The heartbeat is very high and I don't know how long she can live." He couldn't get on his clothes fast enough to return to the hospital. He and the nurse rubbed me down and managed, I think, to get a drink of whiskey into me.

Apparently, you can die of a nervous condition that is treated with the wrong drugs and Dr. Dodge took me off my medication. In a week or two, I was recovered enough to go back home with a nurse. Soon after that, I got over it.

This began a wonderful association with Dr. Dodge. He talked to me about my condition, how I put too much pressure on myself, how I had to learn to relax and how it would be my own fault if I had a breakdown again.

MORE STORIES

I continued to write magazine pieces for the 15 years from 1926 through the early 1940s. In general, my stories were long, quite wordy, and quite profitable. Before I quit, they brought me $1,200 apiece. That was pretty good.

In going North regularly every summer, I always stopped in Philadelphia to have lunch with Mr. Lorimer at the *Saturday Evening Post*. It was an imposing place with a great foyer and an information desk. If you were expected there, you were sent up the elevator to see Adelaide Neall, who welcomed you and escorted you into Mr. Lorimer's office. Miss Neall was both secretary and right-hand woman, and the two of us became good friends. Occasionally, I'd stay the night with her.

Mr. Lorimer had his big desk way down at the far end of his office. He'd get up and stand beside it, while you had to make it across a gigantic floor with whatever dignity you could muster. He had a charming self-pride.

On very lucky occasions, I was invited upstairs to his private dining room for lunch. If you'd just sold a story you sat at his right hand. If you hadn't sold a story recently then you were placed down the table considerably. The first time I had lunch with Mr. Lorimer, I'd sold a story and so I was sitting directly to his right, feeling stiff and awkward. I tried to relieve the tension by telling a funny anecdote. Halfway through it, I forgot the point. Mr. Lorimer laughed uproariously and from then on we got along well.

He was a good environmentalist in his day. He was interested in the birds of Florida and how the Audubon Society sent wardens down into the Everglades to protect them. I told him about all the trouble we'd had with the poaching of birds and he encouraged me to write an article about it. It was printed in a prominent part of the magazine and got some attention.

I turned the poaching idea into a short story about the death of a man who'd tried to protect his timber from poachers. I wrote another short story about an old man and a boy who had to cross the Everglades but I don't remember why.

I also wrote about the West Indies, which I visited with Anne Archbold, one of the richest women in America whose son had a plantation on the island of Dominica. We were there a month or two. There was a quiet beach where we could go swimming without any clothes on, just the women. It was lovely.

We flew to Martinique, and took a car to St. Pierre. This was the beautiful little town that was first destroyed by the eruption of Mt. Pelée in 1902. It blew an ancient plug out of the volanic chimney, spewed burning clouds all over the town, and people who breathed the "burning air" all died. Two prisoners survived in an underground cell, but everybody else was killed. Later there was a second eruption, and the town was never really rebuilt.

An elderly professor by the name of Dr. Perret was setting up a volcanic museum for the French. We visited the museum and I got to know him and knew at once that I wanted to return some day. During the following winter or so, I flew to Martinique, and from there went back to St. Pierre. Dr. Perret got me a room among the ruins, in one of the few buildings that hadn't been destroyed. There was a cafe on the ground floor, a restaurant on the second floor and two or three rooms on the top floor. I liked this queer little ruined town of St. Pierre. I wrote about it both in fiction and as a nonfiction article.

In 1929 or 1930, I did a story that took a second prize in the O. Henry Memorial collection. It was called "The Peculiar Treasure of Kings," about a man on a ship. I worked out the details of the ship from my knowledge of sailing. I made it a barkentine, which I knew was square-rigged on the foremast. The article was illustrated by Otto Fischer. I wanted to have the original painting, but Mr. Lorimer had left it in the art department and Admiral Byrd came along and picked it up. I was mad at Admiral Byrd for taking my illustration. I don't know what he did with it. If any heirs of Admiral Byrd know where that picture is I'd like to get it back. I have a place for it right in my living room.

I wrote stories about Europe during the First World War based on my experience in the American Red Cross. Once, I wrote a story and then lost it. One copy got stolen along with the rest of the mail from my agent's office. He called to ask for another copy, and that was the one I couldn't find. I sat down to rewrite the story, but couldn't remember a word. With the beginning of the second paragraph, I was going crazy. That's when my neighbor Franklin Harris, a very wise man, came over and said: "You're going nuts. Forget about the story. Go out. Get drunk, fall in love, do anything, but forget it for a while. Then come back and write it cold, all over again." He was right. I took a week off and rewrote the story and sent it back to Mr. Hardy. He sent it to Mr. Lorimer and Mr. Lorimer bought it, thank goodness.

In addition to writing for the magazines, I also wrote for the local civic theater. I never did any acting. Saying the same thing for two weeks in a row would have bored me to death. Our star was Joseph Cotten, who'd worked in the *Herald* advertising department. We also had Edgar Lee Hay, who'd been on stage in New York with the song and dance man, Fred Stone. Hay took a job at the *Herald*, too, but couldn't conceal his real talent for long.

In the early 1930s, it was fashionable to put on one-act plays. It was a great time for the little-theater movement and I was on the board of the theater in Miami. We'd plan an evening of one-acts: two comedies and a tragedy. There were plenty of comedies but never enough tragedies. W.W. Jacobs wrote one called "The Monkey's Paw," and another touching tragedy called "The Valiant," but beyond those we had trouble filling the program.

When we decided to do some original writing of our own, I was given the one-act tragedy. It wasn't that I was so good, just that nobody else wanted to do it. The result was a cheery little drama called the "The Gallows' Gate." I based it on a remark my father once made. While he was out West growing up, he'd had to attend one or two hangings. He said the hangings themselves never fazed him, but he was bothered by the creaking of the ropes after the traps were sprung. That always stuck in my mind, so I wrote a play with the creaking gallows. There was an argument between a father and mother over the character of their son, who was about to be hanged.

In the original version, I gave the mother a long monologue in the middle that made no sense and held up the action completely. Later we took the play to Tampa and I cut the monologue, and "The Gallows Gate" took first prize in the state little-theater competition. From there, I blew it up into three acts and it took first prize in a national competition and made me $500. The one-act play was always the better form.

Some years after that, in Roosevelt's WPA days, they revived "The Gallow's Gate," and it played in Florida and in California. Finally I sold the rights to an outfit called Baker's of Boston, and every now and then I would get $5 as my share of the royalties for a performance.

It was thrilling to write for the theater, to see my words brought to life. Our little theater's greatest accomplishment was putting Joe Cotten on the map. After that, I often visited him when I was in New York. It was after that he went on to Hollywood.

It was a sad day when we had to give up the Miami theater. The rent got too high and we tried to continue it in a cheaper place, but it never worked. Its day was done.

A story I wrote about Haiti in 1939 was one of my last magazine pieces. I was 49 years old by then, and had put in nearly 15 years in the magazine-writing business. The Americans were getting out of Haiti and I went down to get the story of the return of the government to the Haitian people. I visited some clinics the U.S. Navy had established that were transferred to local control along with everything else.

I got the sense that Haiti was going to deteriorate very rapidly in the hands of the Haitians. It was already happening around the hospitals we'd built — surgical instruments spotted with rust, etc. I heard things about the drug supplies being sold for private profit. It was a sad realization that things would not go well in the future.

I was invited to travel with a government caravan into the Artibonite Valley south of Port-au-Prince. President Stenio Vincent was riding in a limousine and the rest of us rode in trucks. The government officials had taken over a little house in the village of this dry, sunblasted valley for their entourage. I had lunch with them. Since President Vincent was afraid of being poisoned, Mrs. Vincent and her friends did all the cooking.

Like many Haitians, President Vincent had the manners of an educated Frenchman. I was very correctly put on his left side, and to his right was the minister of education. This man was very important politically, but not very long on education.

Around the table were various other ministers and so forth, and I was the only white person. I don't think they liked me, but they took care of me beautifully. The French are right: It doesn't matter if people are friendly as long as they have excellent manners. These people did.

We drank champagne and ate *pate de foie gras*. I said something about how my grandmother was French, and that was a great bond because it turned out every one of them had a grandfather who was French. As I began to feel more at ease, I told a story about the *loup-garou*. The *loup-garou* is a French legend about a man becoming a wolf. Suddenly, all those black men were staring at me with their desperate eyeballs, and I realized I'd said something portentous. I'd thought I was making idle conversation, but they took the *loup-garou* very seriously. They said the *loup-garou* in Haiti is a wizard, an evil character, and if you wake up in the morning and see a ball of fire rolling down the street, that's him.

After my Haiti story was published in the *Saturday Evening Post*, I went up to Philadelphia to have lunch with Mr. Lorimer. The great editor had already announced his retirement. After lunch, he and I went back to Adelaide Neall's office and ate chocolates. I said something about how I hoped he wouldn't just go off and disappear, that I was sure he could find something productive and rewarding to do. He began to cry and we all began to cry. Our tears dripped down into the chocolate box. What happened to Mr. Lorimer was exactly what I'd feared. He retired, he thought his life had ended, he was a broken man and soon he was dead. I don't think he would have been happy doing anything but editing the *Saturday Evening Post*.

I sensed I was finished with magazine work, and especially the short-story writing. The way I'd written them, short stories were wordy, wandering, deliberate, somewhat diffuse, very complicated, and old-fashioned. I didn't think they were so bad but they weren't the new-fangled concise dramatic short stories of the Hemingway school. Though many of the men who'd served in the First World War had been prepared for that kind of Hemingway writing, I was not a part of it. I didn't subscribe to the Hemingway thinking. I was more or less tied into the mainstream from which Hemingway was estranged. I couldn't write in that bare, stark way in which a story begins like a slap in the face.

Actually, the whole short-story business was coming to a climax in this country and for me the end was already in sight. My last involvement with short stories was when B.F. Ashe, founder of the University of Miami, asked me to teach the short story for the English Department. I didn't think you could teach the short story but I taught the course anyway. You can't teach people to write if they can't write and if they can write, they don't need teachers.

During all this 15-year period of my magazine work, I continued to see my father several times a week. Every other night or so I'd return to his house. We'd play checkers or carry on our running debate about literature. He'd become completely devoted to Abraham Lincoln. I gave him Carl Sandburg's *Life of Lincoln* for Christmas one year and he read the full two volumes, night after night. After he finished the books he wandered around the house for a day or so in a sort of absent-minded stupor. Finally, he admitted: "You know, I'm homesick for Abraham Lincoln." Then he reread the whole thing from start to finish.

I'd already read *War and Peace* and he hadn't but when Hitler went into Russia, we went through the book together. We followed Hitler's earliest advance on a map.

DEATH AND RENEWAL

In 1938, my Aunt Fanny died in Taunton, in the house where she was born and where I'd grown up. I'd depended on her so much for so many things, yet I could never see eye to eye with her about important issues. For instance, there was the attitude she'd adopted from my grandfather: "Never make friends, they'll always cheat you." That was the worst advice I think I'd ever heard from anybody, especially a dear little man like my grandfather, but Aunt Fanny agreed with it, and I was brought up on it.

I was called to Taunton to see her for the last time. I realized then, as I hadn't realized before, that Aunt Fanny really loved me and cared for me. Perhaps I hadn't wanted to realize it because she was such a high-strung and jealous woman. I was glad I could hold her hand at the end. She'd done more for me, in actual physical labor, than anybody else.

My cousins from Connecticut (the daughters of my mother's older sister Aunt Alice) and Uncle Charlie came to the funeral. Uncle Charlie was living outside of Worcester at the time. His wife had died so he was on his own. It was up to me to dispose of the Taunton house, and I stayed on to sell the furniture. It was an unpleasant job, clearing out a place that had been lived in three generations, with all my early memories in it. It was hard getting rid of things. Except for Uncle Charlie, there was nobody left in the family to take anything.

I took a set of Haviland china, 250 pieces which I never could possibly use, but which had belonged to my mother. I still have it, and it must be over 100 years old by now. As old as me, I guess. There was a little sofa that also had been my mother's. I packed it up and sent it down to Florida, along with a little gray-and-white marble table that I later cut to size and installed in my dressing room.

After the house was finally empty, I put it up for sale with an agent. Houses in Taunton weren't selling at all. It took a year or two, and even then it didn't bring much more than a thousand dollars — less than my grandfather paid for it when it was newly built before the Civil War.

When I left Taunton in 1938, it was for the last time. I never went back. There were no surviving relatives in town and none of my old school friends had stayed on. I parted company with the Taunton house in sorrow and in bitterness. There was so much pain connected with the place, I was grateful I wouldn't have to return.

It's sad that my aunt's death should have been the lifting of a burden for me, but that's the way it was. She left about $14,000 which she'd accumulated in all those years by giving music lessons, plus working part-time in a bank. She'd raked and scraped and saved for that. Uncle Charlie, my cousins, and I divided it. My part paid off my mortgage in Coconut Grove, and left me free and clear.

We make such a fetish of the family. I think we've created a tremendous mythology about it. We believe the family must be maintained, it's the basis of society, etc. Yet for a great many of us, the family has been difficult. Many of the troubles of mankind are family troubles, more devastating and more lasting than other kinds of troubles. Almost any well-run orphanage would be better than some families I've known. There are countless unjust and narrow-minded families, and parents who bring up children in hatred for reasons that are invalid.

Just being a family is not enough. There has to be agreement: not a narrowing but a widening, not bitterness and misunderstanding but sensibility and justice.

My father died in February of 1941, the year the Japanese bombed Pearl Harbor. He felt there was a war coming on and said he couldn't take it. He was 84 years old and very tired. Technically, he was killed by a kidney stone, but I think it was really his general decision not to carry on. He'd been working on the *Herald* nearly to the end. The *Herald* had been sold to the Knight family but my father continued as editor-in-chief and wrote all the foreign-policy editorials. He was as clear-headed as ever and wrote just as forcefully. His legs weren't very good because he hadn't exercised them. It's something I've tried to remember: Exercise your legs as well as your brain.

The year before he died, the Carnegie Foundation for Peace sent him abroad with a group of editors to meet the European heads of state. For three months, they toured Europe. He was impressed with Czechoslovakia, and its great leader Tomas Masaryk. In England, they'd asked him to make a speech at the tomb of the unknown soldier at Westminster Abbey where the editors had gone to lay a wreath. He was thrilled by that and sat down and wrote me about it that night. I still have the letter. I think it was the greatest moment of his life, remembering his people, the Quakers, had been driven out of England and now he was back to make a speech at Westminster Abbey. I've since gone there and stood where my father stood, trying to experience what it must have meant to him.

His kidney stones developed because he'd practically lived on milk and eggs without any awareness he was building up a terrible cholesterol content. The trouble came on very quickly, and the doctors said he was too old to be operated on. If it had been up to me, I would have told them to operate so at least he'd have a chance — but they didn't and he died. I was with him in a hospital near our house. I was prostrate with grief, but I stayed to the end. At the last minute, they took him to the operating room and he died on the table. Otherwise, I held his hand, which gave me great satisfaction.

He said, "You'll come with me?" and I said, "Yes, father, I'll be with you." That was it.

I had another one of my psychoses after my father died in 1941. It may have been in 1942. Maybe it was his death that caused it, or maybe some other things. Undoubtedly I had a father complex. Having been brought up without him and then coming back and finding him so sympathetic had a powerful effect. It had a lot to do with my not wanting to get married again.

This time I was wandering around at night in my nightgown, screaming my head off, and my neighbors the Harrises got me into a taxi and took me to Dr. Dodge's place right away. I was put in a room with another woman who had some sort of breakdown. I don't think I was there very long.

Dr. Dodge said I had the easiest kind of psychosis, the manic kind. The depressive kind, he said, is much harder to cure. The manic phase is an attempt of the mind to throw off all kinds of unwanted stuff, which is why it's manic. I hadn't gotten enough stuff off my chest, and it had built up.

I was glad to be under Dr. Dodge's care. Because of him I understood my condition, and could manage it better.

Beyond the grief and in spite of my breakdown, the deaths of my aunt in 1938 and then my father in 1941 left me feeling suddenly healed. The schism between the Northern half and Southern half was erased, and I could think of myself not as two separate parts but as a coming together, a whole of the best of both worlds, and to a large extent, successful. It was the end of my immature life, if one can say that at the age of 51, and the beginning of a new maturity.

After my father died, I inherited his house in name, but of course I understood my stepmother had to have it for her lifetime. Beyond that, there wasn't much inheritance. I don't think my father did very well with the money he got from the sale of the *Herald*. He'd put it into annuities — one that ceased at his death and the other that wasn't really enough to support Mrs. Stoneman. Her cousin, Mildred Shine, had come to live with her and my father, and took care of them as housekeeper and nurse. Mildred wanted to stay in the house, but it was hard going and the money didn't stretch.

As soon as I became aware of this, I convinced the newspaper to buy the house for Mrs. Stoneman and to let her continue to live there. The proceeds from the sale gave her enough money to live on as well. She was maintained comfortably until her own death five or six years later. Even after my father died, I went over once a week to visit her as I'd visited him. She was a lovely woman, and a lovely friend to me. Her death was a great loss as well.

Father also left me a small sum, not much, but I wouldn't have wanted much. It was enough to get me out of the magazine business. Since the magazine business was dying out, I decided to use the money to support myself while I wrote a novel. Like all short-story writers, I'd always imagined I could easily write a novel. In practice, I found it difficult. I'd done the short stories for so long I couldn't get over the idea of limited space. So every chapter seemed to end in a climax, which isn't the way a novel should work.

THE RIVER OF GRASS

A great release of energy seemed to launch me into my most ambitious and important project. The Everglades book, no doubt my best writing, was a product of this personal renewal.

I'd been working on a novel for about six months when Hervey Allen dropped by my house. His own novel, *Anthony Adverse*, was a tremendous success and sold millions of copies. We'd been friends a long time. His aunt lived in Miami — a nice little woman, very English and slightly passe. He'd pass through town occasionally, and we'd all get together. After his great success, Rinehart and Company made him the editor of its Rivers of America series. Well-known writers had been sent out to write books about the Hudson, the Upper Mississippi, the Lower Mississippi, etc.

Allen came to my house to tell me they wanted me to write a book about the Miami River. I said: "Hervey, you can't write a book about the Miami River. It's only about an inch long." But when a publisher visits your house and asks you to write something, you don't let him go casually. I suggested that the Miami River might turn out to be part of the Everglades. I knew it was connected to the Everglades. I can't pretend I knew much more than that. Anyway, I asked Hervey if I could somehow use the Everglades to back up the Miami River and maybe I could get a book out of that. "All right," Hervey said, "write about the Everglades." There, on a writer's whim and an editor's decision, I was hooked with the idea that would consume me for the rest of my life.

I started right away. I think they gave me an advance of a thousand dollars. Not much. What I knew about the Everglades I've already said. That it was there, that the birds were spectacular, that it should be a national park, and that it shouldn't be drained, that there were millions of acres of it. I'd been out in the Everglades no more than 20 times.

The first thing I did was to talk to John Pennekamp, who'd taken my father's place as editor of the *Herald*. I described my predicament — a book assignment on a subject about which I knew next to nothing. He suggested going over to the courthouse, where the state hydrologist, Garald Parker, was working on a study of the ground water of southeastern Florida. Pennekamp said nobody knew as much about the Everglades as Gerry Parker.

For starters I asked him what the Everglades were, and he explained they weren't swamps but rather a subtle flow of water. Wherever fresh water runs and the saw grass starts up, that's where you have the Everglades.

Conscious of my assignment, I asked if the Everglades could be called a river. He gave the official description: "A river is a body of fresh water moving more in one direction than the other." He handed me a horticultural map of the Everglades and I brought it home, pinned it to the door, and sat around looking at it. As I sat, I thought: If it's running water and it comes curving down from Lake Okeechobee toward the Ten Thousand Islands, and if there are ridges on either side, maybe the ridges are an east bank and a west bank, and maybe the Ten Thousand Islands are a delta, and maybe this really is a river.

I went back to Parker. "Do you think I could get away with calling it the river of grass?" I asked. He said he thought I could. Some years later my colleague Art Marshall said that with those three words I changed everybody's knowledge and educated the world as to what the Everglades meant.

Garald Parker continued to help me throughout my three or four years of research. Not only did he give me a great deal of material, he also told me where to look for things. He told me about the one or two early reports on the Everglades that were filed with the Internal Improvement Board in Tallahassee.

Soon I went to Tallahassee to find out what I could. Spessard Holland was governor. I'd known Mary Holland, his wife, in some capacity I can't remember, and she invited me to stay at the gubernatorial mansion. I was installed in the lovely third-floor rooms and could come and go as I pleased.

The Internal Improvement Board was really the governor and the cabinet wearing different hats. For decades, they'd handled all the management of the Everglades and had done a terrible job. I read all the minutes of their meetings going back for years. It was obvious to Parker, and now to me, that they didn't understand the nature of fresh water in south Florida.

In my travels, I met two brilliant and eccentric men who not only contributed to the book, but who became amusing and faithful friends.

One was John Goggin, a professor of archaeology and anthropology at the University of Florida. Goggin was studying the archaeology of Florida's early Indians — not the Seminoles, who were late-comers, but the original Tequestas, Calusas, etc. His was the definitive work. At one time he'd boasted that he'd studied every Indian mound in Florida. I think it was probably true. He spent years studying the Indians, and sent me his manuscript. With his permission, I rewrote it and used it as an entire chapter in my book. He rechecked it for accuracy. The whole thing about early Indians is pure Goggin. It's the first scholarly material on the subject that isn't gathering dust on college library shelves.

Goggin was tall and had one bad eye. He also had a drinking problem. When he was on a drunk, he could be one wild boy. I saw him like that once. At the same time, he managed to graduate from the University of Florida, to get an M.A. in anthropology from the University of Miami, and a Ph.D. from Yale.

He married an older woman who couldn't put up with his drinking and divorced him. Then he married a younger woman and was terrible to her. He'd wake her up in the middle of the night and demand to be served a complete dinner. She'd get up and cook it, and then he'd say he didn't want it. After she escaped, Goggin finally met his match. Her name was Margaret Knox, just as brilliant as he was, and she had him under her thumb. She refused to marry him, but in the end she did, only because Goggin was dying of cancer.

Then there was David O. True. He'd found the Fontaneda manuscript in Spain, edited it and had it printed. It was the diary of the Spanish boy shipwrecked on the Florida coast and captured by Florida Indians, the first personal account ever written about Florida and perhaps about North America. A really important historical document.

David True was the secretary of the Florida Historical Society, and I met him in the course of my research. We went out to dinner together many times. He was a funny-looking little man, short and lightweight but with huge feet. He walked along clumsily. He had bright eyes and a lot of mistresses. In college he'd been a long-distance runner, but as an older person he did nothing more athletic than sit at a desk and peck a typewriter. He had an insistent voice, and very emphatic, since everything he said he believed to be absolutely true.

He'd come into money in a very odd way, the way things always happened with him. He'd been taking care of the daughter of one of his mistresses, who'd gotten very sick. He'd go and get her groceries and find somebody to clean her house. When she died, she left him everything. He went back into her house and found stocks and bonds all over the place, $120,000 worth, all left to him. It made his life comfortable from then on.

He sunk a large amount of this money into searching for sunken treasure. He was obsessed with the pirates of the Caribbean, plus he had a lot of wild ideas about them — that they'd all been Masons, for instance. He was always looking for Masonic symbols on the trees of the Florida west coast.

To help him in his search for treasure, he collected copies of all kinds of early maps of North America. He carried on a correspondence with libraries all over the world and managed to accumulate a remarkable number of maps. He had them carefully filed with all the documentary evidence, plus notes on what he thought of them, which was usually peculiar. For instance, he was sure that John Cabot discovered Labrador in June, 1492, before Columbus landed in the Caribbean. He had John Cabot doing a variety of wonderful, made-up things. I was never convinced, but I was always amused. We spent many evenings in his strange map-filled house. He'd talk about maps with a cat in his lap, while another one of his cats would sit on my lap.

It took me four or five years to complete the Everglades book. It was supposed to have been 120,000 words but it came out longer. I sent it up to the publishers, and they read it over and accepted it immediately. Then I got a wire saying I should cut out 20,000 words. It was one of the worst jobs I ever had. I took those words out almost one-by-one, a phrase here and there. It meant rewriting in some places, but I persevered. I wired the editor: "Cut 19,000. Refuse to cut another word. If you don't agree, I withdraw book from publication." The editor wired back: "We forgive the 1,000 words."

Rinehart printed 7,500 copies and issued the book in November, 1947. To their great surprise the whole edition was bought up by Christmas. They had an entire window in Brentano's, the bookstore on Fifth Avenue, taken up with the Everglades book. They had to reprint 5,000 more copies as quickly as they could. Reader's Digest bought the first chapter. They also printed a summary and asked me to write an article about an unforgettable character. I did very well from all that.

The publication of the Everglades book more or less coincided with the actual founding of the national park, which after 25 years was finally going to happen. When I was on the park committee, I'd gone down many times to see where the park was to be located and where the boundaries were to be drawn. I attended the ceremonies in Everglades City when President Truman formally dedicated the park. Many people were responsible for this great accomplishment, including my old friend Ruth Bryan Owen. She was a representative in Congress when the vote came up. During the debate in a House committee, the landowners who didn't want to sell to the government argued that the Everglades was a swamp filled with snakes and mosquitoes. To prove it, they brought a big snake in a bag and dumped it on the table. Ruth Bryan Owen saw that something had to be done. She'd never picked up a snake in her life, but she grabbed this one, wrapped it around her neck, and announced: "That's how afraid we are of snakes in the Everglades."

Ernest Coe, the first to dream of the park and the man who'd struggled for 25 years to see it realized, was furious at the result. Mr. Coe had thought the park should include the upper part of Key Largo and the coral reef, as well as part of the Big Cypress north of the Tamiami Trail. The politicians said they had to settle for what they could get on the mainland, that they couldn't include the Big Cypress. Mr. Coe wouldn't accept it. He insisted that without the outer areas, the sloughs and marshes, the park couldn't control the water supply it needed to survive.

Our committee had had a meeting in New York to argue the acquisition. Mr. Coe was there in his seersucker suit, as usual, even though it was the middle of winter. When it was obvious that he would lose the argument, Mr. Coe refused to cast his vote and ran out of the building. John Pennekamp, the new editor of the Herald, rushed out after him and put an overcoat around him, so Mr. Coe wouldn't freeze to death.

Mr. Coe resigned and would have nothing more to do with the Everglades. But when President Truman inaugurated the park they persuaded him to show up. He was on the platform with the President and the others. I was invited to sit up there, too, but for some reason I didn't. I sat in the front row below.

All the local Indians were invited. The branch of the Seminoles called Cow Creeks arrived early and got seats on the platform with the Great White Father, Mr. Truman. The Miccosukee Indians arrived a bit later and were offered chairs along the side below the speaker's platform.

They refused the offer and went home angry, because they weren't given equal footing with the Cow Creeks.

There was always that feud between the Miccosukees and the Seminoles. They speak entirely different languages. People don't understand that, and think all south Florida Indians are Seminoles. Sometime in the mid-1950s, the U.S. government said to the tribes: "If you can prove that you were living in a certain area and weren't just migrants, and if you can prove your land was taken by force or fraud, then the government will pay you." This was a remarkable offer after so many years of fraud and neglect on the part of the government. A trial was held in Washington in front of the Indian Claims Commission. John Goggin got me to go up there as a witness for the Indians. The Indians paid our expenses.

The government paid Dr. John Mahon, a colleague of Goggin's at the University of Florida, $5,000 to write a brief for the government's side. Goggin wrote the brief for the Indians. I was supposed to refute the government's argument, after Goggin and Mahon had made their initial presentations. Goggin gave his pitch first, showing how the land was taken from the Indians by force and fraud. Then Mahon read his brief for the government, and it didn't seem to disagree with Goggin's. The Indian lawyer cross-examined Mahon, and Mahon admitted that he agreed with Goggin on almost every point. In other words, the U.S. didn't have a leg to stand on. There was no need for me to rebut anything, so I didn't have to speak. The case was settled immediately in favor of the Indians. Later the various Florida tribes were given large sums of money, and there were some big disagreements and trouble over it.

Anyway, even though the Indians left the dedication ceremonies in the Everglades, the park was finally established.

During the years I was writing the Everglades book, Uncle Charlie came back into my life. Let me bring you up to date on him. For years, he'd worked as an inventor with Brown and Sharpe, a big machine tool company in Providence. He built the first machine that made shredded wheat biscuits. After that, Uncle Charlie always ate shredded wheat for breakfast.

While his wife Aunt Nettie was alive, they'd stay in their cottage at Field's Point until the worst part of the winter, then retreat to a one-room kitchenette in Providence. They were very happy, the first people I'd known to have a good marriage. They were lovers always — a great lesson in what a marriage could be. Since they had no children, I got the benefit of all their care and attention.

After Aunt Nettie died of throat cancer, Uncle Charlie moved in with a friend in the country outside of Worcester, Mass. By then, Uncle Charlie was too old to work. I didn't see much of him since I'd stopped going back to Taunton.

Then once in the early 1940s, when I had to go to Boston, I saw Uncle Charlie in Worcester and invited him to stay with me in Florida. I had the little extra room in my house that Archie the architect had occupied years before. Uncle Charlie didn't want to abandon his friend in Worcester, who was quite sick, but then the man had to be put in a nursing home and Uncle Charlie felt free to come to Florida and stay in my extra room.

He was in his 80s, a little old man clinging to life. For the first couple of years, he'd visit me for the winter and go back to Worcester for the summer. He rode the Greyhound bus, which took several days each way, and said he loved every turn of the wheel. After that, he moved in with me full-time.

He brought several things with him, including the bulk of the family silver and the family mirror that had come from my great grandfather's house in Maine. He was charming to have around, and neither of us wanted to stir up unhappy, far-off things. We suited each other perfectly. He liked to get up at 7 and fix his own breakfast; I didn't want to get up until 9.

Uncle Charlie was a talented tinkerer around the house, just as his father had been. He fixed the roof and did all kinds of repairs. After he was through tinkering around my house, he went over and tinkered for my stepmother, Mrs. Stoneman. I think he painted her place and got a little money for it.

Every day, he'd go down to Coconut Grove village for his mid-day dinner, then I'd give him his late-night supper. He always had a poached egg, hot milk, toast, and tea, and went to bed early. After that, I'd head out for the village for dinner with friends or a party. Uncle Charlie was so jolly and so much fun that he got invited to many of these parties, too.

He'd have his bath Saturday night, get dressed up Sunday morning and go to church. He had a special cafeteria where he ate Sunday dinner.

When he was finished eating, he'd leave the dining room, sit in the corner of the lobby, and smoke his after-dinner cigar. Then he'd walk and sit in the park, eat some ice cream, and come home on the 3:30 afternoon bus.

He'd always bring back some funny story about a man who'd tried to sell him stolen watches, or a woman who'd tried to pick him up. Once, he didn't return at 3:30, and at sundown I was about to call the police. It turned out he'd fallen asleep at the cafeteria, and they hadn't noticed him until it was time to close the place.

Uncle Charlie got along famously with my next-door neighbors, Franklin and Alice Harris. Franklin was the piano player who'd helped the University of Miami get started. His wife Alice spoke beautiful French and had founded the school's French Department. She was a redoubtable woman of great character. Because Franklin couldn't drive a car, Alice had learned to drive.

They were a curious but good combination. To hear them, you'd think they were always quarreling and sparring around. People would say, "Isn't it too bad they don't get along." But they'd rather quarrel with each other than talk to anybody else.

By the time Uncle Charlie moved in, Franklin Harris had suffered a stroke and was hanging around the house. Uncle Charlie would sit with him on the side porch and have a beer. Franklin could hardly speak and Uncle Charlie wasn't very talkative, so the two of them more or less just sat there. They didn't seem to need to talk.

Franklin Harris communicated with me by playing his piano. When I finished the Everglades book, and ran over to tell him, he sat down at the piano and began to improvise a marvelous congratulatory tune. He could express himself very well that way. Often I'd wake up and hear him playing Bach.

IV

A Writing Woman

In 1948, after I began to get money from *The Everglades: River of Grass*, I went West for the first time. Two friends went with me — Archie the architect and a woman with whom she later set up housekeeping, Lillian Fly. We drove around the Gulf of Mexico, stopping over for wonderful food in New Orleans. We spent Christmas in Orange, Texas, with some of Archie's relatives. I stayed a couple of days in San Antonio and was impressed with their river, which had been lined with parks, restaurants, and open-air shops. The Miami River could use that sort of treatment.

I flew to El Paso and walked into Juarez for lunch. I took a train to Phoenix, a plane to Los Angeles, and a bus to Claremont, California, where my father's sister, Aunt Stella, lived. Aunt Stella was a woman after my own heart, a great throwback, Quakerish in her attitudes still. I looked more and more like Aunt Stella as I got older. I had a nice time with her and her adopted daughter Margaret, one of my favorite cousins.

I left with some regret, because I sensed I'd never see her again. That unfortunately turned out to be true.

I made several other short stops and found myself in a lodge at the edge of the Grand Canyon. I returned via New Orleans, sat at the bar of the St. Charles Hotel, had a Sazerac cocktail and toasted my father. He hadn't cared much for cocktails, but he'd always liked a Sazerac at the bar of the St. Charles.

This traveling from coast to coast was the closest thing to a wild spending spree I'd ever had. Spending money like that made me uncomfortable and I retreated to Miami to recover from it. After I'd pulled myself back together, I started work on the novel I'd abandoned in favor of the *River of Grass* book. It was the story of people who'd bought land on the edge of the Everglades and got caught up in the 1920s boom. *Road to the Sun* was the title. Rinehart published it in 1952 and it didn't sell too well, and eventually it was discontinued.

One reason it didn't do better was that it wasn't very good. For me, it was a terrible struggle to write a novel. I'd had too much short-story writing to be comfortable with the form. Probably I could have improved with practice, but I drifted back into nonfiction. In fact, these years of my 60s could be called my full-length nonfiction period, as the 15 years preceding had been devoted to short stories and shorter nonfiction. Most of the topics and assignments were offered to me and I took them, as opposed to my thinking up projects of my own. As a free-lance writer, it seemed to me much more sensible to take on jobs the publishers wanted done, thus avoiding the trouble of selling them on something.

For instance, after my novel was published, I met with a woman named Erick Berry who was putting together a series of books for teenagers. Each book dealt with the year a particular state was admitted into the Union. In Florida's case, it was 1845. At first, the idea of writing for teenagers left me cold at best. I expressed my reservations to Ms. Berry, and she said: "Just write the way you always do but leave out any sex and swearing. The story can be just as good and a lot of adults will read it as well." That satisfied my pride to some extent.

At first, I thought I'd describe Key West in the days of the wreckers. The wreckers were very active around 1845, and when they weren't salvaging sunken ships they were enticing perfectly unsunken ships onto the reefs to improve their wrecking business. I'd heard the Florida wreckers went so far as to hang lanterns around cow's necks and sent the cows out onto the beaches so they'd be mistaken for lighthouses by confused skippers.

I went to Key West hoping to find records of all this in the salvage courts, but the records had been sent for safekeeping to a wooden house in Jacksonville where they'd all burnt up. One of the maddening things about Florida history is that it's gone on for 400 years with almost no documentary evidence and hardly a remnant to prove its existence.

The lack of material forced me to give up the salvage idea, and I decided to write about something I knew better. I concocted a story about three boys: a white boy who was the son of a Quaker abolitionist family, a Miccosukee Indian boy, and an escaped slave. Some of the details came from my own family. What I did, in essence, was to put old Uncle Levi Coffin out on the Miami River.

This was a pleasant project. By writing on Monday, Tuesday, and Wednesday, I found I could produce 5,000 words a week, and take the rest of the week off to play around, go swimming at the beach at night, and think about my next chapter. Soon, I had the required 60,000 words. The book was called *Freedom River* and broke into 13 chapters, which bothered me for some reason, though I'd never had the slightest superstition about the number 13 before. To calm me down, the editor suggested we turn the last chapter into two, so it came out to 14.

Freedom River was published by Scribner and Sons in 1953. It sold pretty well, though some other books in the series were never finished to anybody's satisfaction, and the whole project was discontinued. My book was kept on Scribner's historical list. There's nothing in it I would change, and I like it still. Later I did a similar juvenile book, *Alligator Crossing*, for a series on the U.S. national parks for John Day and Company. It was not well promoted, but I'm not ashamed of it, either.

During this period, I carried on an important correspondence with Marjorie Kinnan Rawlings. I mention it because of the juxtaposition between us: both of us were known as Florida writers, both had migrated here from up North. I was down in southern Florida discovering a region, while Marjorie was up in central Florida discovering a people. I understood her fairly well.

Our correspondence began after I read some stories she'd written for *Scribner* magazine called "Cracker Chitlins". They were old Florida stories. She captured the language perfectly. I wrote and told her what

I thought. After that, we developed a pleasant relationship.

She and her husband Chuck Rawlings bought an orange grove in the center of the state, near Cross Creek. He was an excellent writer, but he didn't like to write. He got her started writing and then he stopped. She went on to write *The Yearling* and *Cross Creek*. They were both remarkable, part of the rare body of genuine Florida literature. She had discovered what sociologists would call an "enclave" of old Florida people. That's where she got that wonderful, true Florida language.

Her great success was accompanied by an equal measure of unhappiness and disappointment. Her marriage with Chuck Rawlings ended in separation and then divorce, and Marjorie was devastated. During that time, she came down to Miami to see me. Then, in her highly-acclaimed novel, *Cross Creek*, she made the mistake of calling one of her characters "the most profane woman in Florida," or some such thing. The person on whom the character was based got ahold of some terrible lawyer and decided to sue for invasion of privacy.

Marjorie's lawyers tried to get her fellow writers to send in letters of support, basically stating that she shouldn't be held responsible because she was a great writer. I didn't send a letter, because I felt that what she'd done was somewhat injudicious, and that she ought to have been more careful in what she said about characters who were identifiable as her neighbors in Cross Creek.

In any event, Marjorie won her case in the circuit court, but the verdict was reversed on appeal to the Florida Supreme Court and she was ordered to pay a judgment — the grand total of $1. In my mind, it was a suitable ending to the trouble. Marjorie, I thought, had been guilty of something, and the women who sued her, mostly wanting money, got just the amount she deserved.

Because of the invasion of privacy suit, Marjorie gave up Florida and went to live in Cooperstown, New York. She began to write again, but it wasn't about Florida. Her later books weren't good at all. One was called *The Sojourner*, and dealt with family betrayal. It was loosely autobiographical. Though she remarried once, she never got over the break-up with Charles Rawlings. It's another example of how that sort of involvement with a man can ruin a woman's life and work.

In the mid-1950s, Stanley Rinehart of the company that published *River of Grass* came to Miami to inform me they had a new subject for me: hurricanes. That piqued my interest. I'd been living in Florida for years and knew something about hurricanes, including the one that damaged my house, but I'd never experienced a hurricane in person. My great-great-grandfather, the shipmaster in the Maine-to-China trade, had gone down in a typhoon in the China Sea. To that extent, I was at least indirectly related to a victim of hurricanes and had inherited a great respect for high winds.

I set about the research in earnest. I gathered material at the weather bureau and the local hurricane service, then hit the road. I travelled around the Florida coast, and up and down the U.S. East coast, visiting anyplace that had experienced a hurricane. I stayed with the veterans of hurricanes on the North Carolina Outer Banks. I made the people in Charleston, South Carolina, furious by saying that their town had been hit by more hurricanes than any other town on the Atlantic seaboard. They said my pointing this out was bad for tourism and for real estate.

Since I'd always loved the West Indies, hurricanes were a good excuse to go back there. In Jamaica, I looked up two distant relatives, both Quakers named White. One was Martha White, who'd married a man named Miller and who lived in Christiania, the highest town in Jamaica. I visited them there. Martha White Miller introduced me to people who'd gone through several hurricanes, including the bad one they'd had in Kingston.

Then there was cousin Mary White. She worked with the East Indians who'd been brought to Jamaica as indentured servants after the emancipation of the slaves. I visited her Quaker meeting house and school in the hills and her own house in Port Antonio. She drove a horse and buggy from one to the other. If the Indians in the hills were sick, she brought them down to the Port Antonio hospital, or she'd nurse them back to health in her own home. She had all kinds of missionaries coming around for tea. I never saw so many missionaries in my life. There were Seventh-Day Adventists, Seventh-Day Baptists, and Seventh-Day a lot of other things.

After leaving Jamaica, I returned to Martinique, where I'd once done the article on the volcanic eruption for the *Saturday Evening Post*. I had kept in touch with Dr. Perret, the charming academic who had been building the volcanic museum for the French. He took me up the volcano to see a French family who'd owned most of the land before the eruption. They'd also had plenty of experience with hurricanes. I did research on hurricanes in the library at Fort-de-France, where everything was in French.

In Cuba, I interviewed the Jesuit father who directed the weather research at the University of Belen. The Jesuits were the first Europeans in the new hemisphere to study hurricanes. They'd posted men on the eastern tip of the island to watch out for storms, and as reports were brought in by ships, the messengers galloped across the country on horses to spread the warning to Havana. At the time, they knew more about hurricanes than the U.S. Weather Bureau did.

Columbus was on his second voyage to the West Indies when he heard about a hurricane in the Windward Passage. (In fact, the word "hurricane" comes from the Carib word *ouragan*.) He was the first European to be made aware of the deadly storms. He sailed west along the coast of Cuba to avoid them.

The hurricane book was published in 1958. It had a steady hardback sale, and eventually came out in paperback through a subsidiary of Ballantine. Unfortunately, Ballantine dropped all the stories about actual storms, and reprinted only the scientific parts. Once the editor complained to me about the poor paperback sales, and I told him it was because he'd cut out all the hurricanes!

NEARLY MY LAST DANCE

I continued to be blessed with good health; though now into my seventies I had to keep up with the problems of advanced age. I had a sensible diet. I never took vitamins, but I did eat calcium tablets and drank three quarts of skimmed milk a week. I always tried to avoid whole milk and eggs. My father had died of kidney stones, which I'd learned are pure cholesterol.

One popular theory these days is that it's particularly healthy to eat seafood. As I mentioned earlier, I've always liked to eat fish, though not the way the Southerners cook it.

One thing wrong with Southern cooking is that Southerners don't understand fish. Having been brought up in Massachusetts and also having lived in Florida, I feel compelled to say this. In New England, fish is an important part of the diet and intelligently cooked. In the South, it seemed the only way they knew to cook fish was to dredge it in batter and deep-fry it in oil until it came out as stiff as a board. Fish is delicate. You can't treat it as starched laundry.

During the times when Mrs. Greatham, Lilla's mother, would visit Lilla at my father's house, I was amused at every meal where fish was served. My father always would say: "Mrs. Greatham, which part do you prefer?" She always answered, "I'd like the tail, please," but the way it was cooked, there wasn't a bit of difference between one end and the other. It might as well have been asphalt shingles. Southerners don't understand there are ways to cook fish without making it inedible.

Fish should be poached or fried very lightly. I used to cook a fillet by marinating it in lime juice — you had to use limes instead of lemons — then plopping a big lump of butter in a pan under the broiler. I'd let the butter melt and simmer a little, then pick up the fish by the tail and kind of swirl it around in the butter. After that, I'd leave it skin-side down, and baste it a couple of times with more lime juice and butter. Sometimes I'd put mayonnaise on it and stick it under the broiler for an extra minute. Cooking a fish in this manner does not insult its delicacy.

I frequently eat Florida pompano, though I don't know why people go on about it as if it's some heaven-sent delicacy. Actually, I prefer yellowtail to pompano, though yellow-tail's a bit soft. Fish from these warmer Southern waters can't compete at all with fish from the cold climates. Up there, the flesh is firmer. We don't have anything down in Florida to match the swordfish steaks you get up North. They have the herring and all kinds of shad. They have the great clams.

The so-called Florida lobster is really a crayfish, not the true lobster of the North. I've eaten plenty of both. These crayfish are usually boiled and overcooked, allegedly to keep them sweet. Actually, they should be steamed. As a matter of fact, I think the Northern lobster should be steamed instead of boiled.

So I don't sound completely one-sided in arguing the superiority of Northern seafood, I have to mention that Florida has excellent shrimp and the wonderful little Florida oyster that grows on the mangrove roots. These funny oysters are delicious either raw or lightly cooked. One of the first times I ate them was 50 years ago, on a trip through the Ten Thousand Islands, on a friend's fancy houseboat with a cook, a captain, and a crew.

In general, I've done a certain amount of cooking in my life, but I could never keep up with the high Southern standards of Miss Jeffy or of my stepmother. Fortunately, I didn't have to. I wouldn't have wanted to spend all my time over a hot stove. For years I've gotten by with a small baking oven and an electric hot plate with a couple of burners. I've never baked a cake and I don't think I ever cooked a leg of lamb, though I've baked a few turkeys.

I've always known how to cook omelettes because my grandmother was French. When I was little, I always had what she considered the best breakfast for a child — hot cocoa and toast and a two-egg omelette. A true French omelette has to be made with a little water, say a teaspoonful to an egg. Then you beat the egg so it's fluffy. You can't make an omelette with cream — a mistake that many people repeat over and over.

Once when my friend Carolyn Percy was sick in New York, I made her one of my fluffy omelettes. First off, she was amazed I could cook anything at all, since in our college years I was the person who built the fire and washed the dishes, but I was kept away from the stove. She was doubly amazed at the quality of the omelette. Carolyn was a good cook in general, but had never learned about good omelettes. That's because she grew up in cream country.

People generally have said my cooking is "flavorous." I guess that's a compliment. I've always believed that if you begin with an onion in butter and you build up from there for flavor you can hardly go wrong. I can make a good bouillabaisse. I learned the tricks of bouillabaisse from Mrs. Charlie Thompson, whose husband was the captain and fishing guide of the Mellon's yacht in Miami back in the '20s. Bouillabaisse is made from five different kinds of fish, and with special seasoning. You give everybody a bowl of that, plus a big spoon and some French bread, and you've had a meal.

My circulation is pretty good. I'd always had cold hands and cold feet, but that's neither here nor there. I began to have a little trouble with cramps in the feet, but the calcium seemed to cure that. Once during this period of my seventies I had shingles around my left shoulder-blade. For that, the doctor prescribed cortisone. He warned about the side effects, and his warning turned out to be prophetic. After taking two cortisone pills, I began to go to pieces. I started to cry, which isn't like me at all. The doctor took me off the cortisone, but maybe it had worked already, because the shingles went away. I've since been told that chickenpox is the same virus as shingles. A Dr. Blank, at the University of Miami, was looking through his microscope, and accidentally saw that the chickenpox virus and the shingles virus are identical.

Occasionally, in cold weather, I would feel a bit of an itchy twinge where the shingles were. That's about all the illnesses I'd had, except for my eyes, of course. My eyes had begun to deteriorate. Oh yes, and the appendicitis attack. That happened back in the 1960s, when I'd just turned 70 years old and nearly danced myself into disgrace.

There was a young man — in his twenties, I think — and an extremely good dancer. I don't remember his name. I was old enough to be his grandmother, but we met at a party, a wonderful dinner, and began to dance. We did some special loopings and twirlings and all that, danced between courses at the dinner, and even far into the night. The next day, I woke up feeling sort of odd. I went out to lunch someplace and felt worse. I came home again and lay down on the bed, and my friend Carolyn, who was living next door by this time, took one look at me and ordered me to call the doctor.

This was Dr. Burtner, the old-fashioned kind of doctor who still came over to see you. He started punching me, and right away he hit McBurney's Point, and I said, "Go no further. I bet I've got appendicitis." He said, "It's worse than that, it's peritonitis. You are a very sick woman and we've got to get you to the hospital right now." I felt as if I were dying. I was just going out like a light.

By 3 o'clock I was installed in Mercy Hospital. By 7, I was in the operating room. My appendix had burst, and the peritonitis had set in. I was in the hospital for nearly a month, what with all the draining. I was fed intravenously. For a long time after, I was still so sick I couldn't eat.

As I got better, I began to enjoy the hospital. It was a Catholic hospital, and the sisters were wonderful. I had a room overlooking the bay. At night, if they left the windows open it would rain in on me. I loved that. I'd learned what it is to be really sick, and to appreciate the fact it hadn't happened very often. And it was those long steps, loopings and twirlings that did it. So much for strenuous exercise at this age.

MORE BOOKS

Every now and then, I've ventured into some form of publishing. The University of Miami Press was organized with Malcolm Ross as director. I was on the advisory board. Shortly, Malcolm Ross gave it up, I think because he got a better job. In the early 1960s, they offered me his position — for less money of course. That's the kind of thing a woman learns to expect.

I had already turned 70, but I was completely prepared to do full-time work. The salaries for me and a secretary, as small as they were, took up all the funds. This was a university press with no money to buy or to print books! It's very hard to run a press without money, as you might imagine. Somehow, we managed to publish a few books, including three of which I'm very proud. One was a collection of essays on the early Florida Indians, written by my old friend, the genius with one bad eye, John Goggin. The book was quite successful.

Another was a book of the portrait medallions done by a distinguished Englishman named Theodore Spicer-Simson. In Europe, he'd made bronze medallions of famous men of letters, like W.H. Hudson and Joseph Conrad, and had continued his wonderful work in Coconut Grove. We printed photographs of the medallions and told about how they were made. It was a pleasant, scholarly collection of characters.

The third was written by a professor from the art department at the University of Miami, Richard Aldrich. He was stone-deaf, which is one of the reasons he got interested in art. He knew everything there was to know about the art and architecture of Mexico and had produced a manuscript on the subject. Whatever state it was in when I first read it, I encouraged him to finish.

Miami Mayor Maurice Ferre, a great fan of Richard Aldrich, put in five thousand dollars towards the completion of Aldrich's book. Then we realized we had no pictures. An art book without pictures is a problem. I enlisted Richard Merrick, brother of the developer of Coral Gables, and famous in his own right as a great American painter of the Ashcan School. Merrick was born in Miami, then lived in New York, and returned to Miami for most of his adult career as a painter.

We sent the two Richards, Aldrich and Merrick, to Mexico. Between the two of them, one as deaf as a post and the other a dashing and adventurous gentleman, it was a riotous trip. The result was *Style in Mexican Architecture*. It discussed the combination of the Catholic imagery and the native Mayan imagery, the kind of thing where there's a crucifix with a snake around it, etc.

Soon, I resigned my post at the University of Miami Press. I was in the wrong place completely. The three books I've mentioned were the only things I remember doing that were useful. Very shortly, the press itself was abandoned and all the projects were turned over to the University of Texas Press.

Due to the proverbial lack of money, plus our lack of managerial ability, the whole thing failed. You'd think I'd have learned by now to stick to my writing.

Sometime in the 60s, I also did some lectures at the Dade Junior College. I never felt like teaching, because when you're a teacher and the students don't learn things it's your fault. When you're a lecturer and they don't get it, it's their fault. I lectured on Florida history in the winter term for five straight years. It was 16 weeks, two classes a week, plus a Saturday seminar. Made $800 a term, which to me was good money. I discovered I could stand and talk for two solid hours, and the only thing that got tired was my feet. I've been talking ever since.

The Rivers of America series, of which my *The Everglades: River of Grass* was a part, was very successful in general. There's something about a river that's a living thing. It's a stream of history as well as water. Rivers are very intimate to man. The publishers tried to duplicate the success with another series on the lakes of America, but that didn't work so well. A lake is more of a static entity.

Harper and Row also thought up a series called Regions of America. Regions are not as inspiring as rivers, but since my book had done so well, they asked me to write about the Florida region. The editor was a likeable man named Buzz Wyeth, or more formally, Marion Sims Wyeth, Jr. His father was one of the architects who built Palm Beach, so he had a keen feeling for the state.

I set myself to work on it sometime after I'd recovered from peritonitis. Of course, I already knew a lot about South Florida, but not much about the rest of the state. I didn't really know the middle, nor did I know the panhandle. Actually, the various parts of Florida have little in common, and trying to lump them together is particularly futile.

But I did the best I could. I took a research trip with an old friend from college, Marian Johnson Murray. She'd come down to do publicity for the Ringling Museum and stayed on in Sarasota after she retired. We had a hilarious time driving around the panhandle in her little car. We went to all sorts of queer little places, to the Chattahoochee River, to the charming old town of Apalachicola. I discovered yet another second cousin I hadn't known before, related to my grandfather's Whites.

It was helpful that my stepmother came from an old Florida family. Her grandfather was Francis Eppes, the grandson of Thomas Jefferson, whom I've described earlier. Also, she was the daughter of Confederate Captain Shine, who had been the tax assessor in Orlando and was part of the committee that planted all those beautiful oak trees. I got plenty of material for the book from my stepmother, who died soon after it was published.

We called the book *Florida: The Long Frontier* — which has a double meaning, since the state has a long coastline and also since it continues to be a frontier to this day. It turned out to be a kind of pop, non-textbook history. There weren't too many good straight histories of Florida. There was *Florida: Land of Change*, written by Kathryn Abbey Hannah at Florida State University when it was still a girl's school. I don't think it's awfully interesting, quite frankly, but the facts are there. Another was the two-volume account written by Charlton Tebeau.

I was particularly interested in the part that Florida played in the Civil War. As you know, I'm a damn Yankee, and my father's people were abolitionists. I still think slavery is the worst crime ever committed against the U.S. and we're still paying for the crime. We're being punished for it. It's been a dreadful problem from the start. The South was stupid in thinking it could maintain slavery by fighting a war over it. The South had those romantic ideas of Walter Scott that all they had to do was get on a horse and wave a sword and the silly Yankees would fade away completely. Of course it didn't work.

The only old Southern part of Florida, in the cultural sense, was the northern part. Actually, Florida wasn't very useful to the South in the war effort, except that the cattle came through here from Cuba. Also, Florida had salt works. Salt was very important for the preservation of beef. The Yankees tried to destroy the salt works, but they'd immediately be started up someplace else. It was a simple matter of putting out a pan and filling it with salt water, then letting the water evaporate.

The only battle of any importance was fought near Tallahassee. In this battle, every able-bodied male, including boys from the West Florida Academy, defended the city. When the Yankees were defeated, the ladies of Tallahassee put out trestle tables in the streets and had banquets for all the soldiers and civilians who'd just taken up arms. In the middle of their wonderful celebration, the news of Lee's surrender at Appomattox reached them. Poor dears. Then they had to suffer the humiliation of Reconstruction.

During that time, all the ladies who had plantations, like my step-mother's people, opened up boarding houses for all the Yankees to come down and spend the winter. This made for good relations and brought Yankee money into the state. Florida has always known how to capitalize on such things.

The early Floridians, as I've said, didn't care anything about documents and my Civil War research suffered as much as my research into the Key West wreckers. In fact, many early Floridians were con men and promoters of dubious reputation who realized that the less that was known of their exploits, the better. Consequently, it was difficult to write good Florida history. I scratched around and found what there was.

I finished *Florida: The Long Frontier* in 1966. It was published in 1967 and had a pretty good sale. Harper and Row was going to remainder the last 920 copies, but I gave a local Miami press, Banyan Books, an option to buy them and Banyan did. Banyan later sold them out.

I wasn't sure what to do next. I wanted to keep writing, but I didn't know about what. As seems to be my custom, I waited for the next project to drop into my lap. This happened as follows. One day, I was talking to Theodore Bolton, a neighbor who'd once been a librarian in

New York. Bolton was an expert on books. He reminded me of some notes I'd made several years earlier when Dr. Frank Chapman, dean of American ornithologists, had come down to Miami to study birds. All that summer, whenever it was, I'd gone to dinner with Dr. Chapman every week. Besides his birds, Dr. Chapman was very involved with W.H. Hudson, the 19th century writer, one of the literary geniuses of the late Victorian and early Edwardian England.

At the time, I'd told Dr. Chapman he ought to write a definitive biography of W.H. Hudson. Dr. Chapman said he was too old for such a project, but gave me all his Hudson notes, and all the letters he'd written on his research trips. This material had been lying around my house for years, and it was the librarian Theodore Bolton who reminded me I still had it.

Then when the editor at Harper and Row, Buzz Wyeth, asked me what I wanted to do next, I told him about W.H. Hudson. He discouraged the idea and told me that literary biographies aren't very profitable. (Later, I chided him about publishing a life of Edith Wharton that was a big success.) I think he also doubted that a 76-year-old woman could take on the years of travel to England, where Hudson did much of his writing, and to Argentina, where he spent his early life.

I decided to take on the Hudson project without his encouragement, without an advance, and completely on my own. That it would take a lot of time and a lot of traveling was all right with me. I still liked to travel, even though my eyes were going bad.

Just a few months before my 77th birthday, I applied for a $7,000 traveling fellowship from the Wellesley Alumnae Association. They turned me down. I got the rejection in December, 1967 — just before Christmas and just as I was about to enter the hospital to have my first cataract operation. I remember thinking, "What a way to celebrate."

After the operation, I had to wear a black patch over my good eye until both eyes were coordinated again. Wearing my black eye patch, I returned home from the hospital to find another letter from Wellesley offering me a smaller stipend of $1,500-$2,000. With that, I was able to go to Buenos Aires for the first time. I carried the old notes and the letters of Dr. Chapman in my suitcase.

An old friend, a retired Marine officer named Captain Bill Cairns, said he'd travel with me through Argentina. He was much younger than me, 22 years younger in fact, and I'd met him when he was renting the house next door one summer. He'd taken me to the movies numerous times. He was a movie addict, as many retired military people seem to be. They live in odd places, and at night their only recreation is movies. He used to drive me down to the little theater that specializes in foreign films. Sometimes, I'd have him over for dinner. Together, we saw what I think is the greatest movie ever made — La Strada, directed by Federico Fellini. It was wonderful.

Captain Bill Cairns had moved onto a houseboat in the marina at Coconut Grove. He took piano lessons and had a beautiful little Hammond on the houseboat. We became better and better friends, so when I told him about my Argentina project he volunteered to be my escort. He'd wanted to go there anyway, and expected to support himself by teaching English at the American cultural center. He spoke good Spanish, and showed me how to use the library and find the English-language periodicals in Buenos Aires. We always stayed in separate hotels. I thought it was very funny.

We met in Buenos Aires, me with the black patch still on my eye, in the spring of 1968. I visited the birthplace of W.H. Hudson in the countryside about seven miles out of Buenos Aires. My guide there was Hudson's niece, Violeta Shinya, the director of this memorial park. I saw the ombu trees, very strange, not a true tree but an enormous weed. They look like trees, but the wood is more like pith, and of no use at all. The Hudson houses were located among these ombu weeds, at a place called 25 Ombues.

I discovered that the first Hudsons who'd gone to the Argentine bought land from the sister of the 19th century tyrant, Rosas. I looked for tombstones of these Hudsons. It seems they died in a great plague epidemic in Buenos Aires and their bodies were buried together in a common grave. A memorial tablet was put up on a wall of the great Buenos Aires cemetery, and Bill Cairns, exploring along it, discovered the names.

I was lucky to find Hubert Rockwood Hudson still alive in town. He let me see the records in the Hudson family Bible. That's where I found out that Daniel Hudson, the father of W.H. Hudson, was born in Marblehead, Mass., in 1804. I also discovered that he and Caroline Kimball Hudson, the mother of W.H., were married in Boston in 1825. Later I went through the Massachusetts records to confirm all this.

After the Argentine trip, I had enough money for a brief trip to

England. It was a rainy and cold September when I arrived. I stayed in the little family hotel, the Whitehall on Montague Street, around the corner from the British Museum.

I went to Hudson's old publishing house, J.M. Dent, and they dug up a whole deskful of packages full of Hudson material, letters, etc., that they might have intended to publish after Hudson's death but they'd forgotten about. I was given an office and a secretary and they told me I could stay as long as I wanted. By the time I discovered this gold mine I'd unfortunately run out of money. I'd reserved a seat on a plane back to America for the next day.

I flew home to Coconut Grove, desperate to turn right around for England. I explained the predicament to Christine Chapman Robbins, whose husband Bill had worked with me on the board of the Fairchild Tropical Gardens and was also president of the American Philosophical Society. Somehow, he was able to get the philosophers to donate $1,500 to my cause, and I was able to return to England that same fall. I started in right where I'd left off.

On my subsequent trips to the Argentine, Hudson's great niece Violeta would always show me around. Once we took a little plane to Cordova, a beautiful old Spanish city, all completely white, up in the foothills of the Andes. The Latins understand how to build cities, as I've said. It's a great pity the Americans haven't learned this from them. Anyway, up there in beautiful Cordova we went over some of the rough manuscript, and Violeta made many valuable suggestions.

In all, I visited Argentina three times, including one trip through Patagonia. I went to England seven times and took many side trips to the south of the country where Hudson had gone in his wanderings, into Hampshire and especially into Cornwall about which he wrote in Land's End. There, high above a little coastal town called Zennor are the great rocks on which "W.H. Hudson often came here" is carved.

On my most recent trip to Argentina my eyes had deteriorated to the point I could hardly see at all. I'd developed a routine about airplanes. I'd get off the plane and a wheelchair would meet me and take me to a taxi. The taxi would take me to my hotel and the concierge would pay the taxi man, and then I'd be all right. I stayed at a familiar old hotel until my friend Violeta arrived to be with me.

I was invited to visit some relatives of a friend on the Rio Negro in Patagonia. I had to take a small plane, which was a bit more complicated.

I'd been told what the taxi fare would be, but when I got to the airport and gave the man what I thought was the right amount of money, he started yelling *"Uno mas, uno mas."* The money down there was either red or green, and I didn't know which was which. I gave him something that must have satisfied him, and he came across with some change.

I got inside the airport, expecting it to be small and quiet, but it wasn't small and quiet at all. It was a big-city airport with lots of lines of people. I got lost and couldn't tell which line to get in. I'd learned some Spanish from my hairdresser back in Miami, so I more or less announced to the crowd: *"Yo no veo bien, ayudame, por favor"*, which translates to "I don't see very well, please help me." A lady stepped up and said, "Oh, I speak English." Given my wonderful Spanish, how did she know that I spoke English?

Anyway, she and her husband were going to the same place I was, so they took care of me. When I got off the tiny plane at an equally tiny town called Biedna, there were my host and his son. They directed me to an even smaller plane that flew us to their farm. They had 20,000 acres north of Rio Negro, devoted to sheep and wheat. There was a simple but comfortable ranch house in an island of trees. The trees were a necessary protection from the wind.

That Sunday, we had a big party for the sheep shearers. There were long tables out on the patio, a half a lamb roasted on a wood fire, gin and tonics and lots of other things to eat and drink. People came on horseback and jeeps and airplanes from all over that part of the country. It was a neighborhood party where the neighborhood stretches for hundreds of miles.

This was Patagonia, where Hudson had written his beautiful book, *Idle Days in Patagonia.* He'd gone down from Buenos Aires on a ship, but the ship had been wrecked on shore in one of the sudden storms. He'd walked ashore and then across the country to this very area where I stayed. I was the oldest person there, and everyone was nice to me.

Back in Miami, I started writing the W.H. Hudson book and had little more than two chapters finished when my eyes began to fail me completely. Gradually my handwriting got worse and worse and I could hardly see to write. To add to the trouble, my dear friend Alice Knowles, who was helping with the typing, was suffering in the same way. Between my terrible handwriting and the bad eyes of both of us, the work became very difficult. Since then, I've turned over the rough draft to my friend

Margaret Ewell, an excellent editor who is going over the whole thing to see what it needs.

SOME SAD GOODBYES

After Franklin Harris died in the house next door, his wife Alice lived on there for several years. Alice shared the house with her sister, Katherine Hill. Katherine had a Persian cat named Sam Hill. Alice didn't care about cats, I think she preferred dogs, but Katherine and I were sympathetic over the question of the cat. She asked me to take care of it, if anything happened to her.

When Katherine died, Uncle Charlie and I took Sam Hill with us. Both Uncle Charlie and I were fond of any kind of animal, but particularly a cat. Actually, Sam Hill was very popular on his own account. He was the imperturbable kind of gentleman cat who is at home anywhere. He was invited to parties and people would talk to him. Eventually, we gave him to my old friends the Gullivers.

Without Katherine, Alice was alone again, but she didn't seem to mind. I was very close to her. She traveled by herself to Guatemala, where she and her husband Franklin had stayed together on vacations. The last time she was there, she had a heart attack, and they cabled her son Stephen to come down and get her. She had another heart attack and died while sitting beside him on the plane home. They covered her up with a blanket and the undertaker had to meet the plane. It was very shocking for her son.

That left the next-door house empty. Alice's heirs didn't want it. They were going to sell it, and since my lot is so narrow, and my house so close to theirs, I worried about who might move in. I called Carolyn Percy Cole and told her about Alice's death. On the spur of the moment, she said she'd buy the Harris house, and that she did, for cash. I was thrilled. She paid $10,000 for the house and put $15,000 into restoring it.

It was the middle of 1957 when Carolyn had the house fixed up. After that, she came down every winter, along with Vida Winkey — her black cook, driver, and general manager. Carolyn fit right in with my friends in Coconut Grove. Having Uncle Charlie over here and Carolyn over there was a wonderful arrangement. Also, when Carolyn went back north to Old Bennington, Vermont, for the summer, I'd visit her up there.

In 1958 or 1959, Uncle Charlie suddenly found he couldn't empty his bladder. He was a little man clinging to life. I got the doctor, who put him in the hospital in the care of the specialists. They operated and put in a tube, which was a great humiliation to Uncle Charlie. He hated having a tube. From then on, he began to give up. Soon, he got seriously ill. The doctor diagnosed it as cancer of the prostate, but a kidney stone is what killed him, just as it had killed my father.

Uncle Charlie's illness didn't last long. He wasn't strong enough to stand very much. I took care of him in the daytime, and a night nurse came in towards the end. I held his hand as he was dying. He died here in my house. The last day or two all he could say was "Swan Point," "Swan Point." I'd say, "Yes, Uncle Charlie, it'll be Swan Point."

Swan Point was the beautiful cemetery in Providence, where his wife Nettie had been buried, and Uncle Charlie was put there as well. He was my last living relative from either of the two families.

His death was a great sorrow. On his own account I missed him, and I regretted also that so charming a life had to end. Yet he was in his nineties, so you can't expect too much. I was alone again in the house. It was a return to a state of being that was my deliberate choice. I don't understand people who go around complaining they're lonely; I couldn't stand not being alone some of the time. One of the reasons Uncle Charlie and I got along was that each of us worked alone in his own framework. Also, we hadn't talked much about the troubled and far-off times in the family's past.

Perhaps I would have felt lonelier if I hadn't been living in Coconut Grove. Coconut Grove was more unchanged than many places, because people in the Grove never wanted to sell their houses. They died off, of course, as many of my closest and dearest friends had sadly begun to do.

After Uncle Charlie died, my friend David True, the eccentric map collector, also died. I'd seen the old bachelor once a week for years and years. He'd lost some of his considerable fortune in real estate, and his ex-wife who had a little house on 27th Avenue between a grocery store and a filling station, let him live there rent free. It was a funny little place, but he continued to live there while he used his money for the things he really wanted to do.

As he began to fail and to get sick, some people from a strange religious cult came over and cared for him, cleaned his house, took him to the doctor, made sure he was comfortable. The money he'd inherited so unexpectedly years earlier while he took care of the sick daughter of his mistress was in similar fashion handed along to the cult.

When David True was very ill and obviously was going to die, he got worried about his maps. Actually, he'd always worried about what would happen to the maps. I'd suggested he leave them to a library or a historical society, but he insisted they'd just stash the maps away and ignore them. After he died, I discovered he'd left them to me. He also left me $10,000.

An upstairs room in Carolyn's house next door was vacant, and I was allowed to convert it into a repository for David's maps. I filled one end of the room with fine bookcases, built with screens on the doors so the central air conditioning would reach the manuscripts inside.

The maps were kept up there for a year or two, and then an old friend of True's, Charles Arnade, came to ask about them. He had some connection to the University of South Florida in Tampa, and made arrangements for the maps to be taken there. I went to visit them and found they were beautifully housed and well cared for by the librarian, Dr. Dobkin.

After that, a Dr. Fuson of the history department was given a sabbatical to study the maps. He came to see me, afraid that I might be mad that he'd concluded that David True had wild ideas. I assured him that David's wild ideas were no surprise to me. He also said that though the maps were copies, there wasn't a better collection on the early discovery of North America anywhere in the world than what David True had amassed. It shows what a retired person can do, when he or she gets interested in a certain subject.

V

A Friend
of the
Everglades

The Everglades surrounded us at the outskirts of Miami and beyond. My book on the Everglades was 20 years old and I was 78 before I got absorbed in the great effort to save them. I hadn't imagined doing much more about the Everglades. There were the beginnings of a national environmental movement, to which I was sympathetic — at first a sympathetic bystander. I found myself drawn into it about the time I started the W.H. Hudson project, about the time I lost so much of my eyesight I could hardly have seen the Everglades outdoors.

There was no organized environmental movement until the late 1960s, and little understanding of what ecology is about. Back in the 1920s, a few of us sensed that water was the key to the health of the Everglades, so perhaps we were untutored environmentalists even then. In my magazine-writing phase, I'd written about the plight of the birds and other animals in the Everglades and occasionally had lobbied in their behalf. I'd served on the committee to establish the national park. But these were the sporadic and disjointed conservation efforts of a full-time freelance writer.

The Everglades were always a topic, but now they promised to become more than that. They promised to become a reason for things, a central force in my existence at the beginning of my 80th year. Perhaps it had taken me that long to figure out exactly what I was able to contribute, and for me to marshall my forces.

Perhaps at my age, the aims should have been clear for some time. Or perhaps it merely took all the building up of resources waiting for the opportunity. In my case, I was always a writer, but had not turned inward. I wrote from emotion but not with that inner absorption that characterizes the novelists. That same love and emotion, I think, which was held somewhat in abeyance in my earlier periods of journalistic voyeurism, was ready to be channeled to the Everglades. It was almost as if the Everglades had waited for me. It was a cool subject, to which I could apply my passion.

On a simpler level, this was another case where a great project seemed to fall into my lap. It happened as follows. In the late 1960s, the Audubon Society in Miami got all embroiled in a fight against a developer named Ludwig, who proposed to put an oil refinery on the shores of lower Biscayne Bay. The environmental movement in Florida owes a great debt to Mr. Ludwig. His idea was so ridiculous and it stimulated such widespread opposition that many people who'd otherwise been sitting back were enlisted into the environmental movement right then.

People who fought the Ludwig project were just about exhausted, but they came out with a victory: the protection of the part of the bay where Ludwig wanted to put the refinery. Since then, there's one thing I've learned about environmental causes: The most dangerous time is after some project like Ludwig's has been stopped. The opposition senses the lull, and uses the occasion to spawn numerous other idiocies that ought to be stopped. As soon as the Ludwig idea was killed, an equally ridiculous idea arrived to take its place: the jetport in the Everglades.

One of the hardest working of the Ludwig opponents was Joe Browder, an acquaintance of mine who headed the National Audubon Society in Miami. Mr. Browder complained publicly that nobody had the energy left to help him oppose the jetport, though a jetport might be more damaging to wildlife, the water flow, and the general well-being of the region than an oil refinery in Biscayne Bay.

There was a gal working for Joe Browder by the name of Wilson. I met her one night in a grocery store and I said, "I think you and Joe are doing great work. It's wonderful." She looked me square in the eye and said, "Yeah, what are you doing?" "Oh me?" I said. "I wrote the book". "That's not enough," she countered. "We need people to help us." To get out of this conversation, I casually mumbled some platitude like "I'll do whatever I can."

You couldn't say "I'll do whatever I can" casually to Joe Browder. He was at my doorstep the next day and asked me to issue a ringing denunciation of the jetport to the press. I suggested that nobody could care particularly about my ringing denunciation of anything, and that such things are more effective if they come from organizations. Without skipping a beat, he said, "Well, why don't you start an organization?" So there I was, stuck with a challenge that began as a polite rejoinder in the grocery-store line.

Mr. Browder also said that since I was identified with the Everglades and yet was not connected to any specific faction or group, that I could help unite the various individuals and organizations that had grown up around the cause of preserving it.

He took me out to visit the site of the proposed jetport, right in the path of the flow of the water across the wetlands. A small landing strip for private planes had been put out there already, and it had stopped some of the flow. He and I both knew we didn't ever want to see a huge airport and industrial park in the Everglades.

I was mulling it over at the Fairchild Tropical Garden Ramble, a sort of outdoor picnic, when I ran into Michael Chenoweth, whom I'd known earlier from Coconut Grove sailing regattas. I asked him what he thought about an organization that might be called something like The Friends of the Everglades — which anybody could join for, say, a dollar. Without hesitation he handed me a dollar. "I think it's a great idea," he said.

Now I had not only the idea of an organization to contend with, but also one member and an endowment. What choice did I have but to carry this further? I enlisted the help of Mr. Pritchett of the Coconut Grove Bank who agreed to be treasurer, and Florence Coey, a faculty member at the University of Miami graduate school of international studies, who agreed to be vice president and secretary. She had to do all the typing, since I was only a two-finger typist.

We became the Friends of the Everglades. Soon, I started making speeches to every organization that would listen to me. My college elocution training from 60 years earlier came in handy here. I got 15 or 20 new members, at $1 apiece, every time I spoke. In a year we had over 500, and in another year over 1,000, and later 3,000 members from 38 states.

I had a friend named Everett Skinner who had a bad leg, and had trouble getting in and out of cars because of it. His mother had bought him a camper, and he volunteered to let us use it in our recruiting drive. We made a big circle around Lake Okeechobee, stopping in little towns where I'd give a speech to a women's club or a garden club or a business club. Five or six of us made this trip: including Michael Blaine, a young man whom I later took to Paris, and Dorothy Rook, a librarian for the British Royal Society for the Protection of Birds. The men among us slept in Everett Skinner's camper and the women got rooms in motels.

The jetport was stopped — not necessarily through my efforts — but through the efforts of many people and the responsiveness of the Secretary of the Interior under President Nixon. The Friends of the Everglades was continued, and soon we turned our attentions from the single jetport project to the general predicament of the water.

Water, as I've said, was vaguely understood as critical to the Everglades by a small number of visionaries, including my father. Since the early part of the century, he and a few others sensed the stupidity in draining the so-called swamps. There was more scientific understanding of it thanks to the efforts of Gerry Parker, who made the great study of groundwater in the late 1940s. Finally there was Art Marshall, with whom I joined forces. He'd come back to Florida after commanding some large division in the Army during World War II and devoted himself to the study of conservation, especially water. In the early 1970s, he'd already begun to make his mark with speeches on the subject, and got everybody interested. He was the leading man, not only in our organization, but in all of the organizations.

I was proud to have contributed to Marshall's education by getting him a copy of Gerry Parker's old study. Marshall had never seen it.

Parker had done a monumental piece of work, but as a government publication, it might have died on a shelf. He had discovered that water in Lake Okeechobee came from as far north as the Kissimmee Valley, and that the same water worked its way south through the Everglades. This great interconnection stretching hundreds of miles from central Florida into the Everglades was the basis of Art Marshall's efforts.

Art Marshall took up where Gerry Parker left off. Although my phrase "River of Grass" first awakened people to the notion of the Everglades as a river, it was Art Marshall who filled in all the blanks. He taught that much of the rainfall on which South Florida depends comes from evaporation in the Everglades. The Everglades evaporate, the moisture goes up into the clouds, the clouds are blown to the north, and the rain comes down over the Kissimmee River and Lake Okeechobee.

Lake Okeechobee, especially, is fed by these rains. When the lake gets filled with too much water, some of the excess drains down the Caloosahatchee River into the Gulf of Mexico to the west, or through the St. Lucie River and into the Atlantic Ocean to the east. The rest of the excess — the most useful part — spills over the southern rim of the lake into the great arc of the Everglades.

Marshall realized the profound importance of keeping the area wet. More than any other person, he stretched our idea of the Everglades and how they interact with everything else, which created the most powerful arguments for preserving the water. Self-interest is a more reliable motivation than environmental pity or *noblesse oblige*, and Marshall accomplished the extraordinary magic of taking the Everglades out of the bleeding-hearts category forever.

THE WATER

Meanwhile, man has been doing his best to drain, plug, stanch, dike, and otherwise remove the water from the Everglades since the beginning of this century. The original road across the Everglades, the Tamiami Trail from which I first saw the ibis and the wood storks, the grassy wet pastures and the cypress strands, cut the flow of water to the wetlands below it. Dry land plants began to be seen where once there were aquatic plants, and the area's character was profoundly changed. By 1947, when the national park was established, the Everglades already had been transformed.

That same year, 1947, the Army Corps of Engineers signed a contract to do something about flood conditions around Lake Okeechobee. The engineers wanted to "correct" the flood plain system, as opposed to understanding it. A political body, the Central and Southern Flood Control District, was established to work with the engineers. They dug canals to drain more water off the land. They did this to please the big agricultural interests around the lake.

The sugar people and others wanted to farm the rich lands immediately below the lake. My father wrote editorials against such drainage in 1906, and nearly went bankrupt as a result. People hated him for saying the Everglades shouldn't be drained. It would be an empire of the sun, a paradise for crops, Governor Napoleon Bonaparte Broward had said. Father was right and the governor and the rest of them were wrong.

Then the sugar people had to irrigate to plant their cane. They backpumped their irrigation water into the lake, along with all the pesticides, fertilizer, dead cats and old boots that the water had absorbed.

As the waters around the lake receded, the rich peat used in raising the sugar cane was depleted from an original 30 feet deep to above five feet. It was gradually eaten up by direct exposure to the sun. There were so many peat fires every spring that you got a reek of peaty smoke from West Palm Beach south to Miami.

The engineers drained to satisfy the sugar people, then drained some more to satisfy the cattle people, who wanted more dry land to support their dairy herds. The dairy herds produced manure, and the manure found its way into the rivers that flow into the lake. Very soon, Lake

Okeechobee was polluted. You could fly over it and see how brown it was. A pernicious weed called the hydrilla began to show itself just below the surface. Hydrilla takes up all the oxygen, and kills the fish.

Three conservation areas were established on the edge of what once was the free-flowing stream of the Everglades, and this cure was worse than the disease. Number one fortunately didn't amount to much, but numbers two and three further retarded the water flow. They created pond conditions, instead of allowing the water to run as it must. Flowing water became standing water. In standing water, the pollution settled in one place, covering the river bottoms and lake beds with an ever-thickening density of polluted ooze.

All this interrelated stupidity was crowned by the straightening of the Kissimmee River with a giant canal. The river no longer meandered, and its beds were dried up. With less water in the river, there was less water for the lake, less water to flow into the Everglades, and less water to evaporate into rainfall to feed the river once again.

Instead of studying the Everglades, the engineers continued to work on flood control. All they cared about was floods. They built more and more canals, and drained more and more water off the lands — wasteful and stupid beyond words.

This was the situation we faced in our new organization, the Friends of the Everglades. It had grown to a few hundred members by 1972. In that year, I attended an historic conference on the water problems. Suddenly, there were people who understood the situation. We worked with the national park to put in some culverts and to partially fill some old canals, thus increasing the water flow. As a result of the conference, the state was divided into five water-management districts.

Johnny Jones, ex-head of the Florida Wildlife Federation, helped us in our efforts. I didn't see eye to eye with him about his hunting, but on the water issue, we were allies. Art Marshall, Jones and I went to Tallahassee to ask the Senate Appropriations Committee to spend some money to clean up the Kissimmee River. They flatly turned us down. As far as we got was a resolution from the Florida House of Representatives, telling a U.S. Senate Committee to tell the Army Corps of Engineers to tell its employees to study the possibility of breaking down the Kissimmee Canal, so the river could meander again. Congress voted $60,000 for the engineers to study this. Of course, they love to study it. They'd keep on studying it until the cows came home. Then they'd ask for more money for another study.

Since 1972, I've been going around making speeches on the Everglades all over the place. No matter how poor my eyes are I can still talk. I'll talk about the Everglades at the drop of a hat. Whoever wants me to talk, I'll come over and tell them about the necessity of preserving the Everglades. Sometimes, I tell them more than they wanted to know.

As more people got interested in the cause, we began to gather talented support through the process of self-selection. A prime example of the virtue of self-selection is Franklin Adams. Years earlier, he'd attended one of my classes on Florida history, and he reintroduced himself to me at a water management conference. He said he'd moved to Naples, where he ran a small rug-cleaning business out of an old hearse. He came to this conference in an unofficial capacity, a private citizen interested in Florida's water problems.

Any private citizen who attends a water management conference without being paid for it already has proven a powerful motivation. It wasn't long before Franklin Adams became chairman of the Friends of the Everglades in Collier County. From there, he's gone on to become one of the most effective environmentalists in Florida. He's also a wonderful speaker, which gives me a chuckle. At first, he insisted he was hopeless as a speechmaker.

People from other counties were recruited in similar fashion. Mostly, they chose themselves. Taking a cue from the way Joe Browder recruited me into the jetport fight, anytime I hear somebody complain about something, I take them up on it. For instance, Marguerite Zapoleon wrote me a letter from Broward County complaining about the backwoods fires that were bothering her and her husband. Soon, she was Broward County chairman of the Friends of the Everglades. A similar thing happened with Doris Henriquez and her husband, Edward, in West Palm Beach. They'd attended various water meetings on their own, and it wasn't long before Doris attended them as a representative of our organization.

This method of finding dedicated people is very successful. For other county chairmen we've had Roy Bazire and then Mary Ann Wallace in Lee County; John Strong in St. Lucie; Marilyn Reed for Dade; Mary Steffee Degtoff in Osceola; Jessie Freeling and Alice Cohen in Hendry and Glades; Bill Pantel, Michael Chenoweth and Pam Pierce for Monroe; and Joe Podgor as our expert on toxic waste. They're all intelligent, emotional, and energetic. A group like this can do remarkable things.

I've also had good secretaries to help me with the Friends of the Everglades correspondence. There was Debbie Lyles, and after she got married, Linda Hardin. Both were indispensable in handling the paperwork that had begun to mount.

It's curious that the ignorance about the Everglades has persisted all these years. I suppose it's partly because Florida gets so many new residents. But with increasing publicity, we're hoping that more people will understand the dilemma and we'll have a great public outcry that necessarily precedes a solution. Until we get the Kissimmee River valley restored, we'll never get all the water in the Everglades we need.

We've got to have evaporation from the Everglades so we'll have rainfall. We need to be constantly on alert against any threat to the Kissimmee-Okeechobee-Everglades basin. It's the central support for our south Florida existence — the drinking water, all our water, all our rainfall. If the flow stops, it would mean the destruction of south Florida.

We've also got to do something about the pollution that threatens our water supply. Canals extend from the Everglades into the wellfields of our urban areas. To counteract the pollution that already has built up in and around Lake Okeechobee, our drinking water is filled with chemicals, so it tastes bad and smells queer. That it costs money to keep our water fit to drink is idiotic. People haven't thought this through at all.

There's always talk about how the state should clean up the pollution. The state shouldn't clean it up. The people who polluted it should clean it up. It's going to be hard to convince them of that, of course. The sugar people are responsible for much of the pollution and they have a terrific lobby in Tallahassee. The dairy farmers on the northeast shore who dump untreated cow manure into Lake Okeechobee have political clout as well. I know they could solve this problem themselves, because I met one farmer who's done it. He explained how he put in polishing ponds so that only treated effluent gets into the lake. Other farmers should be made to follow his example.

Ex-governor Graham decided enough was enough and started a new program to restore the Kissimmee River. Through a state resolution, he got the engineers to break down a portion of their old flood control canal. The engineers didn't want to do it because the canal cost millions of dollars. It was a grand mistake that they don't like to admit to.

In 1985, I went to visit the Kissimmee River at the governor's invitation. He took the first shovelful of earth from the canal and I was standing right beside him. He said to me: "We'll come back next year and see this place all covered with water." A year later, we did return, went out in a boat, and saw exactly what he'd predicted. The water had spread all across that particular jog of the stream. It was a joy to see the river coming back.

Some engineers have balked at restoring any more of the meander, and say they're worried that flooding will return. There are ways to control flooding without their canals.

The three conservation areas in the Everglades should be abolished. All they do is pollute our drinking water. The dykes around these areas should be taken down, which would increase the flow of the Everglades. The Everglades could be 40 miles wide or it could be 80 miles wide, depending on the amount of water it receives. We could protect the surrounding cities and towns by running new dykes to the extreme high water mark all along the East coast.

Dade County in particular has let people move into the so-called East Everglades to build houses. These homeowners now are screaming for drainage. For once, the Corps of Engineers has made a good decision in refusing to drain. They couldn't drain there without destroying the sheet flow of the entire system.

I remember a hearing on the East Everglades, where I was the only speaker for the opposition. I got up and explained why the land shouldn't be drained, and the people booed me. I said, "Can't you boo any louder than that?" and they booed some more. "That isn't loud enough," I said, "Come on, boo me LOUDER." Everybody started laughing. They're all good souls — it's just that they shouldn't be out there. In spite of 500 of them arguing against me, the Dade County Commission ended up supporting my position. It had something to do with zoning.

These East Everglades people are out of luck. Some are squatters. I think many disadvantaged people moved out there. I'm sorry about that, but they're going to have to be relocated. It's not impossible. It's the only way.

Our entire water management system must be revamped, and there must be some new legislation. Recently, we've made some progress, and taken some backward steps as well. They shouldn't have run that interstate highway from Tampa to Naples. They shouldn't have run the new highway from Naples to Ft. Lauderdale. It holds back water from the Everglades. Already they've had problems with the existing Alligator Alley. We need more water in the Everglades, especially in the national park.

One thing we don't need is more studies. We know enough now to go ahead. If we keep on studying the water system, Lake Okeechobee will be dead before we get through studying it. As of my writing this, it's within two years of total pollution unless the state takes steps to clean it up.

THE WILDLIFE

To be a friend of the Everglades is not necessarily to spend time wandering around out there. It's too buggy, too wet, too generally inhospitable for camping or hiking or the other outdoors activities which naturalists in other places can routinely enjoy. When newspeople come down and say, "Let's go out in the Everglades, just like you always do," I often laugh. I hardly ever go into the Everglades. You don't just go out in the Everglades, unless you have an airboat, and those noisy contraptions are no blessing to the inhabitants.

I can't say I've spent many years and months communing with the Everglades, though I've driven across it from time to time. I know it's out there and I know its importance. I suppose you could say the Everglades and I have the kind of friendship that doesn't depend on constant physical contact.

But I've always been an animal lover. I have an innate love of animals that goes back farther than my life in Florida. I remember most of the wildlife I've ever seen, plus all the house cats I've ever met.

Once I was with some photographers. We went out on the Tamiami Trail to a place called Cooperstown. For $50, they hired Mr. Cooper to take us out into the sawgrass on an airboat, one of those above-mentioned contraptions that looks like a car hood connected to an airplane engine. Mr. Cooper jockeyed the airboat out to where a couple of canals come together, and then stopped so we could hear each other talk. The sawgrass was way over our heads. Up one of the canals came a 10-foot alligator. We fed it marshmallows.

We'd throw out a marshmallow and he'd open up his mouth — it was all yellow inside — and then chomp down. I was holding the next marshmallow when a purple gallinule flew into the boat, took it out of my fingers, and flew away with it. Evidently, marshmallows are a favorite food of alligators, not to mention the Everglades birds.

There are a few crocodiles left in the south Florida area. I've seen one or two. They have a nesting area on the mainland of lower Florida Bay, opposite one of the keys. Once we found a crocodile nest there on a high pile of sand. The nest had been opened up by something or other, and what eggs were left hadn't hatched.

Back in the 1960s, I saw a panther. I was staying on Marco Island at Mrs. Tommy Barfield's hotel. Mrs. Barfield had the dirtiest hotel in the state, I think. Before you settled into a room you had to get the dustpan and the broom and sweep up the cigarette stubs, but Mrs. Barfield's food was wonderful so it was worth it.

Anyway, I was staying at Mrs. Barfield's, got up early — which for me was extraordinary in itself — and walked down the old road between the shore and the mangroves. As I sauntered along, a large, handsome panther emerged from the mangroves, moved slowly across the road and disappeared into the scrub brush on the other side. He wasn't 20 feet away. I saw the markings on his face. They weren't really markings, just those long whiskers around the muzzle that cast a shadow. I walked on and saw the tracks of his great, big fat furry footprints in the dust and sand of the road. Then it occurred to me that maybe the panther was looking at me, so I turned and scampered away. He decided not to follow.

They tell me that the panthers used to follow people, though they've never been known to hurt anybody. Laymon Hardy, a friend of mine who grew up around Lake Okeechobee, says that panthers aren't weaned until they're over a year old, when suddenly the mother gets tired and casts them out, with no training in hunting or anything, so they're ragged and hungry. They'd follow anything to get a piece of a ham sandwich.

The Marco panther was the only one I ever saw whole, though years earlier I'd spied a tail disappearing into the bush.

I've never seen a black bear. I know there are supposed to be some in the Everglades, and the Game and Fresh Water Fish people estimate how many still exist, but you never hear stories about anybody seeing one. You'd think somebody would see one if they were there. I haven't seen a bobcat, either. I regret I've never seen an otter, although many people have.

Ospreys I've seen many times, partly thanks to Laymon Hardy, who got Florida Power and Light to put platforms on the top of telephone poles so ospreys could build their nests. And back in the 1920s, bald eagles were flying over everywhere in the Everglades, south to Flamingo. Bald eagles never nested on the telephone pole platforms — I guess they were too shy.

I've seen many wonderful marine animals. We used to watch manatee swim up the Miami River. I've hooked a few fish in my time. I've done some bone fishing, where you stand up in the boat and the bone fish go around and around and you go around and around with them. Years ago, I went fishing in the creeks and bays of the Everglades with Dr. W.J. Matheson, who had dinner parties on his cruising houseboat, complete with cook. He had the whole thing beautifully worked out — a smaller boat was dragged behind and used to catch the fish. We would change from our formal clothes to white canvas jumpsuits and go off fishing at night.

One time we were fishing down by number five trestle, on the way to the Keys. Something as big as a cow hit my line. I almost disappeared over the stern before somebody grabbed me around the waist and pulled me back. I spent an hour fighting the cow — which turned out to be a 90-pound Jewfish. It weighed more than I did. Dr. Matheson somehow kept it alive in the boat's well, then let it out in the canal near his house where it survived for a long time.

The only serious run-in I've had with a snake was at my own back door in Coconut Grove. I'm not afraid of snakes per se, it's the wiggle I don't like. One Sunday morning, when I was taking the garbage out to the garbage can, I stepped on something that felt like a piece of hose and heard a loud rattle. The speed of light had nothing on me as I put my foot back inside and slammed the door. I looked out the window and saw the five-foot rattlesnake coiled on the warm bricks. He'd been frightened, too, so he went off and coiled up by the garbage can. It was almost as if his scales were ruffled, and he was bloated with anger. He was a handsome rattlesnake — big. Archie the architect, who was sharing the house with me at the time, called the police, who came and shot the snake. Afterwards, I was sorry I hadn't called the snake farm; he didn't need to be killed.

Everybody said I'd have to look out for his mate, but I never saw a mate.

I've seen black snakes and of course water moccasins out in the water. When we were fishing out there in the Everglades canals along the unfinished Tamiami Trail, we watched the moccasins swim from one bank to the other. They're quite blind. You can stand near them and let them go by and they won't notice you at all. They're very dangerous, but not aggressive. I suppose they could kill you if you bothered them, but there's no sense in that.

Of course, I've seen opossums. One time my cat came through the cat-flap in my bedroom and made a funny, triumphant little noise. I put on my shoes — you never know what you're going to step into after a cat announces something — and there on the floor by the cat was an odd creature which at first I couldn't identify. I picked it up by the tail and discovered it was a baby opossum. It was playing dead, which is a true state of coma they go into; it's not just a ruse, they're really scared. I put it into a basket, closed down the lid, and went back to bed.

Next morning, I investigated the basket, and two bright eyes were looking up at me. I picked up the opossum with a padded kitchen glove and tried to feed it milk from an eyedropper. I'd put the milk in one side of its jaw, and it just dribbled out the other. I decided it wasn't milk the opossum wanted, so I put some cat food on a toothpick, which was a great success.

I made a house for the opossum by cutting a hole in a cardboard box and placing the box upside down inside a chicken-wire cat carrier. Opossums need shelter; after all, they're not turtles. Immediately he entered his little house and slept there. When I put out food and water, he'd peek out of the box, and then make a dash for the plate. He quickly outgrew the carrier.

Then I installed him in an outside cage, and he got too big for that. He was obviously going crazy. You could see he wanted a mate and had to get out, so one day I just opened the door and let him out. After that, I'd sometimes see a big fat possum in the yard and think it was he. They say that possums make good pets, but I didn't want to bother him to be one, and the yard with its stone fence seemed an admirable place to live.

I don't like to see animals in cages, and especially birds that are strong flyers, such as parrots. I'd hate to have a parrot in a cage. The happiest parrot I ever saw in a cage was in Argentina. He'd fly around all day and then return to the cage, but only to be fed and to have a place to sleep.

Florida has a funny little gray fox. Around Coconut Grove, I could hear them barking at night during the summer, a squeeky little bark. I'd put chicken bones out in the field next to my house and watch, and at night I'd see the little fox sneaking over to take the bones to eat. I still see them occasionally, which would indicate that a few of them have survived.

George Merrick, the developer of Coral Gables, brought the big red fox of the North into south Florida. He and others had the idea of hunting the fox, which is so stupid. I don't know what happened to that variety of fox here.

We've got a number of very interesting rats, something like 15 kinds. There's a fat little brown Florida rat, awfully sweet, a pleasant little rat. I saw the cutest sight on my own terrace one time. I heard an odd squeaking, and went to the door and looked out to find a little convention of brown rats. They were young rats, maybe six or seven of them, facing both ways, running around in a circle. When two would bump together, one would jump over the other. They were playing!

When I was a child, I loved mice, but my grandmother wasn't fond of having them around. My grandmother would catch the mice in a live trap, and then she couldn't bear to have them killed, so somebody would have to put them in Mason jars and let them loose on the railroad tracks. And my grandmother thought she was being humane.

You don't see many other species of animals in Coconut Grove, especially since the area has been built up. We have a regular neighborhood squirrel who squeaks very loudly, and a few rabbits. The last little rabbit I knew, one who'd sit out in front and eat in the grass, was killed by dogs.

Oh yes, and there are turtles all over the place. Some neighborhood children who were visiting from England, picked up a great big one, about a foot square — only round. Somebody had painted its shell red and the paint wore off. The turtle was brought to me. The mother said: "Would you please do something to discourage Alistair from trying to take that big turtle back to England?" I had a long and serious talk with Alistair, who was about nine years old. I said: "Now, Alistair, you're talking about taking Horace to England, which will take him completely out of his normal habitat. He is here in the tropics, a warm climate, and you propose to take him where it is cold and rainy, where he will be very uncomfortable. I don't know if he could live very long in that environment. Think of that seriously. If you want to leave him here, you can put him on my terrace and I will block the stairs so he can't get away, and I'll see to it he has the best things to eat in the way of weeds or whatever he eats, and I'll take care of him if you give up your idea of transporting him to England."

He thought it over very carefully and decided not to take Horace to England. He was a serious little boy.

I had Horace on my terrace for some time, but the poor thing was trying to get off. Finally he did. I wasn't sorry because I figured he was happier out in the open.

I've had many cats. I have a cat door in my bedroom window so they can come and go, and they live in the house. People who don't appreciate cats always say that cats kill birds. But as a matter of fact, the real enemy of the bird is the rat, because the rat can sneak up into the nest and suck the eggs and eat the nestlings. Cats can't get up to a bird's nest, but the cats kill rats and keep the rat population down. So my experience is where you have a good cat or two, there are more birds.

I had a darling cat named Emily, who was a calico. Even people who don't normally like cats liked Emily, because she was very outgoing. They would come to speak to Emily and she'd be sitting on the table listening to them. For years I had Emily. Finally, she killed a large lizard and tried to eat it and it poisoned her. When we finally found her, she was half-paralyzed. There was nothing to do but take her to the vet and have her killed, because she couldn't live like that. It was very sorrowful indeed.

Now I have Jimmy. He's an outside cat except when he wants to come in. People in several houses feed him, I think. They also feed Willie, a stray who is getting fat. There's no way of filling him up. I don't think

Willie Terwilliger is a menace to anything. I think if he met a rat, he'd say, "Hey rat, how's the children?" and things like that. As a matter of fact, the female cats are much more hunting animals than the males.

It was my cat Jimmy who taught me how silly and cruel this business of putting collars on panthers in the Everglades really turns out to be.

I've spent a great deal of time in recent years trying to protect animals from the hunters, as well as from the general stupidity of certain government officials supposedly on their side — including those who collar panthers. This is a big part of my efforts.

The hunter's day is about over. Hunting is a sad consequence of the fundamental male approach to society. The Florida Game and Fresh Water Fish Commission is stacked with hunters, the state cabinet is full of hunters, and for all I know, maybe the governor is a hunter. I'm always going on about this but I rarely get to first base. Hunters are perfectly impervious — they don't hear you at all. It's like talking to the walls talking to Johnny Jones of the hunter's organization about hunting. But I don't stop trying. I've got to keep it up: Sometime I might make some kind of a dent on him.

I'm fond of Johnny Jones. I could wring his neck sometimes, but I'm fond of him. He has a very nice wife and a very fine daughter. I'm fond of many people who hunt — even if I do think they're like backward children who haven't grown up.

We've tried to get a moratorium on hunting deer and wild pig in the government's Big Cypress preserve that abuts the Everglades National Park. The deer and the pig are food for the panther. It's difficult trying to argue this point with the hunters. The hunters are still allowed to go in there, and the government could stop it with the scratch of a pen. But the government is thoroughly dominated by the hunters. The psychology is so ingrained it's almost impossible to fight.

After I threatened to rouse the schoolchildren on this issue, the game and fish people sent a representative to Miami to try to talk me out of it. For the time being, I haven't done anything, but soon I think I will. I don't want the deer and pig left to the hunters. I want them left to the panther. Why on earth people should be allowed to go and shoot animals for no reason I'll never understand.

We're most concerned about the panther. Though it's hard to tell how many are left, everyone agrees there aren't many. Some experts estimate there are 40 panthers and others say 150. Either way, the panthers have been driven into the Big Cypress by the human development around them. They don't live in the Big Cypress because they like it, but because it's the only place that's been reasonably safe for them.

Then along comes the collaring program, which so many government people think is wonderful. They chase a panther up a tree with dogs. They shoot the panther with a tranquilizer and when it falls down — one fell and hit his head and died, so there's one less panther already — they put the collar on it, complete with a battery that beeps. They let the panther go and then they fly up in a helicopter to listen to the beeps. They radio down: "There's a panther behind that palmetto," as if they've learned something of startling importance. Where the panther is is all they've learned.

Because of my own house cats, especially Jimmy, I realized how inhumane and short-sighted the idea of putting a collar on a panther really is. Panthers are cats, too. Every time I think of them out there in the Big Cypress, burdened with those beeper collars, I think of my Jimmy and Willie Terwilliger, and how they wouldn't appreciate having a big heavy yoke put around their necks, and how easily they could get snagged on the collar, choke, and die.

As of this writing, there are four or five panthers with collars. They're going to have be caught again when the batteries run out. If they collar a panther that's still growing, the collar may get too tight and choke the animal. We're rapidly running out of panthers and can ill-afford to lose any more of them.

The collaring people have gotten more money from the federal and state governments to continue their program. I don't care what they say, I think it's stupid. I can't see how its improved the life of a panther one little bit. The only thing that's going to improve the life of the panther is to keep the hunters out of the Big Cypress so the panther can get enough to eat.

It would also be a good idea to keep oil companies out of the Big Cypress. Several have bought mineral rights, even though the oil out there is thick and full of sulfur, more like liquid asphalt, and costs a lot to refine. These companies have to have road access. You can't deny a landowner that right, but at least we've got it boiled down to one road. I hope eventually they'll have a pipeline, so trucks won't have to come and go.

The school children voted the panther the state animal, and they're going to have to be told that hunters are killing the panther's food, and that the collaring program is an outrage. Don't think I'm not going to tell them, because I am.

There are numerous other examples of misguided efforts to protect animals. At one time, the water management board had the bad habit of dumping the excess water from Lake Okeechobee into the Everglades at the wrong time of year. One season the wood storks had just begun to nest when the water poured into the park and covered their food supply. The birds couldn't feed their young, and the nestlings died. Since then, the wood storks have wisely moved up to the Corkscrew Swamp, which is owned by the Audubon Society. There are something like six thousand of them, and I think they are safe there. The national park was the loser.

Several years ago, there was a conflict between the deer, the water, the water management people, and the hunters. In one of the conservation areas, water was held back from the Everglades until the sawgrass was replaced by shrubs and the deer came in to feed. The deer is a browser, and not a grazer. The deer moved into area, attracted by the myrtle and the elder and the willow shrubs. The water managers promptly opened the floodgates, drowned out the food supply, and drowned the fawns. There were deer standing up to their bellies in water. The deer that didn't drown were starving.

There was great debate over what to to about them. The hunters volunteered to go out and kill the deer to save their lives! Other people went out to rescue the deer, but some deer died as they were pulled into rowboats. The whole thing was a mess, because the whole idea of these conservation areas is wrong. They shouldn't be there in the first place. The dikes around these areas should be taken down, which would increase the breadth of the Everglades, and eliminate these artificial dry spots and wet spots. That way, the wrong animals wouldn't migrate into the wrong places.

There's an old Miccosukee Indian named Buffalo Tiger whose son Lee has been a friend of mine for many years. I was out there recently, at their reservation on the Tamiami Trail at the edge of the Big Cypress, where the panthers live. We had an interesting debate about the Seminole Indian leader named Jimmy Billie, who shot a panther and was recently arrested for it.

Jimmy Billie served in the U.S. Army, went to Vietnam, and came back to take over one of the branches of the Seminole tribe. He's very clever. He's the one who got them bingo and cigarettes and all that stuff. And he's the one who shot the panther. He was charged with a crime, but the Indian lawyer appealed to a higher court, where the charges were dropped on the grounds that Indians have a right to kill things on their own property. More accurately, the court decided that the panther issue was outside the jurisdiction of the government. Later, the decision was reversed, and the case is unresolved to date.

The killing of this panther made me mad, which is why I brought it up with Buffalo Tiger. Having a discussion with a Miccosukee is like meeting the Statue of Liberty or something. If you're sitting at a table with a non-Indian and one Indian, it's really a party of two. The Miccosukee doesn't say anything. You buy him a Coke, and pretty soon he drinks it and gets up and goes off.

Anyway, I carried on this one-sided discussion about the killing of the panther. "Mr. Tiger," I said, "I want to speak very frankly about this business. I recognize the Supreme Court says you have every right to do what you want on your own property. But this is bad publicity for the Indians, for your people. You're supposed to be great conservers and save all wildlife, and then you go and shoot a panther when you know we haven't got many panthers. Mr. Tiger, why did Jimmy Billie shoot the panther?"

Mr. Tiger didn't answer, but I'd already been told by his son that the panther was shot to get the whiskers for the medicine bundle for the medicine man. I continued on this tack: "Now, Mr. Tiger, is it all right to kill the whole panther just for the whiskers? I don't think so. You're giving people the impression you don't care about panthers, when we know you do. If it's the bristles you want, let me make a deal for you with the people at the University of Florida who get the dead bodies of any panthers killed on the road. I'll guarantee you they will send the bristles if you promise not to kill any panthers."

Buffalo Tiger seemed to think that was a good arrangement, though it's always hard to tell. "Harrumph. Very good," I think he said. I've been in the process of trying to organize the bristle thing. Recently I found out they do it with eagle feathers in the West.

VI

Human Nature

POLITICS

I met Bob Graham for the first time in the 1960s, at one of the annual and futile attempts to clean up the Miami River, celebrated with a regatta. They asked me to be queen of the regatta, and Mr Graham, then a state representative, was king. We had fun. We came down the river together on a boat with a band and made speeches from the boat about cleaning things up. Nobody paid any attention to us. Then we got off the boat and wandered along the riverbank, listening to the music.

Maybe I'd met him casually at some earlier time, back when he was a boy, back when I served on various committees with his mother. Or maybe he wasn't even born then. His mother was a very silent woman. His father, Ernest Graham, came down from Chicago and turned a Miami dairy farm into a real estate fortune at Miami Lakes. Ernest Graham's oldest son — by his first wife — was Philip Graham, who married into the Washington *Post* and later committed suicide. Bob

Graham is Philip Graham's half-brother — so in this way he's connected to the great newspaper.

After we were queen and king of the regatta, I lost track of Bob Graham. He got very involved in politics. After he became governor, I always had his ear on environmental matters — though I didn't always get what I wanted. One time I didn't was when I went to Tallahassee to convince state agencies to prohibit industrial development around the northwest wellfield area in Miami. This wasn't just my doing — it was a Friends of the Everglades project inspired by Joe Podgor, who runs the toxic water and pollution branch of our organization.

The county already had approved the development, but the state's Department of Community Affairs had appealed the county's decision. The state Cabinet had to rule on the appeal. When I went up and spoke to Governor Graham and the Cabinet they absolutely shot me down. I was upset; on the whole, Governor Graham (now a U.S. Senator) had been very good on the environment.

As it so happens, I was staying at the Graham townhouse in Tallahassee when the appeal was heard. He and his wife made me this gracious invitation and couldn't have been nicer. Mr. Graham is a political animal, so sometimes he's got to do the expedient thing, as he did in siding with the developers in the northwest wellfield dispute.

Every now and then I go to a meeting and some man in shirtsleeves comes up and kisses me and I say, "Who is it?" and the voice says, "Bob Graham." I'm always delighted to know it's Bob.

I'm glad he was elected U.S. senator. I never met his predecessor, Paula Hawkins. She's a Republican and I'm a registered Democrat, so I didn't like her on general principles. I didn't have to have anything against her specifically.

I don't know Claude Pepper very well, though we call each other by our first names. We never had any deep feelings personally.

I'm a good friend of Lawton Chiles's sister, and I correspond with the senator by letter. I only recently met him in person, but he's always writing me and every now and then I trouble him with some special request. He's very kind about trying to accommodate whatever it is, or else he tells me why he can't. One good thing he's done is to get the steel hunting traps outlawed in Florida.

Of the other Florida governors, I knew Caldwell the best. Spessard Holland helped me when I was writing the Everglades book, and later when he became a senator he was a big supporter of the national park. I stayed in the gubernatorial mansion with Spessard and Mary Holland, and once I had a dinner party with the LeRoy Collinses. Collins was one of my favorite governors.

I knew Governor Askew quite well. He was too religious for my taste, but otherwise we got along. He was an intelligent, high-minded governor and very helpful with the Friends of the Everglades.

We've had some simply terrible governors, such as Sidney J. Catts. He was dreadful, a Ku Klux Klanner type from Georgia. Then there was Claude Kirk. He was a Republican, which wasn't as bad as a Ku Klux Klanner. Actually, Mr. Kirk did some very good things, especially when he listened to Nat Reed, his excellent advisor on the environment. Come to think of it, we've had several governors that were much worse than Mr. Kirk.

On the local level, I've known Maurice Ferre, the once perennial Miami mayor who helped us finance the Richard Aldrich book at the University of Miami Press. He's a man of the world, a delightful and charming host. I wouldn't trust him exactly — but he's charming.

He came down to see me when he was running for Miami mayor this last time. He wanted me to be honorary chairman of his committee. I told him I couldn't get political or else the Friends of the Everglades would lose its tax-exempt status. I think he understood. I wish I'd advised him to tell the voters he was running for the last time. If he had, I think he might have won. As it is, he lost. After six terms, people were afraid he'd be around forever.

His opponent Masvidal also came to see me, and other candidates did, too. It was funny. In these situations, I can be a two-faced woman. I treat them all so pleasantly, like I'm so glad to see them and then I don't do a damn thing after that. Well, I can't be political as the head of the Friends of the Everglades. I would have liked to come out for Bob Graham for senator, but I couldn't even do that.

I like the present mayor, Suarez, very much. He's Miami's first Cuban-born mayor. With Havana cut off now, Miami has taken its place as the gateway between the two Americas, a position it will never lose. Probably it will be one continuous metropolis from Homestead to Palm Beach.

They say this is a Cuban city, or that the Cubans are taking it over. I don't despair about this. Cubans are becoming Americans. It is still a melting pot and people will melt. The only thing that concerns me in this regard is that the people from Latin America do not have the sense of civic responsibility we've developed in the U.S. There is a difference. They've been satisfied down there in Latin American with dictators. I don't know why they like dictators, but they do. Theirs has been a government of elitism. In many instances, they've neglected to support the writ of habeas corpus, which is the basis of our liberties. People complain that the poor start all the revolutions. The reason they have revolutions down there is that the rich people do not understand democracy, and nobody but the rich has the opportunity to prosper.

That's my worry about the first-generation Latin Americans in Miami. They will have to acquire a sense of civic responsibility. If they don't it's going to be just too bad. Then their children will have to.

Mayor Suarez understands civic responsibility. He's done some good things for us in Coconut Grove. He came out against the Treister development we've been fighting so hard. I've known Kenneth Treister for years, and he's done some terrific things himself. But he got this idea of developing the land next to the oldest house in Coconut Grove, and the money went to his head. Fortunately, the mayor of Miami is on our side.

I've never run for office. I wouldn't be very good at it. If you run for office you stick your head in a noose. You give up free will. My father kept out of politics for the same reason, and I learned from him. You can wield just as much power with a newspaper.

Speaking of the newspaper, I've met the present editor of the Miami *Herald* and we have a friendly relationship, but I think the paper suffers from the fact it's part of a chain. So many editors come in here knowing nothing about Florida, plus they can be very opinionated and sometimes have trouble learning. Quite often I feel they've taken the wrong tack. But they've been good on the environment. We usually get good support from the *Herald*.

As for the current local celebrities, I've met Isaac Bashevis Singer and talked to him in private. He's a very distant and impersonal man. His books are beautiful books. Well, he didn't know me from a hole in the wall and I came up to ask him about the book *Shosha*, about whether it was autobiographical. He answered my questions, but he wasn't too excited about talking to some strange person. He did tell me that the part about his running away with his dying Shosha as the Nazis were coming into Poland, that part was autobiographical. I asked him about how Shosha died on the trip, and what they did with the body. "We couldn't take it," he said. "We were running for our lives. We had to leave her on the side of the road."

I never met the artist Christo when he came down here to wrap the islands in Biscayne Bay. I thought that was perfectly ridiculous. A foolish waste of time and money. I've heard he did an even stranger thing out West. There he set up miles and miles of washlines with sheets hung on them all across the country. It was crazy, but had a terrific effect. They say you could see the wind.

Of course, I continue to meet hundreds of people at meetings and I serve on numerous honorary boards. I started the Friends of the University Library in 1959-60, and continued as president until 1966. I also chaired a lecture series which brought to the University such notables as Alistair Cooke, John Ciardi, Hodding Carter, Robert Frost, Arnold Toynbee, Louis Untermeyer and Philip Wylie. I was also on the board of Fairchild Tropical Garden until very recently. I got an unexpected visit from Nell Jennings (widow of Colonel Montgomery who established the Fairchild gardens), a delightful woman and totally incapable of any kind of deception. She and another friend called up and said they wanted to see me. I thought to myself — "Now, why do they want to come and see me? I'll bet a nickel they want me off the board. No personal reason, but they can only have so many people on it, and they'd prefer somebody who's rich."

So they came, and Nell said to me, "Well, Marjory, you've been on the board a long time." And I said, "Yes, Nell, I think it's time you retired me." And she said, "Oh, oh . . . do you want to retire?" I said, "I'll retire cheerfully and I am now retired. Please accept my resignation." They made me an honorary member of the board and I don't have to go to meetings anymore. Everything works out for the best.

MAKING DO

Since building the house and making do with the money that I've made or that was left to me, I've gotten along well. I'm not rich but I'm comfortable. Travel has been my chief extravagance, and my finances have been in very good shape.

After my wonderful and lifelong friend Carolyn Percy Cole died in 1973, she left me the house next door to use for my lifetime. I've rented it to a delightful man, Don DeHut. He balances my checkbook and reads me my mail and worries about sending my clothes to the cleaners so I'm not going around with spots on me. He's a bachelor and loves cats, and has all the other great virtues as well. I don't look on him as a son, I look on him as an heir. I have no other heirs, no other relations left. Between you and me, I'm leaving him my house.

I can still make new friends without much trouble. For several winters I did some lectures down at the Dade Community College. One of my students, a young man named Michael Blaine, asked me how I got to the auditorium. I said it was difficult sometimes, and he volunteered to drive me back and forth. We became good friends. Later he drove the van around Lake Okeechobee on our speaking tour for the Friends of the Everglades.

We went to Europe together in 1977. I was 87, and he was about to turn 27. When he told me about the birthday, I invited him to Paris to celebrate. We stayed in a little hotel I knew over on the Left Bank. I took him down the Seine on a wonderful *bateau mouche*, the fly boat, for lunch. He loved Paris. He would have been speaking French if he'd stayed there for any length of time.

Though I appreciate my friends, I certainly don't wish to share the house with anybody full-time. I'm always happy when Sister Smith, my cleaning woman, comes over — but then I can't wait until she goes. I want to live alone and I must be alone a good deal of the day. I've never been lonely, just alone. I think people who can't stand being alone are silly. How do they know who they are or what they're like if they're never alone?

My closest friends are those I've known over a long period. One, Kitty Harwood, was in the group of beautiful young people I swam with in the early days of Miami Beach. Another, Margaret Schoonover, I've known for 40 years. Her mother and father moved to Miami very early. I often see Kay Sweeney. She bought the Fairchild place. She's very well-to-do and has old money. Old money is quite different from new money.

I've known Dr. Henry Truby for years. I always liked him. He's amusing and we have a great deal to talk about, and we mull over old mutual friends like Henry Field. Helen Muir lives just up the street. Her husband Bill was 20 years younger than I am, but we did many things together. He and I wrote the play for the civic theater called *Storm Warnings*. It must be 45 years I've known Helen. She's a writer herself, and did the wonderful book called *Miami, U.S.A.* Bill died some years ago.

I've known many black people, especially through my work with Elizabeth Virrick. There was Father Gibson, the rector of Christ Church, and B.J. Guilford the policeman. B.J. was very quiet, but when he spoke, it was with the still, small voice of conscience. He always said the right thing. I got a call from him recently. He's living up in Lakeland, which he said is "quiet." If I went to Lakeland, he'd be the first person I'd look up.

Then I have my Latin family, Manuel and Maria Arroya. He's from Peru, she's from Colombia. I go to their house in the evening every couple of weeks. He washes my hair, she does my feet. I can't see to do my feet anymore. He comes for me, takes me out there, brings me back. It couldn't be nicer.

I met them through my former hairdresser in Coconut Grove. After she died, Manuel bought the business, so I started going to him. They raised his rent so much that he set up shop in his own garage. During the week he works at a shopping center, while his wife works with indigent people in some sort of program for the police department. On weekends they both do hair and feet.

Manuel is very serious and hard-working. He's in the third year of high school night course. We get into long philosophical arguments. I always end up saying: "Oh dear, Manuel, life isn't like that." But he's serious about his beliefs. He says everybody should be happy and I say: "Look, dearie, that's not the way the world was built."

I was fortunate to find Katheryn Witherspoon, who helps me out by taking dictation. For some years now, she's been coming to the house twice a week, which is all the time I've had to give to the Hudson book. We've produced a kind of a rough draft. Lately we've been going over it and rewriting it. It's much too long and wandering. We've rewritten up to the point where Alfred Russell Wallace discovers Hudson's book on the Argentine and praises it in the English literary magazines. There's a long way to go and I've been working on this project for 19 years.

Mondays and Fridays, I have a personal secretary, Martha Hubbart, who helps with the correspondence and reads to me. Every day but Wednesday and weekends I have one secretary or another from 2 to 5. That's how things get done around here.

OLD AGE

As I write this in 1986 I am 96 years old. It may seem strange, but I'm very comfortable in the nineties. I like the nineties. I don't seem to remember much about the eighties, but in the nineties I have a sense of achievement and a sense of leisure as well. I'm not pushed as much as I was.

I think I enjoy old age more than I enjoyed middle age. Being let off of the responsibility of middle age is a real pleasure. Middle age is the age where everything's got to be done. Old age can be more relaxing, more contemplative.

I've already said that I'm ambitious and my superego is always pushing me around, making me want to do more things. I still have complexes about what I haven't done, but in the nineties these have eased off a bit.

We hear a great deal about old age nowadays. Of course, people are living longer because they aren't dying as readily. I was down at East Ridge, a retirement village, having lunch with a friend and I had a chat with the girl at the desk. "I'm sure you have a few people down here in their nineties," I said. "In their nineties?" she answered. "We have eight people over a hundred." I didn't ask if they were vegetables in beds, but I gathered that they were pretty spry.

It is much easier to be old these days. That life in general is easier is one reason there's more of it.

At the end of the last century, there was a great preoccupation with the idea of death. Death seemed to be a release for everybody. Christina Rossetti wrote: "When I'm dead, my dearest, sing no sad songs for me." Swinburne wrote:

From too much love of living
From hope and fear set free
I thank with brief Thanksgiving
Whatever gods that be
That no life lives for ever
That dead men rise up never
And even the weariest river
Winds somewhere safe to sea.

We don't have much of a death cult today. Instead, we have a youth cult. Youth has become the great period of release that death once was. If you're old as I am, somebody's always saying: "Oh, but you're young at heart." What in the heck do they mean by "young at heart"? My heart is just as old as I am — if not a month or two older. To be young at heart means absolutely nothing. I enjoy being 96.

Death is just over the hill somewhere, but what of it? We've known about death all our lives. I don't think the young are aware that the old accustom themselves to the idea of death as a welcome companion. You can still be glad that no life lives forever.

My father had had enough at the age of 84, and he said he was glad to be going. He left with tranquility, which is the way to do it. I think you live longer if you're relaxed about death. In fact, relaxation is the most important factor in longevity. People who get all twisted up inside get cancer and have nervous breakdowns.

I consider myself lucky to have been taught to relax after my nervous breakdowns, or mental fugues, or whatever they were. Relaxation has been the key to my health. I was in New York one time, after I'd been pretty cleared up of my psychoses by Dr. Dodge. I went to have an interview with old Dr. Smith Ely-Jelliffe, who was famous for having introduced Freud into this country. I saw him just for an hour but he put his finger exactly on my problem. He said my conflict was between my ego and my superego, which was completely right.

I've been very ambitious, always trying to do more than I could, and that's where the conflict came in. It disturbed me that couple of times until I talked to Dr. Dodge, but it was Dr. Jelliffe who gave me the idea of the ego versus superego that made the most sense. I haven't had any trouble since.

Moderation in all things is equally important. If you can acquire it before you're old, it's even better. It's hard to acquire new habits when you're old because you don't want to bother. So if you haven't been moderate in your ways of living before your nineties, you'd better look yourself over and see where you can moderate some of your excesses, things that you know should be changed. If you're in your nineties, and you're still doing something overindulgent or stupid, you'd better stop it. If you haven't got will power to stop it in your nineties, maybe you'd have been better off to have died in your eighties.   Good health you can't do without. Not everybody enjoys it, but the more you can do to improve your health the better. Without good health, no age is any good. I've never had anything much the matter with me, but I get a checkup every year. I continue to have a sensible diet, and avoid whole milk and eggs. When you're old, you have to watch your cholesterol.

A doctor once told me to take aspirin, because as you grow older the blood thickens and the aspirin tends to thin it out again. For years, I've taken two aspirin a day, and at my recent checkup, they told me my blood pressure is that of a teenaged girl.

In cold weather, I still feel a bit of an itchy twinge where the shingles once were. I've had a little trouble with cramps in the feet, but calcium seems to have cured that. That's about all the illnesses I've had lately, except for my eyes, of course.

Now, I suffer from this hereditary thing called bilateral macula deterioration of the retina. Nothing can be done about it. Sight isn't everything in the world. Somebody once said to me, I thought tactlessly, that one of the worst things that can possibly happen is to lose your sight. That's not true. The worst thing that can happen is to die young. The second worst is to lose your mind. I'd much rather lose my sight than either life or mind.

Because of my poor sight, though, I don't enjoy traveling as much as I once did. When I can't see where I am, there's not so much pleasure in it. I've been traveling recently, but it's tiring. I'm pushed around in a wheelchair to the airplane, and out of the airplane in another wheelchair to the taxi, but sitting around in a wheelchair is tiring also. It is no final answer to keeping me from being tired. I've travelled enough, and I remember where I've been. I don't think I'm going to bother much anymore.

Don't forget your legs. Women particularly give up on legs very early. They want to sit around, but when the legs give out then you're pretty well done for. I'm very concerned about keeping going on my legs. I can't take the long walks I used to take because I can't see, but I walk as much as possible around the house and around the yard. Keeping up the legs keeps your heart going, and keeps the body in balance. Too much sitting around will impair the whole system.

One of the unfortunate things they do in nursing homes is put people in wheelchairs. It's easier to push people around that way, but people in wheelchairs lose the use of their legs. It opens you up to all kinds of trouble with the bones.

There's the whole business of osteoporosis, where the bone has been affected. It happens to people, especially women over 60, who don't eat right. They don't keep up their protein and calcium intake. People have gotten silly about their diets. They won't eat this, they won't eat that, they cut down on their protein, and the bones are jeopardized as a result. A great deal of this trouble has to do with our cult of vegetables. This vegetarian nonsense has caused more osteoporosis than people can imagine.

To be prepared for life in the nineties, you have to eat right. Then if you have the right diet, the right medical advice, and the right attitude, you can be healthier in the nineties than you were in the eighties. There's no reason you have to be physically handicapped in the nineties.

There's no reason you have to be soft in the head, either. If you've made it into the nineties, you're probably not. You probably have an accumulation of good sense. If you haven't got good sense, of course, it's too bad — but maybe it's not too late to acquire it. Your brain is like any other part of the body. If you neglect it, it's going to deteriorate.

They say you can't teach an old dog new tricks, but you can. I am remembering some things better now than I did before. I can remember a few telephone numbers, and I never used to remember telephone numbers. That's an improvement, isn't it? There's nothing inherently wrong with a brain in the nineties. If you keep it fed and interested, you'll find it lasts you very well.

Keeping up your mental activity is very important. There's no reason you can't continue to be interested in ideas, in reading, in talking about things, in seeing what's going on. Maybe you can't read. But there's a wonderful service called the Talking Books for the Blind. There's a local office in every big county in connection with a library. The government sends you a record player and a cassette player and all the records and cassettes you could possibly use. It doesn't cost a cent. I couldn't do without the talking books. I use them all the time. There's an extraordinary talking book library. It's one of the greatest things that our Library of Congress has ever done.

You can't listen to music all the time. You can't even listen to talk radio all the time, although I tune in often. You've got to stretch your mind. You've got to keep on reading books that will stimulate you.

Old people that are bored by the way their lives are going must be fooling themselves. There are too many things in which to be interested, too many things to know about for anybody to be bored or unhappy in that way. You have to do things for yourself.

When you do things for yourself, you'll have more people to come see you because you'll have something to talk about. And you won't be complaining, which is a bad habit to acquire. Complaining about being old, nobody loves you, nobody comes to see you is a big mistake. Maybe people don't come to see you because you bore them to death. Reading books and having something to talk about will save you and your friends some trouble.

I wish we would get over this peculiar American schism between youth and old age. Youth is afraid of old age because it thinks old age is going to blame it for everything. Old age is afraid of youth because it thinks youth is going to reject it. If we could all realize each has something the other lacks, we might do much better. This could be a role for middle age. Middle age could do more to bring old age and youth together, in a new reciprocity.

BELIEFS

When people ask "What is your philosophy?" I have to object. "Philosophy?" After all, we don't live by a philosophy, or even a complex of philosophies. We live the best we can, working our way through life, trying to learn what makes sense and what doesn't, proving and disproving things as they come along.

As to formal religion, my breakaway to Florida and divorce from my husband somehow divorced me from Episcopalianism as well. I gradually came away from the feeling of religion completely. Since college, I hadn't known any concept of God that I could understand or adhere to. Of course, there are different concepts of God. There's that concept of God as a kind of Santa Claus, the giver of every good and perfect gift. Another concept is that of Eastern potentate, who must be praised and flattered in order for one to get what one wants from him. That's an aspect of God I particularly dislike.

Frequently, I review my religious history, to try and make some sense of it, to put it into context. My grandmother on my mother's side, my French grandmother, was not a member of any church until after she got married and had children. Then she and my grandfather went to Methodist meetings. Later, my grandmother joined the Episcopal church and took us children there.

As a child, I had the habit of earnest and passionate prayer about my mother's condition. That went on for years, and the prayer was never answered. My mother died dreadfully with cancer anyway, and I began to feel that what she had suffered was more than any God could possibly inflict on a lovely, gentle and blameless individual. I felt that so deeply, I was in revolt against the secular idea of religion even as a young woman. Since, I've been in revolt against all the popular concepts of God.

My father, as I've said, converted to Episcopalianism after having been brought up a Quaker. For as long as I can remember, he was senior warden of Trinity Church in Miami. He and my stepmother were devout church-goers, and they were always having ministers and bishops to breakfast.

I think about all this years later, because as one gets older, one is faced with the necessity of thinking about it. And I've decided that one of the great troubles with religion in general is that it hypothesizes a dual universe. They're always talking about body and soul, about things material and things spiritual. Dualism pervades practically all Western religious thinking, and I'm unable to believe in it.

I don't care whether the universe is all material or all spiritual, those are only words. I believe that whatever it is, is all one. I don't know what it is, how can I know it? Time, the heavens, the galaxies, it goes far beyond our ability to understand it, and I'm not even going to try.

People have all these theories about life and the universe, the dual nature of things, but there's no possible way of proving it. A lot of theories, beliefs, creeds, legends have been built up by mankind to explain things that are practically unexplainable to the human mind. I don't particularly like the label, but I suppose I am an agnostic, because in the ultimate sense I just don't know what's what. I don't see how I could possibly know.

I do believe in one universe. That's one philosophical tenet on which I really and truly can stand. I don't know how the universe got started. I don't believe in the old man with a long gray beard who started things. I know too much about the Bible to believe that every word was written by God. But I'm completely convinced that whatever it is — maybe matter, maybe spirit — is all one. Therefore, I call myself a monist.

On the other hand, I don't believe there is a soul. The soul is a fiction of mankind, because mankind hates the idea of death. It wants to think that something goes on after. I don't think it does, and I don't think we have souls. I think death is the end. A lot of people can't bear that idea, but I find it a little restful, really. I'm happy not to feel I'm going on. I don't really want to. I think this life has been plenty. It's just about all anybody could take, really. I'm cheerful about the feeling the end will come — let it come.

This may seem harsh, but actually it's an important part of a positive attitude and a sense of human fulfillment. I believe that life should be lived so vividly and so intensely that thoughts of another life, or of a longer life, are not necessary.

Index

Italic page numbers refer to illustrations.

effect of mother's breakdown on, 47-48, 56-57

engagement to Frederick, 124-125, 126

as environmentalist, 13-14, 20-23, 159, 176, 190-195, 223-242

on exercise, 178-179, 259

on extramarital sex, 111, 128

on family, 187

on feminism, 23, 78

on Florida politicians, 107, 245-248

fondness for cats, 21, 149, 218, 233-234, 238-241

as Francophile, 19-20, 33, 110, 114

Freudian influences on, 23, 253-254

on friendship, 177

health of, 206, 208-210, 254-256

home in Coconut Grove, 146, 149, 150, 161, 171-178

on independence, 17, 179, 219, 250, 256

interest in geography, 74-75

interest in the sea, 65-65, 111, 115

as journalist, 101-113, 124, 127-128, 133-135, 166-168

on Latin Americans, 247-248

love of reading, 16, 18, 49-50, 52, 100-101, 173, 256

marriage of, 84-92, 95

on marriage, 89, 127-128

on moderation, 254

moves to St. Louis, 82-83

as Navy yeoman, 112-114

nervous breakdowns of, 167-168, 179-180, 188, 253-254

in Newark, 83-87

in New York, 88-90

on old age, 220, 252-256

on pacifism, 112

on philosophy, 76-77, 257-258

physical appearance of, 14, 43-44, 96, 201

poor eyesight of, 214, 216, 217, 254

as public speaker, 51, 77-78, 211, 226, 230

as publisher, 210-211

on refugees, 116

relationship with Andy, 110-112, 114, 116-117, 126-128

relationship with father, 42-43, 56-57, 99-101, 111, 167-168, 185, 188

relationship with mother, 30, 44, 47, 53, 56, 69, 78-79

relationship with stepmother, 97, 100

religious training and views of, 44, 52, 60-62, 74, 101, 105-106, 257-258

researches Florida, 212-213

reunion with father, 95-101

self-assessment of, 17, 50, 61, 73-74

on sexual relations, 23, 65-66, 72, 85, 89, 128

theater work, 182-183

travels to West, 201-202

travels with Red Cross Society, 18, 114-124

and wildlife conservation, 233-242

as writer, 23, 67-68, 70, 154, 168-170, 180-185, 189, 190-193, 202-206, 224

Dredd Scott decision, 19, 20, 38

Dualism, 258

East Everglades, 232

Ecology. *See* Environmental causes

Edwardt, Captain, 120-122

Eichberg, Julius (musician), 34

Eliot, George, 20

Ely-Jelliffe, Dr. Smith, 253-254

English Composition (Matthews), 70

Environmental causes. *See also* Everglades; *Everglades: River of*

Addendum

To be half-blind is a very inefficient situation. You think you can see without realizing that you can't see everything. When I dictated *Voice of the River*, I left out some very important people and experiences:

When I first came down to Florida in 1915, the Miami Women's Club was the center of activity for the area's women. I met so many women who were very intelligent, college graduates who had come here to live because they wanted to live in a warm climate. The Women's Club was the center of a great deal of activity in those days. We reviewed books and put on plays.

Before World War I, I founded the Business and Professional Women's League. Later it changed to a club and became a chapter of a national organization. It got business and professional women together to pursue various causes. It was part of the women's movement. Women were loners in that era. It gave them a great deal more sense of stability and belonging. I'm still honorary president of it.

I got to know Charles M. Brookfield soon after he came to Coconut Grove from Philadelphia in 1926. He made a great study of Florida birds and wrote a book with Oliver Griswold about the Keys, *They All Called It Tropical*. During World War II, Charlie was a naval officer. After the war he became the Audubon Society bird warden in the Big Cypress Swamp and the Everglades, working out of Everglades City. We had done away with poaching here in the U.S., but we still had trouble with the Cubans coming over and killing the birds for their plumes. That went on for some time, even after the national park was established. Earlier, some of the local residents on the west coast had been the worst of the poachers. That was one of the main reasons for establishing the park. I remember several trips with Charlie in which we saw impressive flights of as many as 40,000 birds at one time.

Nancy Brown (Mrs. Roy Brown), who lives in South Miami, is one of the most intelligent women I've known. She understands and remembers all of the environmental legislation. Her counsel is most awfully important. If Nancy is for something, you know that's it.

Minna Burnaby was Uncle Barbour Lathrop's niece and Henry Field's mother. She came down and bought an estate on the bayfront in Coconut Grove. Chauncey McCormick of Chicago and Coconut Grove sent me a letter to say she was coming to live here in the winter. She at once looked me up. Henry Field came down and inherited the place when she died.

Mae Knight Clark was on the faculty of the Cushman School, a very good private school for girls in North Miami. Mae didn't like the textbooks for the beginning classes in English and mathematics, so she wrote her own. Miss Cushman, the head of the school, was so much impressed by them that she showed them to the Macmillan sales representative when he came around. He took them to New York and showed them to the Macmillan editorial board. They asked her to come to New York to write some new arithmetic textbooks. She didn't want to work in New York, but they made it worth her while. They rented an apartment for her, gave her a secretary, and paid her very good royalties. After Mae retired, we took several trips abroad together between 1959 and 1977. In 1965, she was being treated at the Moorfield Eye Hospital in London for a severe virus infection of the eyes. Her ophthalmologist took a 10-day vacation and said she might go where she chose during that time. We flew to Paris, secured a car with a 19-year-old driver, and spent the 10 days in the chateau country. Our driver was the son of a nobleman who had just died, and he took us to his family's ancestral estate. Mae's eyes were bandaged, but periodically she would lift the bandage to look around.

In 1988, something very strange happened to Don DeHut, my tenant in the house next door. He took me out to dinner and told me he was in a bad state of depression because of his mother's death, and was under a psychiatrist's care. I regret that he hasn't spoken with me since. He resigned as treasurer of Friends of the Everglades but didn't bring over the books. After we got a court subpoena on July 26, 1988, he brought them over. I've revised my will so my house won't be left to Don. Negotiations are going on now for the state to buy it and make it a museum.

Mabel Dorn was a great student of tropical horticulture. She became interested in subtropical gardening, taught herself, and helped to organize 14 garden clubs. She also served as president of the South Florida Garden Club and vice president of the Florida Federation of Garden Clubs. I said anybody who was that involved in gardening ought to write about it. The result was *The Book of Twelve*, a South Florida gardening book published in 1928. I edited it and wrote a foreword.

Ellen Edelen was responsible for the Banyan Books edition of *The Everglades: River of Grass* in 1978, which appeared before the Mockingbird Book paperback edition. Now Pineapple Press has a new revised hardcover edition.

Ed Goodnow had a stock company of actors in Boston. He came to Miami and lived in Coconut Grove. Somebody gave him a letter of introduction to me. Ed was a good friend; we went to plays together a lot. He was on the board of the Civic Theater, which did all kinds of plays with local people as actors. For a while in the 1950s he managed the Coconut Grove Playhouse for its owner, George Engle, and brought down some extremely good plays. One of those plays was *The Solid Gold Cadillac*, with Billie Burke. The play has a last line which someone comes from the wings to deliver. Ed Goodnow recruited me to play that last line for two weeks, so I was an actor every night plus Wednesday and Saturday matinees. He sent a taxi for me and paid me Actor's Equity fees. It was a lot of fun, but waiting for my cue was so boring. I did enough acting and was a good enough actress, but I would never live the life of an actor. I would be bored to death.

After the war, when I was at the UM Press, I got Kitty Harwood, with whom I swam in the early days of Miami Beach, started doing a book on Vizcaya. She worked on it for 20 years. I had the county commissioners appoint her as archivist for Vizcaya, with access to all the records. She discovered a lot of James Deering's letters and did years of research abroad, visiting the historic places from which Deering and his interior decorator, Paul Chalfin, brought so many fine things to Vizcaya. The book came out in 1987 and has been a great success. Ellen Edelen at Banyan Books published it.

Marjory Leposky is my very first namesake. When she was born in 1974, about two weeks after my 84th birthday, I was flabbergasted to learn she was named for me. Nobody had ever done that before. I was so honored that I sent her my own baby spoon to use. She's 14 now. I hope to follow her life and career for many years. Marjory is the daughter of George and Rosalie Leposky, a husband-wife team of writers. George helped me prepare this addendum to *Voice of the River*.

George Rosner was head of circulation at the University of Miami library. He was a young man of Austrian parentage. Fortunately for him, his mother and father were visiting in New York when he was born, so he is an American citizen. He spent his early years in Austria. He attended the University of Miami and the Columbia University library school in New York City, then came back to UM as head of circulation. I met George when I set up the Friends of the Library. He was the executive secretary and right-hand man who did all the hard work. Since he retired, he has been my chief man of business. He takes care of my checkbook, sees to my mail, and brings me wonderful dinners.

Jack and Bertha Ward came to Miami to retire with his father, Charles

Ward. They had lived in several South American countries. Jack was an engineer who built roads and other things.

I was in on the very beginning of the University of Miami. In 1924 or 1925, a group of ministers of local churches got together and decided we should have a university. It would be religiously oriented, but non-sectarian, and it would grow to serve people from South America as well as North America. I attended one of the early organizational meetings. They got Dr. Bowman F. Ashe down here from Pittsburgh to put it on its feet. Dr. Ashe said in a meeting that he never wanted to be associated again with anything for which he had to raise the money, but very soon the ministers found that they could not finance their idea. Although real estate was booming, nothing else was doing well. I told Dr. Ashe, "You're trying to organize this when there's a depression coming." The ministers couldn't seem to raise any money, so they gave up the whole thing, which left Dr. Ashe alone with it. By this time he was so interested in the idea of the University of Miami that he put all his savings and his life insurance into it.

The university was established on a shoestring, with Dr. Ashe's money and whatever he could collect from the community. One year a good many of us on the faculty gave up our salaries so the university wouldn't have that burden of indebtedness.

George Merrick, the developer of Coral Gables, gave the land, and they raised enough money to put up the skeleton of the classroom building. It stood there for years, unused, while the university itself was carried on in the Anastasia Building in Coral Gables. The Anastasia Building had been half built in the boom. It was turned over to the university, and repaired sufficiently so classes could be held in it, with gypsum board enclosing the frame and forming the interior partitions. They called it "the cardboard college." Eventually, when the country recovered from the bust and the shortages of World War II, the university was able to raise more money and grow to become an institution of real strength and great importance.

I was on the original faculty as a lecturer in English composition. Among my colleagues in those early days was Bertha Foster, a very distinguished musician, who headed a local musicians' club and was asked to found the department of music. Mana Zucca also was on the music faculty. That was always a very strong department.

My grandmother on my mother's side was French; my grandfather was completely English and Cornish. He was a mild-mannered man, but he laid down the law that he didn't want French spoken in his house. He spent weekends down on Naragansett Bay at his son's house. When he left, we got out the French books and had a good go of it. What I speak is a book French; I don't know all the local idioms. I wish I spoke modern colloquial French. I did use my French a good deal when I was in France for the Red Cross and when I was in the Argentine. Many of those rich South Americans had been to Paris and spoke French. When I was in Buenos Aires, the man at the front desk where I stayed spoke no English, and my Spanish was very bad, so we spoke French.

For several years in the 1960s I had a hive of bees in the eaves of my home. Those eaves curve, and there's a hollow space under them. Once you get bees and they start making honey, it's very hard to get rid of them. Bees are amazing characters. They can burrow their way through cement. They burrowed their way down through my fireplace floor. I was sitting here one night when something tickled my knee. I slapped it and it stung me. Bees don't bother me, even if they sting me. I like working with bees. I could have been a bee mistress. But I had to have these bees killed. There are people who cannot stand bee stings. It might kill them, and I would be liable.

In the early 1970s I found out what to do from a man named David Strong. He and his wife are here in the winters and go to Wyoming in the summers. Now, every year, David Strong comes and puts into the eaves dabs of this mustard gas compound he buys from the drug store. I still have streaks on the unpainted plaster inside the house where the honey leaked through. The plaster shows the entire history of the house. It still has long streaks from the 1926 hurricane.

January 1990
Coconut Grove, Florida